THE FUTURE OF SUCCESS

THE
FUTURE
OF
SUCCESS

ROBERT B. REICH

ALFRED A. KNOPF   NEW YORK   2001

THIS IS A BORZOI BOOK

PUBLISHED BY ALFRED A. KNOPF

Copyright © 2000 by Robert B. Reich
All rights reserved under International and Pan-American
Copyright Conventions. Published in the United States by Alfred A. Knopf,
a division of Random House, Inc., New York, and simultaneously
in Canada by Random House of Canada Limited, Toronto.
Distributed by Random House, Inc., New York.
www.aaknopf.com

Knopf, Borzoi Books, and the colophon are
registered trademarks of Random House, Inc.

Library of Congress Cataloging-in-Publication Data
Reich, Robert B.
The future of success / Robert B. Reich.—1st ed.
    p.   cm.
Includes bibliographical references and index.
ISBN 0-375-41112-7 (alk. paper)
1. Work.   2. Information society—United States.
3. Quality of work life—United States.
4. Work and family—United States.
I. Title.
HD8072.5.R45 2001
306.3'61—dc21   00-040552

Manufactured in the United States of America
First Edition

To my students

CONTENTS

THE FUTURE OF SUCCESS

Introduction

A FEW YEARS AGO I had a job that consumed me. I wasn't addicted to it—"addiction" suggests an irrational attachment, slightly masochistic, compulsive. My problem was that I loved my job and couldn't get enough of it. Being a member of the President's cabinet was better than any other job I'd ever had. In the morning, I couldn't wait to get to the office. At night, I left it reluctantly. Even when I was at home, part of my mind remained at work.

Not surprisingly, all other parts of my life shriveled into a dried raisin. I lost touch with my family, seeing little of my wife or my two sons. I lost contact with old friends. I even began to lose contact with myself—every aspect of myself other than what the job required. Then one evening I phoned home to tell the boys I wouldn't make it back in time to say good night. I'd already missed five bedtimes in a row. Sam, the younger of the two, said that was O.K., but asked me to wake him up whenever I got home. I explained that I'd be back so late that he would have gone to sleep long before; it was probably better if I saw him the next morning. But he insisted. I asked him why. He said he just wanted to know I was there, at home. To this day, I can't explain precisely what happened to me at that moment. Yet I suddenly knew I had to leave my job.

After I announced my resignation, I received a number of letters. Most were sympathetic, but a few of my correspondents were angry. They said my quitting sent a terrible message; it suggested that a balanced life was not compatible with a high-powered job. Many women on the fast track were already battling a culture that told them they were sacrificing too much—and here I was, they said, essentially telling people the same thing. Others complained that while it was easy for me to leave my job and find another one that paid about as well while giving me more room for the rest of my life, they didn't have that choice. They had to work long hours, or the rent wouldn't get paid and there would be no food on the table. So I was sending the wrong message to people like them, too. Still others wrote to inform me indignantly that I shouldn't think myself virtuous. Hard work was virtuous, abandoning an important job to spend more time with my family was not.

Perhaps I should have expected that my career decision would carry symbolic weight—I had, after all, been the Secretary of *Labor*. In fact, I'd had no intention whatsoever of sending a message about how other people should lead their lives. Certainly I didn't think there was anything virtuous about the choice I'd made. But until that time I had been making a different choice, an implicit one, without acknowledging it. *That* was the problem. The wake-up call my son requested was a wake-up call for me to make an explicit choice, and make it consciously.

The experience made me notice a lot of things I hadn't seen before, even though I'd spent most of my adult life examining work and the economy. It focused my attention on the struggles most of us are having over paid work and the rest of our lives—men as well as women, young people setting out on their careers, middle-aged people who in years past would have already resolved these matters—including choices that sometimes are posed starkly, but more often are subtle, and appear in various guises. And it caused me to want put together what I've observed about the large-scale changes occurring in the global economy with these small-scale personal dramas. This book is the result.

I am writing here about making a living and making a life, and why it not only seems to be but actually *is* getting harder to do both. Acres of paper and oceans of ink have been expended in detailing the dizzying exuberance of the emerging economy. Yet there has been almost no discussion about what it means for us as *people,* and about the choices that lie before us for the kinds of lives we wish to lead. The deepest anxieties of this prosperous age concern the erosion of our families, the fragmenting of our communities, and the challenge of keeping our own integrity intact. These anxieties are no less part and parcel of the emerging economy than are its enormous benefits: the wealth, the innovation, the new chances and choices.

My purpose here is to invite a debate that's larger than the admonition to "slow down and get a life." To view the struggle for a better balance between paid work and the rest of life only as a personal one, waged in private, is to ignore the larger trends that are tipping the scales. It's not just a personal choice; not simply a matter of personal balance. It's also a question of how work is—and should be—organized and rewarded. It's a question of a balanced society.

The central paradox is this: Most of us are earning more money and living better in material terms than we (or our parents) did a quarter century ago, around the time when some of the technologies on which the new economy is based—the microchip, the personal computer, the Internet—first emerged. You'd think, therefore, that it would be easier, not harder, to attend to the parts of our lives that exist outside paid work. Yet by most measures we're working longer and more frantically than before, and the time and energy left for our non-working lives are evaporating.

Why should this be? If what we do for pay is making us richer, why are our personal lives growing poorer? Why can't we dedicate more of our material gains toward making our lives *outside* paid work richer? The British economist John Maynard Keynes, writing in 1930, during the darkest days of the Great Depression, cheerfully predicted that in a hundred years England would be eight times better off economically, so that its people would choose to work only fifteen hours a week. Their material needs satisfied, they would see the love of money as "one of those semi-criminal, semi-pathological propensities" that affluence had cured. Keynes probably will be correct about most people being far better off materially in 2030, but incorrect about their working fewer hours, at least if Britain keeps going the way of the United States, and we keep going the way we have been.

Of course, not everyone is far better off materially than a quarter century ago. Some aren't better off at all. And many people are working harder because they have to. But here's the strange thing: The richer you are, the more likely it is that you are putting in long and harried hours at work, even obsessing about it when you're not doing it. A frenzied work life may or may not make you better off, but being better off definitely seems to carry with it more frenzy.

Consider some counterintuitive statistics: In America, college graduates earn on average 70 to 80 percent more than people with only a high-school diploma, which is twice the premium accorded to a college degree twenty-five years ago. So you might suppose that people who have graduated from college would feel they have to work somewhat less intensely than high-school grads. You'd be wrong, of course. It's the college-degree holders who are working the longer hours. And maybe you'd also think that, with the college premium having doubled, college students themselves would be somewhat less concerned about being well-off financially than they were twenty-five or thirty years ago. But you'd be wrong about that, too. Surveys show they're far more focused on financial success than ever before.[1]

What's happened? Have college grads become greedier, more obsessed by money? Maybe, but there's no good reason to assume so. Has our national character changed in just a few decades? It seems unlikely; the character of a people doesn't alter so quickly.

The typical American works 350 more hours a year than the typical European, more hours even than the notoriously industrious Japanese. You might then suppose that more Americans would prefer to work a bit less, sacrificing some earnings. But only 8 percent of them say they would prefer fewer hours of work for less pay, compared with 38 percent of Germans, 30 percent of Japanese, and 30 percent of Britons.

Do we have a workaholic gene that the citizens of other advanced nations lack? Or is work so much more satisfying and enjoyable here? Both seem doubtful. We didn't used to work that much harder than they did, decades ago. Why have we started to?

We hear a rising chorus of American voices resolving to slow down. Yet more of us seem to be speeding up. We say with ever more vehemence that we value family. So why are our families shrinking and family ties fraying—fewer children or no children, fewer marriages, more temporary living arrangements, more subcontracting of family functions to food preparers, therapists, counselors, and child-care givers? We talk more passionately than ever about the virtues of "community." And yet our communities are fragmenting into enclaves filled with people who earn similar incomes—the wealthier, walled off and gated; the poorer, isolated and ignored.

Are we engaged in mass hypocrisy? Mass delusion? Probably neither. Most Americans seem genuinely to be seeking more balanced lives. The problem is that balance between making a living and making a life is becoming harder to pull off because the logic of the new economy dictates that more attention be paid to work and less to personal life.

Introduction

Here is my argument, in brief:

The emerging economy is offering unprecedented opportunities, an ever-expanding choice of terrific deals, fabulous products, good investments, and great jobs for people with the right talents and skills. Never before in human history have so many had access to so much so easily.

Technology is the motor. In communications, transportation, and information-processing, the new technologies that gained momentum in the 1980s and 1990s are now racing ahead at blinding speed. They are making it easier to find and get better deals from anywhere and allowing us to switch instantly to even better ones. These technologies are radically sharpening competition among sellers, which in turn is provoking a staggering wave of innovation. In order to survive, all organizations must dramatically and continuously improve—cutting costs, adding value, creating new products. The result of this tumult is higher productivity—better, faster, cheaper products and services of every description.

Economically, all of this is to our great and unequivocal benefit. But what it means for the rest of our lives—the parts that depend on firm relationships, continuity, and stability—is acutely problematic. There's no diabolical plot here, no trap cunningly devised by evil corporations and greedy capitalists. It's a matter of straightforward logic.

The easier it is for us as *buyers* to switch to something better, the harder we as *sellers* have to scramble in order to keep every customer, hold every client, seize every opportunity, get every contract. As a result, our lives are more and more frenzied.

The faster the economy *changes*—with new innovations and opportunities engendering faster switches by customers and investors in response—the harder it is for people to be confident of *what any of us will earn* next year or even next month, what they will be doing, where they will be doing it. As a result, our lives are less predictable.

The more intense the competition to offer better products and services, the greater the demand for people with insights and ideas about how to do so. And because the demand for such people is growing faster than the supply, their earnings are pushed *upward*. Yet the same competition is pushing *downward* the pay of people doing routine work that can be done faster and cheaper by hardware and software, or by workers elsewhere around the world. As a result, disparities in earnings are growing steadily larger.

Finally, the wider the choices and easier the switches, the less difficult it is for people to *link up* with others who are just as well educated,
wealthy, and healthy as they are—within residential communities, businesses, schools, universities, and insurance groups. And the easier it is
for them to *exclude* the slower, less educated, poorer, sicker, or otherwise more disadvantaged, all of whom have greater needs. As a result,
our society is becoming more fragmented.

In short, rewards of the new economy are coming at the price of
lives that are more frenzied, less secure, more economically divergent,
more socially stratified. As buyers switch more easily to better deals, all
of us have little choice but to work harder to satisfy buyers. As our
earnings become less predictable, we leap at every chance to make hay
while the sun shines. As the stakes rise—toward greater wealth or relative poverty, highly desirable communities or patently undesirable
ones—we'll do whatever we can to be in the winner's circle and to get
our children safely there as well.

For all these reasons, most of us are working harder and more frantically than we did decades ago when these trends were just beginning,
and than do citizens of other modern nations where these trends are
not as far along.

The price may be worth it. The terrific deals are benefiting all of us
in myriad ways. But even if the price is acceptable today, will it still be
worth it in the future as the stakes continue to rise?

There is, undeniably, much to celebrate about the new economy.
American capitalism is triumphant all over the world, and with good
reason. Neo-Luddites who claim that advancing technologies will eliminate jobs and relegate most of us to poverty are wrong, even silly. Iso-
lationists and xenophobes who want to put up the gates and reduce
trade and immigration are misguided, often dangerously so. Paranoid
populists who say global corporations and international capitalists are
conspiring against us are deluded, possibly hallucinating. We—you and
I and most Americans—are benefiting mightily from the new economy. We are reaping the gains of its new inventions, its lower prices, its
fierce competition. We are profiting from the terrific deals it's offering
us as consumers, and to a large and growing portion of us as investors.
We are driving the new economy forward.

And yet . . . As wondrous as the new economy is, we are also losing
parts of our lives to it—aspects of our family lives, our friendships, our
communities, ourselves. These losses closely parallel the benefits we're

gaining. In an important sense, they are two sides of the same coin. And as the new economy accelerates, both the gains and the losses are likely to increase. Working ever harder in order to compete within a system where competition is growing fiercer; selling ourselves with increasing determination within a system that's turning almost everyone into a self-promoter; sorting by wealth, education, and health in a system that's making it ever easier to sort—these phenomena are self-propelling. The more people join in, the more imbalanced the situation becomes, and the harder it becomes for any individual to choose a different path.

In the pages ahead, I explore these trends and their implications in detail. Part One of the book is about the new work. In it, I explain how new technologies are changing the way work is organized and rewarded. Part Two is about the new life. There, I explore the consequences of the new work for ourselves, our families, and our communities. Part Three is about the personal and social choices all of this implies.

The trends I discuss are powerful indeed—but they are not irreversible, or at least not unalterable. We can, if we wish, reassess our standard measure of success. We can affirm that our life's worth isn't synonymous with our net worth; that the quality of our society is different from our gross national product. We can, if we want, choose fuller and more balanced lives, and we can create a more balanced society. The question is: Do we really want to?

PART ONE

THE
NEW WORK

CHAPTER ONE

———————————

The Age of the Terrific Deal

W E ARE ENTERING the Age of the Terrific Deal, where choices
are almost limitless and it's easy to switch to something better.
This is the first principle of the new economy. Understanding it is the
first step toward understanding what is happening to the rest of our
lives. All else follows.

And who doesn't want a better deal? Only the indolent, insane, or
congenitally complacent would pass up a product that's obviously better (and costs no more) or cheaper (and of the same quality), an investment with a higher return, a more rewarding job, a more comfortable
community. You owe it to yourself, your family.

You owe it to capitalism. The system works only if people are pushing for the best deals. Otherwise, producers fail to innovate or invest,
or they squander money and effort on the wrong things. When millions of people are constantly seeking something better, the market
disciplines all players. Everyone has to do his or her best in order to satisfy everyone else. All resources are put to their best uses. People work
hard. Economies surge forward.

This has long been the American way. It is now rapidly becoming
the world way. America was founded by people who left places and
abandoned old ways in search of a better deal. And if they didn't find it
where they landed, they kept moving until they did. Subsequent generations of immigrants added to the restless brew. The freedom to exit is
not explicitly listed in the Bill of Rights, but it's among our most precious.[1]

We're still moving. "Where are you from?" has become a difficult question to answer. Each year, 17 percent of Americans change residences. By second grade, almost 40 percent of American children have already attended more than one school. Almost 3 percent of families move to another state each year; about 20 percent of workers change jobs.[2] A growing number are changing their spouses or partners, although not usually on an annual basis. More are lifting their faces, amplifying their busts, reinvigorating their erections. If people are not getting makeovers, they are *starting* over. The very idea of "settling"— settling down, settling in, settling for second-best—runs against the national grain.

When I travel abroad, I'm always asked: Why aren't you Americans ever satisfied with what you have? I tell them it's in the genes, maybe the water. The American historian Frederick Jackson Turner saw the American frontier as "the great escape from the bondage of the past," and rued its closing in the last decade of the nineteenth century as a constraint on the American spirit.[3] But Turner barely lived to hear of the automobile, and never contemplated the Sunbelt, the suburbs, television, and cyberspace. The American cannot be contained.

We never cease to talk about *going*. "Go West, young man," urged Horace Greeley, the editor of the *New York Tribune,* a century and a half ago.[4] A generation ago, someone with notable ambition was said to have "get-up-and-go"—among the highest of compliments. A "go-getter" is admirable; he or she doesn't wait for opportunity to knock. Express hesitation about doing an ambitious thing, no matter how rash, and someone is sure to urge you to "go for it." (I once briefly considered a bungee jump. The portion of my brain governing judgment won out after a few seconds, but in the brief interval of equipoise a stranger shouted these three words so loudly that I almost dropped off the precipice anyway, minus cord.) Not to "go" when the going is good is a sign of moral weakness, a lack of gumption and grit. The characters of Horatio Alger's popular novels went for it—from rags to riches.

The insistence on a better deal didn't begin in America, nor is it this culture's exclusive province. It's just more extreme here. For most of its history, humankind lived in small villages surrounded by dense forests, deserts, wide savannahs, nearly impassable mountains, or otherwise dangerous and mysterious terrain. Travel was perilous, information scarce. Most people died in the village where they were born. The history of modern Western civilization—the great waves of exploration, expansion, and invention that commenced in the fifteenth century—can be understood, in part, as the continuous pursuit of better deals.

Motivated by a mixture of curiosity and greed, Western capitalism grew and spread. The historic steps constitute well-known chapters of history books: The Age of Exploration, the Age of Imperialism, the first Industrial Revolution, the Age of Mass Production that ushered in the great industrial consolidations at the start of the twentieth century. But the chapters oversimplify. History was never this neatly sequential, nor as innocent as these titles suggest. There were periods of confusion and backsliding, of reaction and bloody repression. All that can be said with confidence is that those who wanted something better, and had the best tools at their disposal to get it, gained ground. If history is written by the winners, it is won by the most ambitious.

THE WORLD IS in the midst of another great opening: the Age of the Terrific Deal. It started in America several decades ago and has been gathering momentum ever since. It's about to accelerate very sharply. It's based on technology and imagination. Combine the Internet, wireless satellites, and fiber optics, great leaps in computing power (through circuits no wider than a few atoms), a quantum expansion of broadband connection (transmitting more and faster digital data into homes and offices through networks of fiber-optic cables and constellations of satellites), a map of the human genome and tools to select and combine genes and even molecules—and you've got a giant, real-time, global bazaar of almost infinite choice and possibility.

Finding and switching to something better is easier today than at any other time in the history of humanity, and in a few years, will be easier still. We're on the way to getting exactly what we want instantly, from anywhere, at the best value for our money.

EXACTLY WHAT YOU WANT

Until recently, the major difficulty in getting exactly what you wanted was oftentimes the extra cost of making one-of-a-kind. I'm all of four feet ten inches tall, with a waistline significantly larger than that of a ten-year-old boy, which means that if I'm to look even vaguely respectable, anything I wear has to be custom-tailored. It is a royal pain, and often I don't bother. But recently I discovered the Web site of a clothing manufacturer on which I can enter all my size specifications and select the shirts and trousers (along with fabrics and styles) I want. Within days the garments arrive at my front door. When I first ordered, I expected the tailor who received my improbable measurements to assume they were mistaken, and change them (this had happened before). But the shirt and trousers fit perfectly. And then it hit me: I wasn't dealing with a tailor. I was transacting with a computer that had no independent judgment.

In the pre-industrial era, craftsmen made almost everything to order, but this was expensive. Then came mass production—giant machines powered by electricity; large looms capable of weaving great sheets of cloth; machines that spit out tens of thousands of matches, cigarettes, and nails; giant vats distilling and refining petroleum, sugar, alcohol, and chemicals; huge furnaces for making steel; big molding and stamping machines turning out auto parts; and then vast assembly lines. As the scale of production grew, the cost of each item produced plummeted.

But the logic of mass production dictated sameness. The first mass-produced shoes in America were called "straights," because they didn't distinguish between left and right feet. Henry Ford's assembly line lowered the cost and democratized the availability of the automobile, but did so by narrowing choice. "Any customer can have a car painted any color that he wants, as long as it's black," he famously offered.

In order to ensure a profit, mass-producers had to invest up front and then predict how many identical items could be sold and at what price. Accuracy of prediction brought high reward; inaccuracy could mean bankruptcy. Improving the odds by stabilizing the market became the core managerial task of the twentieth century. There were essentially four rules: (1) To avoid the possibility that suppliers might unexpectedly raise prices or competitors might overtake their own product with new inventions, producers bought or merged with other producers—enabling the few survivors within each industry to coordinate plans informally thereafter. By the midpoint of the twentieth century, economists spoke with awe and no small discomfort about "oligopolies," such as the Big Three automakers and the five major steelmakers. (2) Where oligopolies didn't evolve on their own, regulatory agencies set prices and standards. That such agencies protected consumers from fly-by-night operators and unpredictable service was not inconsistent with their simultaneous roles as guardians of industry stability and bulwarks against excessive competition. (3) To avoid wildcat strikes and work stoppages, producers eventually, grudgingly, accepted organized labor. By the middle of the twentieth century, almost 40 percent of America's working people belonged to a union—often organized by industry so that no individual company would be at a competitive disadvantage relative to others, and so that wage and benefit increases could be conveniently passed along to customers in the form of higher prices. (4) Finally, to reduce the risk that consumers might fail to buy as many items as were planned, producers embarked upon campaigns of mass persuasion. Madison Avenue burst forth with jingles, contests, and, by midcentury, that great monument to American ingenuity—the thirty-second television commercial. Thus was the American consumer—eventually the world consumer—lured into wanting that which was made available in large quantities. Mass persuasion did not always work, as evidenced by the Edsel and the New Coke, but the occasional failure did not detract from the effectiveness of the overall approach.[5]

As a result of all this effort to guarantee a large and stable market for what was mass-produced, consumers got many more things, more cheaply. It was a virtuous cycle: Mass production begot mass marketing, which whetted appetites for more mass consumption, which, in turn, enlarged the system of mass production. But notably, choices were limited in order to reap the full efficiencies of large scale, and products didn't change much from one year to the next. It was a small price to pay for the boon.

The emerging system is starkly different. I have detailed elsewhere the shift, starting in the 1970s and escalating since, from high-volume to high-*value* production, from standardized to more customized, rapidly improving products and services—in steel, plastics, chemicals, telecommunications, transportation, finance, entertainment, and many other industries.[6] Increasingly, digital technologies now enable sellers to tailor products to suit particular buyers while still keeping production costs down. There is no need to guarantee a large, stable market for every item.

How did I get my made-to-order shirts and slacks so cheaply? It was thanks to programmable robots, numerically controlled machine tools, computerized routing systems, and the Internet. Unlike the old machines and assembly lines that could do only one thing over and over, these new systems can instantly make one-of-a-kind, and then just as quickly make a different one-of-a-kind. My order went directly into a computer, where it was turned into digital symbols and then sent to a machine that took a piece of fabric, cut it to my specifications, and sewed it together in a flash. Then the finished product came back to me. Human beings along the way programmed the robots, designed the software, devised the Web site, and marketed it. I suspect that a few people still cut and sewed some of the pieces by hand, in barely sanitary conditions and for third-world wages.

The new global bazaar is connecting unique buyers with sellers who can meet their needs directly, eliminating the high-volume bottleneck in between. Made-to-order is becoming the rule. You can already custom-order your computer, your daily (or hourly) news, your car. Last Christmas, Nordstrom.com offered a choice of several million styles of shoe, tailored to customer specifications. A builder friend custom-orders the doors and windows he needs; the mill at the other end uses laser-guided machinery to cut the wood to my friend's exact specifications. "On-demand printing" will soon allow you to get any out-of-print book that is stored on a publisher's computer database. Soon to come: customized appliances, personalized music, made-to-order vitamins, medicines tailored to your genes.

Economies of production scale still matter, but less than they did. And the trend is away from making a large amount of the same identical, unchanging thing. In fact, in an era when customers crave what's new and unique, large-scale production can be risky. Any enterprise dedicating itself to just a few lines is competitively endangered. The "shelf life" of products is continually shrinking. New software renders older software obsolete. So-called "killer apps"—fundamentally new ideas, products, and ways of doing business—alter the terms of competition for entire industries suddenly, without warning.

Yes, companies are merging into giant telecommunications-entertainment-Internet-financial behemoths, and the range of retail outlets continues to shrink. But, in most cases, the advantage of this sort of concentration is not in production scale; it's in marketing and brand recognition—an issue to which I'll return in the next chapter. Large size and a stable market are no longer prerequisites for low-cost production. Few companies any longer aim to sell a fixed volume of anything. This means they're less dependent on a steady source of supply, and on a predictable mass market. And fewer industries are dominated by oligopolies. Competitive strength now turns on being better, faster, and cheaper than rivals. Mass marketing and advertising are giving way to pinpoint marketing directed to unique customers (like abnormally sized middle-aged men). Network-television audiences are dropping off. Mass-market magazines are losing readers.

Nimble businesses now jump into new markets, because they don't need large production scale to succeed. Musicians connect up with individual listeners directly over the Web, circumventing the high-volume record companies that used to intercede between them. Sellers of antiques and junk and items in between find buyers through e-auction houses. E-traders circumvent stock exchanges and brokers and, if they wish, trade online twenty-four hours a day, withdrawing from the rest of the human race. Magazines exist for every taste, a number of them utterly tasteless, almost three new ones launched *every day*. And you can find a vast array of one-of-a-kind products designed to order: the music of Wales or eastern Kentucky or eighteenth-century Korea, love poems of the Renaissance containing the name Clare. I recently read of a Web site featuring photographs of comely models who were auctioning off their eggs to the highest bidders (federal law prohibits trafficking in human organs, but not in eggs, at least not yet).

Micro-businesses hire Web designers to set up sites and pay an Internet service provider a monthly fee to house them; rent software for ordering and billing; contract for shipping and delivery; rent a secure-server line for credit-card transactions, and have a bank manage them. If such businesses need it, they can tap into a global reservoir of expertise. They can find all these services on the Internet, where they find their customers as well.

Regulatory barriers have been disappearing largely because upstart businesses and leading-edge innovators want in—and are gaining enough economic muscle to open the regulatory gates, or hop over them. Feisty discount airlines, innovative banks and financial institutions, and entrepreneurial telecommunications cable and wireless companies have all seen opportunities to profit. The old walls are tumbling.

This is not to argue that all large-scale commodity businesses will vanish and all the routine work that supports them will disappear. My claim is about the direction of change. One of the major effects of the new communication, transportation, and information technologies is to alter the terms of competition—reducing the advantages of mere production scale, and rewarding producers who can quickly improve products and services and invent new ones that delight customers even more. Buyers are getting far better access to exactly what they want.

FROM ANYWHERE

Distance used to be the second big constraint. Most of what people used came from nearby, and if they lived far from others, they had to do most things for themselves. In the eighteenth century, as Adam Smith observed, "[i]n the lone houses and very small villages which are scattered about in so desert a country as the Highlands of Scotland, every farmer must be butcher, baker, and brewer for his own family."[7] Even by the mid-nineteenth century, most economies were still local. Connections were difficult. A letter sent from New York arrived in Chicago ten days later.

Then came the modern industrial era of steam engines, railroads (along with refrigerated boxcars), and the telegraph. Food could be delivered at longer distances without perishing. Messages could be sent across the nation in minutes. Materials could be gathered from thousands of miles away; shipped to central locations, where they were processed, boiled, bent, or bolted in large quantity; and emerge as finished products to be sent to all corners.

The twentieth century added cargo ships, interstate highways pummeled by gigantic haulers, jumbo jets carrying freight in railroad-sized containers, overseas cables, and eventually fiber-optic cables and satellites bouncing electronic signals from one continent to another. Giant factories could be placed anywhere labor was cheap and transportation adequate. Mom-and-pop shops gave way to department stores, followed by large chains, giant discount houses, "super stores," and 1-800 numbers attached to sprightly catalogues whose sundries arrive on doorsteps—overnight if required—via United Parcel Service or Federal Express.

In the emerging global bazaar, distance itself is on the way to all but vanishing. The economy is moving away from things toward weightless services that can be transmitted anywhere around the world at almost no cost. More of the market value of almost everything bounces off satellites or moves through fiber-optic cables at the speed of light. In 1984, about 80 percent of the cost of a new computer was hardware, 20 percent software. Now the ratio is reversed, and it keeps widening. Eventually hardware will all but vanish too, replaced by wafer-thin devices that are little more than software downloaded and upgraded from anywhere.

The real value of my shirt-and-trouser order lies in the system that translates it into digital instructions along the way, monitors every step to make sure it's done quickly and correctly, and then speeds it back to me. The apparel industry that departed New England in the first half of the twentieth century in pursuit of cheaper labor in the South, and then promptly moved on to Southeast Asia, where labor was even cheaper, is being transformed largely into design, marketing, and software systems located wherever the designers, marketers, and software engineers reside. Only a small fraction of the price of a final garment has anything to do with routine sewing and cutting. I'm mostly buying intangible services.[8]

With everything a click away, there's less reason to shop locally. Local economies won't vanish any time soon, but the Internet will steadily erode them. Your selection of books used to be limited by what the local bookstore had in stock or could order for you; then came the giant chains with more selection, discounts, and speedier special orders; then, Internet e-tailers like Amazon.com, from which you can get virtually any book in print within a few days even if you live a hundred miles from a bookstore. Now, "e-books" can go directly from the author to your computer. Soon, the contents of books will be downloaded off the Web into your own digital book device. You'll be able to curl up at night with a good byte.

You no longer need the local pharmacist to fill your prescription, or even a local doctor to give you one. Web-based cyber-docs advise and dispense more cheaply (though they're sometimes less interested in your medical condition than in the condition of your credit card). And if your cyber-doc won't cooperate, you can get hormone supplements, steroids, aphrodisiacs, and almost any other pill your mind or body desires over the Web without a presciption, from anywhere around the world (a prospect that should thrill neither the Food and Drug Administration nor the parents of rebellious teenagers).

Films and videos will go directly from editing rooms to your home screen by way of the Internet; they're already starting to go to movie theaters this way. Educational lectures, seminars, books, materials, and tests will emanate from learning centers located anywhere, delivered to students residing anywhere.

You'll circumvent local car dealers and garage mechanics. Already much of the value of a new car lies in the tiny electronic devices that tell it how best to follow your instructions when you innocently press on the accelerator or turn the wheel. The rest is a plastic-and-steel container—a body without a brain. In a few years, technicians will be able to repair these tiny car brains from anywhere, much as telephone-company technicians can now fix your line from remote locations. You'll be able to upgrade your car's brain—getting more power, better fuel economy, higher performance overall—without even taking it to a shop for a brain transplant. You'll get a menu of new functions over the Internet, click on the ones you want, and—presto—a functionally new car will be waiting in your driveway. It may look like your old one, but its upgraded brain will make it perform better. The cost of shipping it to you, from anywhere, will be minuscule.

Similarly, refrigerators eventually will emit tiny electronic pleas for help when something goes wrong, and will then be repaired online. Computer systems will be repaired, reconfigured, and upgraded through the Internet. The readouts from tiny electrocardiogram devices implanted in your chest will be checked by online doctors.

Once, people lent money to one another within the same town or city. Remember the scene in *It's a Wonderful Life* when Jimmy Stewart tries to explain to panicked depositors who want to withdraw their money that their savings aren't in the bank but are financing one another's homes and businesses? "The money's not here! Your money's in Joe's house . . . next to yours!" That was then. Now, the residents of Bedford Falls are putting their savings into a vast reservoir of global capital that sloshes this way and that, seeking the highest return at the lowest risk all over the world. In recent years, the volume of global trading in financial securities has grown much faster than the national products of rich nations. The biggest profit comes from correctly guessing where all this money will slosh to next.

TRADE BARRIERS have been falling for decades, but the bigger trend is that fewer things are being traded relative to intangibles. An ever-larger portion of international commerce comes in the form of videos, music, film, television shows, news, designs, software, and business services (management consulting, marketing, financial, legal, engineering) that no longer need be located near their clients.[9] By the end of the twentieth century, a dollar's worth of imports and exports weighed, on average, only about 30 percent of what it did thirty years before,[10] and the weight loss is accelerating.

You often hear about technology and globalization as if they are separate trends, but they are becoming one and the same. Global trade and finance depend on technological advances that can move digital symbols instantly; and technologies are advancing because of intensifying competition from all over the world to do all sorts of things better, faster, and cheaper. Both the English language and widely utilized software standards are emerging as universal systems of worldwide communication because so many new technologies depend on them.

That people in an advanced economy spend more on weightless intangibles than on three-dimensional objects causes some folks of literal bent to feel vaguely uncomfortable, but the trend should be of no concern. The vast majority of those living in the midst of advanced economies don't have serious difficulty acquiring adequate food, clothing, shelter, and the other tangible necessities of life. The greater value, and more eager expenditure, comes in the psychological domain: speed and convenience, entertainment, intellectual stimulation, feelings of well-being, and financial security. It's the rare human being who can obtain enough of these; greater wealth only whets the appetite for more.

A neighbor of mine with a satellite dish atop her garage now claims to receive 1,500 television channels. I don't know how she manages. It must take her several days just to surf through them, and the better part of a day just to read through a schedule of what's showing. She seems delighted with her acquisition nonetheless. At this writing, there are 2.8 million Web sites, totaling 800 million pages. The most sophisticated search engine plumbs no more than 16 percent of them.[11] By the time you read this, the number of sites may have tripled. Anyone who attempts to surf this ocean risks drowning. Yet my younger son and his teenage friends spend several hours every day exploring it, downloading music, trading video clips, chatting endlessly to one another—all of these operations occurring simultaneously, at a switching speed so fast as to be incomprehensible to anyone over the age of thirty.

AT THE BEST PRICE AND HIGHEST QUALITY

The third old constraint, also disappearing, is lack of information about where a better deal can be found. Comparison shopping used to be a hassle. I remember traipsing after my parents around Peekskill, New York, on a hot summer Saturday afternoon in the early 1950s as they went from one car dealer to the next, seeking the best possible deal on a sedan. Whenever they had almost reached a decision, my father would want to check "one last time" with a competing dealer to see if he could get a better price. By the end of the afternoon, my parents were confused and exhausted, and I had a headache. Everyone knew that the "manufacturer's list" price was only a starting-place for haggling, and that the dealer's lament—"Sorry, that's the best I can do"—got you only halfway to a final offer. For less pricey items—home appliances, hardware, white goods—you could rely on ads in the local newspaper announcing special sales, but they lasted only a "limited time" and were for a "limited supply." Big discounters swore they wouldn't be "underpriced" and would match any deal you could get anywhere else, but to hold them to that bargain, you had to find that better deal somewhere else.

Comparing quality was even more of a challenge. Big-ticket items were alike in many respects, thanks to mass production and oligopolies. But items often came with different frills, add-ons, and options. Automobile dealers were known to advertise sales on cars stripped down to almost a bare chassis. A "vacation package" including five nights at a "luxury" resort in Bermuda turned out to be less than anticipated: the flight was in an ancient DC-9 that had to be refueled twice on the way, the resort was last refurbished in 1948, and the bedsprings were shot. More recently, the HMO that looked like health-care heaven in the brochure was less than heavenly once you enrolled: The doctors had the bedside manners of short-order cooks, and they wouldn't refer you to a specialist until you showed signs of imminent demise.

Not even a diligent buyer could comparison-shop among more than a handful of sellers—usually those in the vicinity that advertised in the local newspaper or were listed in the Yellow Pages, or were known to neighbors and friends. You knew that if you stuck with familiar national brands, you wouldn't go far wrong. But if your search involved products or services that were complicated, or unique, or to which people were likely to react differently depending on their tastes and temperaments, you stayed close to home, where you could inspect it for yourself and get information firsthand.

Until quite recently, most high school seniors contemplating higher education had their sights on the local college or, if more ambitious, the state university. Even those who might otherwise have qualified for scholarships to the world's fanciest ivy-infested citadels didn't venture too far away. They and their parents simply didn't know enough to weigh the advantages. The same principle governed your choice of hospital: It was the one close by, or in the region—even if you needed a heart bypass. That would apply in your choice of lawyer, mortgage lender, and car dealer as well.

But all this is changing as new communication, transportation, and information technologies allow readier comparisons. Through the Internet, buyers are beginning to get reliable data on prices and quality on a wide range of products and services from all over. Universities, hospitals, law firms, banks, and car dealers are competing for customers at far greater range, sometimes nationally, occasionally internationally. It's as if all sellers of all products and services have suddenly been placed next to one another in a global bazaar in which all prices, and all information about quality, are immediately apparent to all buyers. The more sellers who appear in the bazaar—who post their own Web sites, offer goods and services online, participate in online auctions, contribute information to various portals—the more isolated and marginalized are those who don't. Join the bazaar or die. But if you join, be ready for fierce head-to-head competition.

You can shop for a car loan or negotiate the terms of a mortgage loan on the Web. Several students have told me they (or their parents) made their final college selection on the basis of which institution gave them the best tuition deal—negotiations made easy over the Internet. Business customers are requiring their suppliers to bid against one another in Web-based auctions. And e-clearinghouses are becoming as ubiquitous as summer garage sales. Sellers are starting to offer deep discounts on remaining items that otherwise would be thrown away—aircraft about to depart with empty seats, trucks returning from a delivery with near-empty containers, hotels reaching the end of the day with empty rooms, radio stations about to broadcast with advertising time still unfilled, colleges about to begin the term with empty slots.

There's a race to provide useful ratings and reviews, as in comparisons of insurance agencies (premiums and payouts); of universities (tuition and fees, and placement of graduates in good jobs); of hospitals (the number and kind of successful operations performed in each, their mortality rates and costs); of law firms (the ratio of cases they've won relative to those they've lost, the average amount of money they have gained or lost in settlements, their hourly fees); of wages for people with certain skills; and of the price and quality of countless new digital, molecular, and genetic creations.

Someday we'll have our own personalized "bots"—the electronic equivalent of golden retrievers—that can be programmed to run into cyberspace and fetch the best deals for us. And as more and more of us sell our own services in the open market, the global bazaar will offer buyers comparative data on our backgrounds, skills, and past performance. *We* will be that which is retrieved.

EYE-POPPING DEALS and bargains, opportunities never dreamed of—exactly what you want, from anywhere, at the best price and value. We are not there yet, and may never be entirely, but the trend is unmistakable—and it is accelerating quickly. It is happening because new technologies are expanding choices and making it easier to find and switch to something better. The wider choices and increasing ease of switching are intensifying competition among sellers. This, in turn, is putting ever-greater pressure on them to offer terrific deals. As a result, the choices continue to widen and improve. The deals are getting even better, the opportunities bigger, the possibilities seemingly limitless. It's a virtuous circle, and we buyers are the beneficiaries.

Were this the entire story, we would live happily ever after, and this book would be very short. But there's more to life than getting terrific deals. We're not only buyers and investors. Most of us also have to work for a living. In addition, we have relationships that are important to us, that help define who we are and what we want from life—our families, friends, and communities. The emerging economy is altering these aspects of our lives as well. And our working lives and our lives outside paid work are not being altered for the better in every instance. The Age of the Terrific Deal comes with a catch. Herein lies the dilemma of our time.

CHAPTER TWO

The Spirit of Innovation

A S NEW TECHNOLOGIES GIVE all buyers wider choice and easier access to something better, they render all sellers less secure. Most people would rather feel secure than insecure, but insecurity is not bad for an economy. It spurs innovation, the other major principle of the new economy. Understanding it is the next step to understanding what's happening to the rest of our lives.

THE NEO-LUDDITE FALLACY

First, though, we need to dispense with a myth. Some future-gazers confuse insecurity with joblessness, and fret that advancing technologies eventually will eliminate jobs.[1] They are as wrong as their forebears, the Luddite machine-breakers of early-nineteenth-century England who destroyed power looms that were forcing weavers out of work. New technologies surely will force people to change or alter their jobs, but they won't reduce the amount of paid work. There's no natural limit to what people want and are willing to pay others to do for them. Nor is there a finite amount of human intelligence and imagination capable of discovering what can be done, or done better.

As societies become richer and as technology makes all sorts of things more affordable and accessible, an ever-larger portion of personal income will be spent on insatiable wants that extend infinitely beyond bare needs for adequate food, clothing, and shelter. No matter how much people possess of these insatiables, they will always want more. It's in these domains that you can expect the economy to grow and future jobs to multiply.

Health. Regardless of how good human beings feel and how long they live, they will always want to feel better and live longer. So there will be no end to the demand for advice, medications, gadgets, treatments, and exercise regimes that prolong bodily existence and well-being.

Entertainment. Regardless of how much people already enjoy life, they will want more fun, thrills, surprise, suspense, titillation, excitement, and aesthetic pleasure. Hence, there will be no limit to the demand for entertaining films, videos, theatrical presentations, music, sporting events, travel, and stories, or for death-defying experiences like hang-gliding, bungee-jumping, or visiting a theme park with a three-year-old.

Attractiveness to others. No matter how lovely people are, most of us want to be more appealing. As a result, there will be a limitless market for such things as fashionable apparel, cosmetics, breath fresheners, straight teeth, tummy tucks, tanning creams, hair dyes, diets, and inexhaustible advice for how to become more sexy, charming, persuasive, or otherwise enticing.

Intellectual stimulation. Despite the psychic damage done by dreary years of formal education, most human brains still yearn to be provoked. So there will be no natural limit to the desire for news, information, explanation, historical description, and insight into why things happen the way they do.

Contact. Hermits and misanthropes aside, humans are social animals with an insatiable need to connect with other humans. Hence, there will be a limitless market for faster, easier, cheaper, and more convenient means of connecting, and also of being pampered, cared for, massaged, and sexually delighted.

Family well-being. Humans are hard-wired for altruism, especially toward those whose genes most closely resemble their own. Family feuds notwithstanding, there's no natural limit to the happiness or health most people desire for their children and closest kin. Hence, an abundance of products and services to care for, educate, inspire, and otherwise ensure the welfare of loved ones.

Financial security. Money doesn't bring happiness, but it is a means of acquiring any of the above, which can. As a result, there will be an almost limitless market for financial advice and planning, schemes to maximize returns on savings, and insurance against bad luck.

These wants can't be "satisfied" in the sense that hunger or sleep or even ambition can be. But with the possible exception of attractiveness, gratification doesn't depend on acquiring more than others have acquired; it can be achieved regardless of relative position. And since the supply of these wants depends more on good ideas than on scarce resources, one person's enjoyment doesn't necessarily come at the expense of another's.

These seven areas represent fast-growing markets within which a large proportion of the workforce will be creating and distributing products, services, and advice in the decades ahead. Such work will find its way into computer software, engineering designs, Web pages, financial services, statistical analyses, musical scores, film scripts, and advertising. Advancing technologies will help idea generators accomplish all such work better and quicker, giving them greater leeway for their imaginations.

Another portion of the workforce will respond to these wants in person. Such work will include the pampering of bodies and minds through what are now called recreation specialists, aerobics instructors, personal trainers, massage therapists, tour guides, spiritual guides, personal coaches, teachers, drivers, waiters, and the like. It will also include caring for infants and children, the sick and the mentally disabled, and, increasingly, the elderly. By the second decade of the twenty-first century, millions of corroding baby boomers will need a lot of personal attention. The boomers will not go quietly. Expect an outcropping of "Med-Meds"—the equivalent of Club Meds with medical facilities built in. Scuba in the morning, emergency oxygen in the afternoon.

The biggest difference between the old work and the new is the sharply accelerating pressure to do it all better, faster, and cheaper. How much better, faster, and cheaper? There's no necessary limit. Even scientific barriers once thought impervious are yielding.

THE NECESSITY OF BETTER,
FASTER, AND CHEAPER

The economic system that dominated most of the twentieth century allowed producers and sellers a fairly relaxed existence. Economies of production scale and stable markets (with their corresponding oligopolies and regulations) protected large enterprises against unruly competition. Small, neighborhood sellers competed only with other local shops and services.

With enterprises, as with people, a comfortable existence tends to weaken motivation to work hard. The old industrial economy did not, for the most part, ignite great entrepreneurial zeal. Big companies maintained research and development departments that produced a steadily respectable output of patented invention, but major breakthroughs were rare, and intended to be so. Too much change would threaten the capacity to plan, and might destabilize the system. Most innovation occurred at the margin, in cosmetic design rather than in the basics. Automobile tail fins grew longer, but the quality of suspensions and engines improved only gradually. "New and improved" dishwashing detergents and kitchen appliances appeared with predictable regularity but were never especially new, nor very improved.

By the middle decades of the twentieth century, sellers could be relaxed about controlling their costs. With unions negotiating wage rates for entire industries, wage increases could be passed along to consumers in the form of higher prices without imperiling any particular company. Nor were sellers interested in squeezing their suppliers unduly. Any change of supplier threatened the efficiency of large-scale production, whose smooth flows required long-term contracts and stable relationships.

As a result of these accommodations of employees and suppliers, wages and prices tended to spiral upward. Price increases raised the cost of living, which caused workers to seek additional wage increases. Occasionally, government sought to control wages and prices directly by establishing official wage and price ceilings or by "jawboning" industrial and union leaders to keep prices within bounds, but to no great effect. Inflationary cycles gathered momentum until the Federal Reserve Board raised interest rates and plunged the economy into recession.

The emerging economy provides a telling contrast. As noted, buyers are less constrained by production scale, distance, or information. With access to a widening choice of products and services coming from almost anywhere on the globe, and armed with better comparative data about price and quality, buyers can more easily switch to something better. The easier it is for buyers to switch to a better deal, the harder sellers have to work to attract them and to keep them.

Some researchers credit the recent upsurges in innovation and productivity exclusively, and simply, to new technologies. But they're leaving out the crucial steps that explain *why* sellers feel far more compelled to innovate. New technologies of communication, transportation, and information are empowering buyers to find and switch to something better. This, in turn, is putting pressure on sellers to produce better. In order to survive and prosper, sellers must continuously cut costs and add value, faster than their rivals. Not only do they have to offer better products and services, but they also have to continuously improve their organizations, to make them capable of generating whole streams of better products and services faster than the competition.[2]

This trend helps explain why inflation has become less of a threat, even during periods of low unemployment. Sellers continuously have to find new ways to slash costs and lower their prices in order to stay competitive. It also sheds light on why, after slumping in the 1970s, productivity (output per unit of labor input) has been rising. Companies have been under increasing pressure to do more with less.*

Fiercer competition has spread to nonprofit institutions as well. Even the stuffiest, most hidebound universities, hospitals, museums, and charities must now innovate, because they're subject to the same underlying dynamic that's affecting the rest of the economy. Attendees, patrons, and donors have an increasingly wider choice from

---

* Productivity grew at an anemic 1 percent per year in the 1970s, increased somewhat in the 1980s, then accelerated to 1.5 percent a year between 1990 and 1995, and almost 3 percent annually between 1996 and 2000. Even these official numbers may underestimate the recent gains. Productivity gains were easier to measure in an industrial economy in which products stayed roughly the same from year to year; it was just a matter of counting up how many more items were made per unit of work from one year to the next. But now that so many new products are better, faster, and cheaper than the ones they're replacing, such a simple tally doesn't reveal how much more value buyers are getting. On the other hand, the productivity gains of recent years may also be *overstated* somewhat because, as we shall see, most Americans are working longer hours than before—especially managerial, professional, and "creative" workers, who are putting in many extra hours at home and during travel. To the extent that these extra hours are not included in the calculation of output per unit of work time, there's an upward bias in the productivity data.

which to pick, better information about how each institution is performing, and greater capacity to switch to one that satisfies them more. So nonprofits have to be better, faster, and cheaper, too.

THE LOGIC OF INNOVATION

To understand this dynamic, it helps to go back to the musings of Joseph Alois Schumpeter. Schumpeter was a professor of economics at, successively, Graz (Austria), Bonn, and finally, Harvard, and also served as finance minister of Austria after World War I. Wherever he went Schumpeter cut a dramatic figure—aristocratic, romantic, and not unduly burdened by modesty. (Later in his life he said he had always had three wishes—to be a great lover, a great horseman, and a great economist—and that two had been granted.[3]) In *The Theory of Economic Development*, originally published in 1912, Schumpeter conceived of a world in which the entrepreneur played a central role.

Most economists still focus on how supply and demand come into balance, and how scarce resources are allocated most efficiently. Imbalances in supply and demand are considered to be inconvenient exceptions to the economists' model of perfect competition, caused by some external force like a flood, plague, or politics. But Schumpeter assumed that a healthy economy is never in tidy equilibrium; it's continuously wracked by invention and change. Innovation will occur most readily, he reasoned, when entrepreneurs are rewarded for their brave efforts by gaining a temporary monopoly on something for which consumers are willing to pay extra—but only temporary. Unless entrepreneurs feel threatened by new competition, they will have no incentive to continue to innovate. Economies, therefore, cannot progress without the "gales of creative destruction" wrought by such entrepreneurial *Sturm und Drang.*

As the twentieth century wore on and large-scale production came to dominate modern economies, Schumpeter became gloomy about the prospects for entrepreneurship. Everywhere he looked he saw businesses more interested in stability than in change. He failed to see, or to value, the benefits of mass production and mass marketing. Instead, Schumpeter dwelled on the lackluster managers and risk-avoiding paper-shufflers who were running large-scale enterprises. He gloomily predicted that capitalism would disappear into a static morass of bureaucratic socialism.[4]

But at the start of the twenty-first century, Schumpeter's dire prediction is being proven wrong. We're moving quickly into a neo-Schumpeterian world.

Try this mental experiment. Suppose you offer to sell X for the price of $Y. Assume you've already figured out how to make X better, faster, or cheaper than anyone else. Maybe no one else even imagined there was a market for X, and you're the first to sell it. Buyers begin flocking to you because you are offering them a terrific deal, and you start to make a lot of money. Schumpeter would be proud.

But now not only do additional buyers find out about the deal you're offering, but other sellers learn of it as well. Your prospective rivals may not know exactly how much you're pocketing, but they can probably deduce it because they can discover how much you're paying for all the ingredients that go into X, including labor. Information is cheap and readily available—and more so all the time. Soon a rival comes along who offers buyers the same deal, and draws off some of your profits. And then another rival, and another, until your profits shrink to almost nothing.

You might try to protect your newly invented X with patents or copyrights. These legal protections for "intellectual property" are similar to those that prevent people from stealing your three-dimensional property. But intellectual-property protections are of only limited help in the emerging economy. Simply by producing X and gaining a positive reaction from buyers, you've already revealed to your rivals that there's a market for X—and *that* particular information is often more valuable than any other. So, sooner than you'd like, one of them will figure out how to make or do X just as cheaply without infringing on your intellectual property. (Maybe he "reverse engineers" your X—takes it apart, and rejiggers it just enough to come up with another way to make it that circumvents your patent—or, if your X is a piece of software or a recipe or an artistic composition, he devises another way to express it that bypasses your copyright.) Perhaps he simply disregards your legal claim altogether and dares you to take him to court; he's much richer than you, and can afford a lengthy court battle. And even if you can afford it too, there's no guarantee you'll win: The heist of an idea can never be proven with the same certitude as the heist of a car. Courts increasingly are clogged with contentious brawls over who invented what and when.[5] (Calvin Klein alleges that Ralph Lauren's "Romance" fragrance infringes on Klein's best-selling "Eternity" cologne—but what, exactly, is an aroma, and is it possible to own one? A scent is also a mood, an image, a style. How to distill it from all that surrounds it, and turn it into property?)

Your profits shrink. Now you have three options: (1) You can figure out how to cut your costs and offer X for less than $Y. (2) You can figure out how to produce a much better X for the same cost. (3) You can use whatever expertise you've gained along the way to be the first out with an entirely new product (Z), which is something that buyers will like even more than they liked X and will pay a premium for. Any or all of these strategies will restore your lead—for a time. You should try all three, because you have no way of knowing in advance which one will work best. But beware: They're all costly, and risky.

The first strategy, to cut costs, is the least risky, but it will cost you in the short term because you'll have to pay to figure out how to make your operation more efficient. Say you hire a management consultant who recommends that you install new software that can accomplish more with fewer steps and fewer people on the payroll, outsource anything else that can be done more cheaply by a subcontractor, and cut the wages of your remaining employees—maybe give them a share in the profits instead or the option to buy shares of stock. You accept his advice and pay his bill. It occurs to you that you should have become a management consultant.

The second strategy, to improve the product, requires money for research and development, and then for marketing. It's a riskier strategy, because you can't be sure that what you consider a newly improved X will be perceived that way by customers. When it comes to product improvements, even Coca-Cola can blow it. But at least you know that your customers like X, so you can have some confidence they will respond well to a faster, more powerful, lighter-weight, tastier, or prettier X-plus.

The third strategy, coming up with a whole new product Z, is the costliest and riskiest of all. It requires more basic research, which, in the end, may yield nothing of value. Z is sufficiently different from X that you can't even be sure there's a market for it. On the other hand, if your gamble turns out to be on the money, the payoff from Z will be the highest of all. You're likely to have the Z market to yourself for a long time before your competitors can figure out how to produce their own versions.

Hopefully, at least one of these strategies will restore your profits long enough for you to recoup the costs of pursuing the others and still come out ahead. But here's the bad news, and I have saved it until now because I didn't want to discourage you: You will never reach a point where you can relax. Even if you succeed, your success will be temporary, because your competitors are sure to follow quickly. Years ago, in the industrial era, competition was more restrained because producers were tied to large-scale production. But now that rivals are nimble, there's no coasting. You may make a nice profit for a while, but in order to survive, you'll need to sink most of it back into the three strategies.

If you do well at this game—keep cutting costs, adding value, and inventing—you'll be able to attract partners or investors. You may even be able to issue a public offering of shares that makes you very rich, but you'd be wise not to count on it. More likely, your new partners or investors will provide just enough cash to allow you to place more bets on a wider assortment of innovations. The greater the number of bets you can make, the more likely one will pay off big enough to cover the other bets and allow you to keep a step ahead when rivals catch on.

Still, even with the additional capital, the race will never end. That's what Schumpeter liked about it. Every producer and seller is running scared—placing bets, working his tail off, watching his back. Andrew Grove, the voluble chairman of Intel, famously quipped that only the paranoid survive in the new economy. He could have added the obsessive and the compulsive. You may exhaust yourself, but thanks to your nonstop efforts the economy is brimming with innovation. Consumers are far better off.

THE NEW ROLE OF BRANDS

Even if you provide the best X at the lowest $Y, you may still starve. That's because there's so much "noise" in the marketplace—so many competitors jockeying for position, so many products and services contending for space, so many messages and solicitations vying for attention—that customers may never find you. You occupy but one booth in a giant worldwide bazaar in which tens of millions of other sellers are trying to lure customers their way. With millions of Web pages, 1,500 television channels available by satellite dish, plus the distractions of instant messaging, e-mail, fax, cell phones, videos, personalized mailings, an almost infinite capacity for custom design, and, soon, exponentially more of everything through broadband—how do you get yourself noticed amid the clamor? Or, to put it in Internet-speak, how do you attract traffic and eyeballs?

Your potential customers have the same problem, only in reverse. They're overwhelmed with information—sales pitches, commercials, bids, choices, visual clutter, noise. The emerging economy gives them great power to get what they want, if they can find it. As their choices escalate, so does their confusion. They need trusted guidance about where to find what they're looking for.

Word of mouth is surely helpful, to you and to them. A satisfied customer may tell her best friend or first cousin about the great deal she got from you, and this conversation may well lead to other sales. Sometimes Internet gossip can generate a powerful "buzz," creating almost instant demand for a particular movie or CD. But gossip is not especially reliable. Besides, by the time word spreads like this, your rivals will be on the move. Anything consumers learn, your rivals can learn just as quickly.

Mass marketing is inefficient because there's not likely to be a mass market for what you produce. You might try direct marketing—advertising in places where people who are apt to buy Xs and Zs are likely to lurk, or telemarketing to computerized lists of people who have bought similar products or services in the past. But this, too, is an expensive way of finding customers. You're still reaching a lot of people who have no conceivable interest, and you're missing many who would be interested.

Your best bet for finding your customers—and for them finding you—is to link up with a big brand that has a reputation for reliability. Trustworthy brands are becoming consumer guides through the jungle of the new economy. Their profits come from pocketing a portion of what consumers pay for what they find.

A well-known brand (including Internet portals and Web sites) may *appear* to have a large organization behind it, because its reputation is large. But in the new economy it need not have many—or any—tangible assets or employees. In the old industrial economy, large enterprises controlled large-scale systems of production and depended on economies of scale. In the new economy, businesses depend on economies of trustworthiness. Their economic value comes not from assets they own or employees they supervise but from the domain of trust they've established with buyers. The only thing the new "large" enterprise needs to control and continuously enhance is its most valuable asset: its reputation for getting customers the best buy. The more buyers who come to rely on it and are delighted by what they receive, the greater its reputation for leading buyers to the best deals—which, in turn, attracts more buyers.

The "largest" enterprises will thus be the brands that enjoy the largest economies of trust, which translate into large profits and high market value. At this writing, the company value per employee at General Motors—a company still largely based on economies of scale—is less than $100,000. But the value per employee at Microsoft, which is rapidly becoming a brand-portal relying on economies of trustworthiness, is more than $12 million; at Yahoo, a pure brand-portal, it's more than $22 million.[6] Although many "dot-coms" are now worth less than they were when investors' enthusiasm knew no bounds, it's likely that market valuations per employee will continue to rise for the leading-edge businesses of the economy.

Disney is a trusted guide to family entertainment. Its brand-portal leads customers to family vacations, films, videos, books, music, sporting events, and family activities online. The people whom Disney employs directly and the assets over which it has direct control contribute only a fraction of these offerings, and that fraction will decline in the future. Most "Disney" products and services will be produced independently. Disney will preselect them to be consistent with—and thus enhance its reputation for—high-quality family entertainment, and will take a small commission (or licensing fee, or markup) on the sale of each. If managed well, the Disney brand-portal will continue to develop greater economies of trust while depending less on its own economies of scale.

Dell has become a brand-portal for computers, and could easily extend its franchise to include other office equipment, telecommunications devices, and anything else that helps buyers work more efficiently. Dell makes none of its computers directly. It links its growing customer base with its widening base of suppliers over the Internet. Dell's subcontractors then assemble to order. Dell only attracts the customers—the eyeballs—and controls for quality. Then it collects a commission on each sale.

Most movies today are produced by small entrepreneurial groups that contract with "big" Hollywood studios to market and distribute their creations. At this writing, CBS/Viacom owns Nickelodeon, which produces the popular, cheerfully repellent *Rugrats* cartoons. But the actual work of creating them is done by a small independent group of animators that contracts with Nickelodeon. That is very much the case for the Rugrats movie, book, Web site, and other seemingly inexhaustible manifestations as well. Independent groups of workers create almost every other entertainment product, too. More than 90 percent of the roughly seven thousand entertainment firms in the Los Angeles area employ fewer than ten employees.[7]

Soon, record companies will no longer be in the business of manufacturing and distributing anything. What's the point, when music flows through the Internet like water through plumbing? If they're to survive, big brands like Warner Music, EMI, and Sony will have to specialize in finding great recording artists, and in marketing themselves to customers as great guides to the music customers will enjoy.

Every big brand is on the way to becoming a Web site or portal that electronically links the right buyers to the right sellers. Yahoo is a major gateway to Internet content; Charles Schwab, to financial services; Amazon.com, to books and music (and, most likely in the future, to any other intellectually stimulating or entertaining product that can be readily packaged and delivered). Other "large" businesses that once made things are transforming into matchmaking brands. IBM is making less of what it sells; more of its business is providing advice and technical assistance, and much of it over the Internet. Cisco's outside contractors take orders directly from its customers, and ship data-networking equipment without a Cisco employee's ever seeing it.

Harvard University is becoming the world's preeminent brand-portal for learning. It's the second most widely recognized brand in the world, just behind Coca-Cola, although McDonald's is closing in. Harvard confers its prestigious franchise on a wide range of research centers, institutes, executive programs, shirts, hats, pillowcases, stuffed animals, a health plan, a hospital group, magazines, journals, and a publishing house. It employs directly only a small fraction of the people who produce these goods and services; it collects royalties or commissions on the work of the rest.

Several years ago, I wrote a book that was published by Harvard University Press, and I still occasionally receive modest royalty checks from its sales. From time to time I write articles for the *Harvard Business Review* and am paid a small sum for them as well. So in this sense I'm still selling some of my services under the Harvard brand. Harvard retains most of the income paid by the recipients of my efforts, and remits the rest to me. The pay is not much, to be sure, and more erratic than it was when I once served on Harvard's faculty, but I profit from the institution nonetheless.

As major nonprofits become brand-portals to a wide range of profit-making enterprises, the distinction between nonprofit and for-profit is breaking down, although the Internal Revenue Service has yet to catch on. Nonprofit museums house for-profit retail stores and restaurants; they promote online for-profit gift shops, featuring knick-knacks made by for-profit knickknack makers; they rent their rooms and galleries for corporate functions and license their trustworthy names to a range of products sold for profit. Harvard is well positioned to be Harvard.com—a leading brand-portal for a wide range of educational services through the Internet, gathered from suppliers all over the world (some of them for-profit) and sold to people all over the world who have come to the Harvard brand as a trustworthy guide.[8] Some nonprofit brands are shedding their nonprofit cloaks to reveal what they're really selling. The New York Stock Exchange, nonprofit since its inception, is being reborn as a for-profit corporation. It has no other practical option. Electronic markets have been drawing customers away from it. The only way the Big Board can compete is by turning its brand into a profit-making portal, and becoming an e-market itself.

A CAUTIONARY NOTE ON
THE FRAGILITY OF TRUST

In the older economy, brands stood for particular products or services. Everyone understood that Ivory was a soap, and Disney a particular kind of filmmaker. The purpose of the brand was to induce consumers to buy particular, identifiable things. A company with a well-known brand name might extend its product line, but buyers still used the brand as a means of identifying specific goods or services. But in the emerging economy—with all its choice, noise, and clutter—buyers often don't know what they want, and use the brand-portal as a means of discovering it. Major brand-portals represent *solutions* rather than specific products. Disney is no longer a kind of cartoon. It's a guide to good family entertainment, available from a vast array of providers.

Brand-portals can keep their reputations for trustworthiness only if they continue to act as agents for buyers rather than sellers. They cannot be double agents. If a brand-portal directs buyers to a bad deal, or even a good one that's substantially inferior to one buyers might find elsewhere, buyers will lose confidence in the brand-portal as a whole—and that loss of confidence will harm all other sellers who depend on it for access to buyers. Every seller naturally wants to be linked to a highly regarded brand-portal, but the brand-portal's continuing value depends on its being linked only to sellers who can deliver. A brand's value deteriorates when it's no longer a terrific guide to what's terrific.

A brand-portal may, of course, advertise or promote particular products and services. But if it wants to preserve buyer trust, the brand-portal must distinguish between promotions and advice. When Amazon.com told its customers that certain books were "destined for greatness," or were "what we're reading," because the publishers of those particular books paid Amazon.com a handsome fee in return for such encomiums, buyers had reason to be skeptical about everything else Amazon.com recommended. When the AltaVista search engine places certain Web sites at the top of its search results because those sites paid for the privilege, it subverts buyer faith in the quality of the search. When drkoop.com—billed as "Your Trusted Health Network"—recommended certain hospitals and health centers because they paid drkoop.com to recommend them, visitors to drkoop.com may have appropriately wondered whether they were receiving the best health-care advice. Even the Harvard brand would lose some of its luster if buyers came to suspect that it could be used by any seller willing to pay the price; Harvard's lawyers, seeking to protect the value of the brand, know that Harvard Beer and the Harvard Diet would not burnish the Harvard image.

A brand-portal may also lose its identity if its scope becomes so broad that buyers no longer know what to trust it *for.* Disney can build up a trustworthy reputation for family entertainment, but not for beer and soft drinks. Amazon.com might be able to extend its trustworthiness to music and videos, but probably not as readily to vitamins and toothbrushes. Few would trust Microsoft to do their family finances (although they may well trust Microsoft as a source of financial software).

LARGE OR SMALL?

The dynamic I'm describing—the competitive necessity for small, entrepreneurial sellers to link up with large, trustworthy brand-portals, and for the large brand-portals to shift from making things to becoming one-stop buyers' agents—explains a seeming paradox of the modern economy. This is the simultaneous explosion of "niche" businesses along with a new wave of mergers and consolidations.

In fact, the two trends perfectly complement each other. Small, entrepreneurial groups are continuously finding new ways to produce better Xs for less $Y, and invent new Zs. These small enterprises are at the heart of the Schumpeterian process of innovation. Large brand-portals, meanwhile, are providing buyers with convenient, one-stop guidance through what's becoming an increasingly complex thicket of products and services. To survive and grow, brand-portals, too, must continuously find better ways of guiding.

The merger boom of recent years is fundamentally different from the boom that occurred between 1885 and 1910, which created General Motors, General Electric, AT&T, U.S. Steel, and the giant trusts, as well as similar consolidations abroad, such as Germany's Siemens. Then, the goal was to stabilize the market and gain economies of production scale. Now the primary goal is to market global brands. Today's media, telecommunications, and financial giants will succeed to the extent that they offer more convenient, recognizable, and trustworthy brand-portals—giving buyers better one-stop access and quality control, while giving entrepreneurial sellers more information about buyers' needs. Mergers will be less successful, perhaps calamitous failures, if their main purpose is to gain economies of scale for making a particular product. Speed and cleverness now count far more than production. In this, the giant bureaucratic organization cannot hope to match the small, entrepreneurial business.

The emerging relationship is symbiotic. Entrepreneurial groups specialize in creating great products. A comparatively few large brands (not necessarily owning many tangible assets or employing many people) function as trustworthy consumer advisers. It is possible, of course, that an entrepreneurial group may become so well known for a superior product that it eventually reverses the relationship. ESPN, the sports network, used to pay cable companies to carry it; now cable companies pay ESPN for the privilege. ESPN has become, in effect, a brand-portal all its own. But most of the time the two kinds of enterprise will complement each other—the first providing content, the second attracting the eyeballs. These alliances are the organizational building blocks of the new economy.

DESPERATELY SEEKING STICKINESS

Even when you attract a customer, your challenge as a seller is not over. You will have to keep the customer. She is able to abandon you instantly—click, surf, graze, roam, switch, and you're history. You're more dependent on her than she is on you, because the cost to you of winning a new customer is much higher than the cost to her of finding a new seller. The lyricist Oscar Hammerstein put it more succinctly than any modern business strategist: "Once you have found her, never let her go." Figure out how to make her stick with you.

There are several techniques to enhance your "stickiness." The simplest is to continue to reduce your price and otherwise add to the value of what you offer, so the customer won't have any reason to switch. Monitor your rivals carefully. If they find a new way to cut costs or improve quality, or invent something better, do the same immediately. Above all, pamper your customer. Delight her. Surprise her with your solicitude. Offer her special benefits if she remains loyal to you. Repeat purchasers of the 1950s were treated to endless quantities of S&H Green Stamps that they dutifully licked and pasted on thin rectangular pages into booklets that, when accumulated in sufficient number, could then be traded for toasters or carpet sweepers. But the Internet gives sellers many more options for rewarding loyalty. You can give buyers a wide range of discounts by sharing data with other sellers—airlines, car-rental companies, hotels, and theaters. Loyal Harvard alumnae (read: repeat donors) are rewarded with special trips, seminars, and visits with doddering faculty; loyal members of the Metropolitan Museum (repeat donors), with exclusive invitations to preview the next exhibit of Impressionists or antiquities; loyal hotel guests, with VIP check-in by the concierge instead of a line at the registration desk.

Encourage her to give you more details about herself so you can custom-tailor goods and services more exactly to her needs. The more data she gives you and the more you do with them, the closer your relationship will be—and the harder it will be for any rival to intrude. By now, my clothier (note the "my"—the ultimate sign of stickiness) knows the size of my head, neck, chest, waist, even my feet; my favorite fabrics, preferred colors, tastes in patterns and styles; where I have shopped before; my occupation; my favorite leisure activities. With every transaction, the company's software "learns" more about me—and can respond better to my needs next time, even anticipate them. I am bound to my clothier not out of loyalty or affection, but by its increasingly better-tailored responses to my every sartorial wish.

British Airways greets its frequent flyers with their favorite drink and newspaper, based on their choices on prior trips. An online florist maintains a list of birthdays and anniversaries its customers have celebrated with flowers in the past, alerts them by e-mail when the dates are again pending, even remembers what arrangements they purchased on the last occasion, and lets them send off a new arrangement at the click of a mouse. A hotel chain remembers that a guest played golf at one of its facilities, and when he reserves a room at another, automatically asks if he'd like to book a time for golf.

So-called "intelligent agent" software can cement the relationship. Amazon.com greets repeat purchasers at its Web site with customized recommendations for other books and music they may enjoy, based on analyses of previous orders. With additional data, an intelligent agent can deduce deep-seated preferences for a whole range of items. If a customer displays a preference for a particular kind of music, food, and book, for example, the agent can suggest a movie that may be equally appealing—by comparing the music, food, and books she has chosen to those of other people with similar tastes in music, food, and books, then noting which movies these others have enjoyed and deducing which of these movies she might enjoy, too. Your customer isn't as unique as she may prefer to think; somewhere in cyberland exists another person with her identical tastes. The more data the agent can gather about her, the closer it can come to finding her taste clone.

Big brands are ideally suited to aggregate such data. Customer databases will be another of their valuable assets, providing a means of linking repeat customers to sellers most likely to satisfy them. Should anyone be concerned about privacy, the market is likely to respond, at least in part. Presumably buyers who prefer that only certain purchasing data about them be used, and only for certain purposes, will be attracted to brand-portals that respect their preferences. And brand-portals sensitive to the possible misuse of such data will gain a competitive advantage over others.*

Of course, while stickiness is good for you as a seller, it's not necessarily good for your customers. Although they can get better-tailored goods and services as a result of the information they give you about themselves, such stickiness makes it harder for them to switch to one of your rivals. From your point of view, needless to say, that is exactly the point; if a rival had as much information about them as you do, he might be able to offer them even better deals. What is likely to happen eventually is that buyers will catch on to the commercial value of their own personal data. They'll "warehouse" it in data banks of their own making—"Me.com's"—which will give them the option of downloading the data to any seller in order to get the best deal. The emerging economy gives consumers power they have no reason to cede, and rivals for their business will ensure that they won't.

ULTIMATE STICKINESS

If all else fails, there's a final technique to help induce consumer loyalty: Create a system of interconnectivity that becomes so widely used that every seller has little choice but to use it, and every buyer who wants access has little choice but to buy from it. Ultimately sticky systems are like languages: If many people use one, others in the vicinity must do the same if they want to communicate efficiently. English is becoming the world's first universal language, because so many buyers and sellers are using it that other buyers and sellers around the globe have to use it to be part of the global market. Unlike real languages,

---

* I do not mean that laws or rules guarding privacy are unnecessary, but only that competitive forces will motivate sellers to be more responsive to customers' concerns about privacy than otherwise. Of course, in order for the market to work on its own, buyers would need to be aware of how personal information about them was being utilized. It can hardly be assumed that they will always know.

ultimately sticky systems are owned by private firms that can charge a fee to use them or advertise on them.

Initially, America Online wanted to create a closed system whose content (news, entertainment, and so forth) would be available only to those who paid for it. But it turned out that AOL's purchasers were less interested in AOL's content than in the ease with which they could communicate their own content through AOL's chat rooms and "instant messaging" system, which alerts e-mail users when one of their friends is also online and available to chat. So AOL changed strategy, connected its closed system to the Internet, and provided unlimited access for a fixed monthly fee. Soon, its system became a standard for online communication. And the more people who used it, the more of a standard it became. Stickiness resulted from the simple reality that consumers could not easily switch en masse to another e-communications system—even one that might be superior.

It's the same with marketplaces. When enough buyers and sellers congregate at any specific location, other buyers and sellers must go there as well in order to have an efficient means of trading. This ancient process—which gave rise to towns at natural ports, river forks, and mountain passes, and created specialized districts for trading particular things (stocks and bonds on Wall Street, diamonds in Amsterdam, pork bellies in Chicago)—is operating in cyberspace as well. When enough buyers and sellers of memorabilia, ephemera, and attic junk congregate in eBay's electronic auction house, other purveyors are drawn there because it's the best place to find good trades. Thousands of other Web sites are competing to become marketplaces specializing in the buying or selling of shares of stock, cars, homes, and sex, among other things.

But even ultimate stickiness is limited. Rivals will try to "unstick" your customers by offering a better or cheaper means of communicating. Some may offer free connectivity. In the summer of 1999, Yahoo and Microsoft began distributing software that could connect with AOL's popular "instant messaging," thus giving all Yahoo or Microsoft users access to the AOL system without paying AOL, and making AOL significantly less sticky. AOL executives claimed that Yahoo and Microsoft were infringing on its property, and muttered vaguely about a lawsuit. But in the end AOL relented; Yahoo's and Microsoft's deep pockets made litigation too costly, and besides, many of AOL's customers wanted to connect with Yahoo's and Microsoft's.

．　　　　．　　　　．

EVEN IF YOUR rivals don't unstick your consumers, the government may. Excessive stickiness can hobble innovation. That's why, under the laws of the United States and of most other capitalist nations, owners of brand names lose their exclusive trademarks when the brand becomes so widely used as to become part of the general language. Otherwise, continued private ownership would prevent rivals from offering competing products because the rivals wouldn't have words to describe them. "Aspirin" was once a trademark, but when buyers began using it as a generic description of a kind of pain reliever, it moved into the public domain, so that any competitor could sell its own brand of aspirin.

American antitrust enforcers are turning their attention to excessive stickiness, and away from mere size or dominance over a given market. The economy is changing so quickly that size and market dominance pose less risk than does ownership of a system of interconnectivity. Here's a case in point: At this writing, Microsoft owns the basic operating software going into almost all computers—Windows. When it sells Windows, Microsoft includes other products for free, such as browsers and e-mail servers. In 1998, the Justice Department sued Microsoft for monopolization. Microsoft objected. Surely, it argued, a single operating software standard is easier on consumers than many different, incompatible standards. And, besides, what's wrong with giving away browsers, servers, and other software? Consumers get a great deal this way, said Microsoft.

The problem was that Microsoft's Windows had become so ubiquitous that buyers and sellers of computers, browsers, and other software had little choice but to license it from Microsoft if they wanted to connect with everything else. This gave Microsoft power to effectively block new products using a different operating system. Arguably—and this was the real concern—it also gave Microsoft power to deter innovation by rivals. So ruled a federal judge.

To see why, imagine what would have happened a century ago had a company named Electrosoft patented the design of electrical plugs and sockets. Say its design has four prongs, arranged vertically—perhaps not the most efficient design possible, but Electrosoft is the first and biggest company in this new market for electrical appliances, so its four-prong vertical design becomes the standard. Soon all homes have

Electrosoft sockets in their walls, and all appliance makers have to use Electrosoft plugs.

The advantage of a uniform standard is obvious. Commercial chaos will reign if there are different kinds of sockets and plugs—some two-pronged, some five-pronged, some arranged horizontally and others on a diagonal. Houses will have to be equipped with all of them. Manufacturers will have to make, and retailers to stock, all kinds. Consumers may even be reluctant to buy new electric toasters or lamps because of the difficulty of matching plugs and sockets. Electrosoft's four-prong vertical standard has avoided all this confusion, and boosted the fledgling electric-appliance industry. Sales of electric appliances are soaring.

Because Electrosoft holds the patent, appliance makers and building contractors have to pay it a royalty every time they make or install a new plug or socket. As the money mounts up, Electrosoft becomes one of the most profitable companies in America, and the net worth of its president soars to a level approximately equaling the total net worth of the bottom half of all American families. But let us not indulge in envy. Electrosoft has invented something that makes all our lives easier, and is reaping the reward. Schumpeter would approve.

Now suppose Electrosoft starts marketing its own electric appliances along with plugs and sockets—and uses its huge profits to price the new appliances extremely low. It even gives away a free toaster or lamp with the purchase of any Electrosoft plug or socket. As a result, other manufacturers of toasters and lamps are wiped out. And potential inventors of future electric appliances don't even try. They figure, Why bother? There's no money to be made (unless they sell their invention to Electrosoft—but at a fraction of what it could have earned otherwise).

A few years later, the prices of Electrosoft toasters and lamps start rising because Electrosoft has no competition. Buyers have no alternative but to pay the higher price. Nor, for that matter, is there much new invention. Refrigerators and electric stoves don't make an appearance for two centuries, and when they do, each costs a small fortune. The lesson should be reasonably clear. What begins as a convenient standard can end up as a barrier to innovation.

Hence, the tradeoff: The Windows operating system, as a common standard, is a boon to buyers, as are the software "appliances," such as e-mail servers and Internet browsers, which Microsoft offers at no extra cost. Yet these won't be boons over the long run if they wipe out competitors. And Microsoft's strategy will be even more costly if it discourages future entrepreneurs who would otherwise create even better and cheaper software appliances: voice-recognition devices, video mail, three-dimensional Internet, and whatever else lurks just beyond imagination.

This trade-off isn't new. Every period of rapid technological change creates opportunities—and needs—for new products to help people use and make the most of new inventions. In the early 1880s, when lightbulbs were first invented, bulbs and sockets came in 175 different sizes. The threads on hoses, screws, and other industrial parts that were supposed to fit into one another were almost as varied. By the time a portion of Baltimore was already in flames, the city's governors discovered, too late, that almost none of its fire hydrants and fire hoses matched up with one another.

Common standards were needed. But rather than one company setting them, the standards were set by emerging industries as a whole, and made freely available to all comers. A standard for lightbulbs and sockets emerged in 1884, the two-prong plug and socket shortly thereafter. Standards for industrial threads were developed by the first decade of the twentieth century (a bit late for that section of Baltimore). In the early 1920s, Herbert Hoover, then secretary of commerce, created the National Bureau of Standards to hasten the development of all sorts of industry standards, free of charge. It was one of Hoover's finest achievements (several years later, he had the misfortune to be President when Wall Street crashed, and is remembered for little else). As a result, America got the best of both worlds. Uniform standards, combined with a lot of innovation and competition, created a steady steam of inventions that now fill homes and serve businesses.

Stickiness can be excessive if it slows technological change. Hence, it's important for laws and rules to prevent this from occurring. Even without the antitrust decree, Microsoft would still lose its highly sticky position if a competing language (like Java) or operating system (like Linux) gained enough followers. But in the meantime, it's not unreasonable that a product like Windows, which has become a basic standard, should be licensed by a different company from the one that sells software applications which run on it, or that it be available to everyone free of charge. It has become part of our common language, like aspirin.[9]

REPRISE: INNOVATE OR DIE

A brief summary is in order. The first principle of the new economy is that choices are widening and it's becoming ever easier for buyers to switch and get a better deal. The second principle is that such breadth of choice and ease of switching is rendering all sellers less secure and more vulnerable to competitors—thus spurring innovation.

The American economy is moving from a system of stable, large-scale production to one of speedy and continuous innovation. Big brands are guiding customers to sellers who offer them the best deals. Rivals are doing whatever they can to "unstick" buyers and offer even better deals. Governments are turning their sights on excessive stickiness—private standards or protocols for interconnectivity that become so universal they stifle new ideas.

The winning competitors are quickest to provide lower prices and higher value through the intermediaries of trustworthy brands. But "winning" is temporary, and the race is never over. Those in the lead dare not stop innovating for fear of falling behind. The result is similar to the ideal Joseph Schumpeter envisioned, before the era of large-scale production made him cynical about entrepreneurship. We're witnessing an explosion of innovation, leading to better products and services. Productivity is rising, and inflation is moderating. Buyers are enjoying lower costs and better values.

The trend must not be overstated. There remain many sectors of the economy where large-scale production still prevails. Efficiencies of production scale will probably never entirely disappear. Innovation is occurring most rapidly where technologies are giving customers the widest choices and easiest means of switching to better deals: in entertainment, finance, new media, software, and Internet-based communications. Not incidentally, these also are the fastest-growing sectors of the economy. But others are also changing. Much of the retail sector is about to be transformed by the Internet. Old, heavy industries like autos, chemicals, and steel are shifting from high volume to more customized products and using Web-based business-to-business auctions to find the best suppliers. Construction, health care, publishing, and education (including higher education) remain far removed from the cutting edges of innovation.

You are also cautioned against confusing the longer-term trend I'm describing with the expansionary phase of a business cycle or with gains in the stock market. At this writing, the American economy has experienced the longest expansion in history, according to available historical data, and stock-market values are still high. By the time you read this, the expansion may have ended and the stock market may have corrected itself with a bruising thud. But the underlying structural trend discussed in these pages is likely to continue nonetheless. It depends less on overall levels of supply and demand, or on the exuberance of investors, than on technological innovation.

To the extent that technology is destiny, the spirit of innovation will eventually extend throughout the entire American economy, and to other economies around the world. This is unambiguously good news for every buyer who seeks a better deal. But the news is more ambiguous for other aspects of our lives, as we shall see. And although technology is setting the pace, our destiny is not beyond our control.

CHAPTER THREE

Of Geeks and Shrinks

Recently I received an e-mail from a former student who's working for a small company in New York. She's devising games that thousands of people can play with one another simultaneously over the Internet. "I'm spending six hours a day coming up with new ideas and twelve hours selling them," she wrote. "Cool stuff! And with my stock options, at the rate things are going, I'll be a multimillionaire in three years! Best to you!"

My former student may well be disappointed three years from now. But undoubtedly the demand for creative and innovative people like her is growing because of the increasing importance of innovation to the economy. Enterprises whose members discover the most imaginative possibilities, for which there's the greatest demand, generate the highest profits—at least until rivals catch up. Their brand-portals inspire the most trust. They are likely to be the "stickiest." And the people who contribute the most to them have (or have a shot at) the most lucrative and often the most interesting jobs found anywhere.

The demand for creative innovators continues to exceed their supply. As buyers switch more easily to better deals, competition is spreading and intensifying. Innovation is occurring in more places, among more products, inside more organizations. And wherever it occurs, it creates the competitive necessity among rivals to innovate as well. The supply of creative innovators, in other words, ignites still more demand for them. And as the demand for them grows, their economic rewards grow in tandem, because the supply can't keep up.[1] My former student, and legions of twenty- and thirtysomethings like her, are the direct and immediate beneficiaries.

There is a common misperception that today's innovators are particularly adept at using new information technologies, especially computers. I may have inadvertently contributed to this view by once using the term "symbolic analyst" to describe the top tier of workers, almost all well educated, who apply systemic thought to identifying and solving problems. Because the new technologies involve symbols and speed analysis, and because the advent of the personal computer roughly coincided with the time when the incomes of well-educated workers began to rise quickly relative to less-educated workers, it seems a logical inference that computers and related technologies are directly responsible. Further, it would seem likely that an education stressing analytic skills of a sort that would complement the new technologies is the best preparation for the work of the future. But these assumptions were, and are, incorrect.

In fact, many of the people who are gaining the most value in the new economy aren't especially skilled in using computers or other information technologies. Their value is only tangentially related to their computational prowess or capacity to solve complex problems. They are not even any longer accurately described as "knowledge workers," because any particular body of knowledge is now so easily encoded into software. The real value these people add to the economy derives instead from their creativity—their insights into what can be done in a particular medium (software, finance, law, entertainment, music, physics, and so on), what can be done for a particular market, and how best to organize work in order to bring these two perspectives together. They are *creative* workers.

My former student has no particular technical expertise. She majored in art. But she apparently has a wellspring of good ideas about how people might want to be linked in cyberspace through giant games they can play together. Her value turns on her inventiveness and her insights into the market, rather than her knowledge of digital technology.

The new information technologies are important, but their effects are indirect: They magnify good ideas. Technology increases the value of creativity by allowing it to be spread quickly throughout an organization's network and, ultimately, to consumers. As noted, it also gives consumers more choices, and thus increases the pressure on all sellers to innovate. Great ideas are the new currency of the realm. Information technology is the bank that circulates the coins ever more efficiently.[2]

Some people may be more creative than others owing to innate talents, perhaps found in genes somehow linked to creative insight. But much of creativity has to do with the families and circumstances you're born into. Parenting is important. Later, I'll share with you evidence about the long-term effects on infants and toddlers of receiving a lot, or a little, caring attention, and I'll present some tentative evidence about the effects of the community in which a child is raised. Surely, education is crucial. Despite the unfortunate fact that most schools are still organized around the old industrial model in which children are treated like unfinished auto parts moving along a conveyor belt, which teachers try to bang, twist, and mold into shape as they pass, formal education does at least teach most of us to read and thus gain access to a world of ideas. It also links us to history and to methods of argument and means of experimentation, all of which are useful in the pursuit of new ideas. Some of us have been lucky enough to be inspired by a great teacher who opened our minds and eyes to new possibilities around us and inside us. Higher education gives us tools to discover even more. And as I will explain later in fuller detail, a good university also connects us with people who can utilize our ideas and profitably direct our energies. Undeniably, the incomes of people with more years of schooling continue to rise relative to people with fewer years.

GEEKS

At the core of innovation lie two distinct personalities, representing different inclinations, talents, and ways of perceiving the world. The first is that of the artist or inventor, the designer, the engineer, the financial wizard, the geek, the scientist, the writer or musician—the person who, in short, is capable of seeing new possibilities in a particular medium and who takes delight in exploring and developing them. The medium may be highly technical, as in computer software or finance, or more fluid, as in the fine arts. This person finds pleasure in stretching the medium as far as it can be stretched, testing its limits, discovering and solving new puzzles within it. I'll call him a geek, because that's how he's often caricatured in the new economy, but he is in fact more than a geek; he's a dreamer, a visionary, sometimes a revolutionary. And his vision is not limited to technology. The true geek can be inspired by any means of expressing innovative ideas.

When the geek bestows his highest accolade on some software—that it's *cool*—he is making an aesthetic judgment. It is cool because it is original and beautiful; it has crossed a conventional boundary, and solved a problem in a surprising way. Cool software is, perhaps, elegantly simple, or it can perform an operation that no one had previously thought of, or it is lovely in the sense that only one steeped in software design could fully appreciate. It reflects insight and dexterity on the part of its designer. The pleasure in devising or beholding it has nothing to do with its likely market value, and everything to do with its artistry—its cleverness, its acuity, its perfection. It is the same pleasure the artist (or an art critic) takes in a painting that is both original and powerful, or the musician takes in a musical composition (or in her performance) that takes the medium to a new level of intensity, grace, and mastery. It is an *insider's* appreciation. "Cool" was, after all, the term used by jazz musicians of the bee-bop generation who broke through the melodious conventions of the age and introduced a new aesthetic—a new rhythm and sound.

A geek's pleasure is linked to novelty, and discovery. Harvard psychologist Ellen Langer, an expert on creativity, terms this attitude "mindfulness." Someone who is merely analytic, rather than mindful, maps out current options and seeks to optimize outcomes. The mindful person seeks out new possibilities. "From a mindful perspective," Langer writes, "one's response to a particular situation is not an attempt to make the best choice from among available options, but to create options."[3]

Creating something that's new and intrinsically beautiful or "cool" entails a process of discovery. You don't know what you'll find when you set out to find it, nor are you completely clueless. Writer Annie Dillard explains it like this:

First, you shape the vision of what the projected work of art will be. The vision, I stress, is no marvelous thing: it is the work's intellectual structure and aesthetic surface. It is a chip of mind, a pleasing intellectual object. It is a glowing thing, a blurred thing of beauty. . . . Many aspects of the work are still uncertain, of course; you know that. You know that if you proceed you will change things and learn things, that the form will grow under your hands and develop new and richer lights. But that change will not alter the vision or its deep structures; it will only enrich it.[4]

The creation of new possibilities can be all-consuming. The geek melds with the software he is designing; the musician is enraptured by the sounds and tempo; the research scientist is absorbed by samples and measurements. Put one of them alone in a room with the right equipment, and he can summon an almost inexhaustible store of enthusiasm for finding new possibilities. The inventor is not antisocial, certainly not misanthropic. But empathy is not his strong suit. He often finds greater satisfaction in interacting with the technology, or with the music, the film, or another medium. What pleasure he derives from interacting with people comes from ensemble work, from the excitement of shared invention, and the sparks that fly when minds collude and collide in the same medium. It is the shared artistry of the musical ensemble, the acting troupe, the research team, the writers' workshop— the joy comes in joint mastery, from the collaboration in achieving something even more beautiful, ultracool.

SHRINKS

The geek is a necessary, but not sufficient, source of commercial innovation. A second personality is essential to it as well. It is that of the marketer, the talent agent, the rainmaker, the trend spotter, the producer, the consultant, the hustler—the person, in short, who can identify possibilities in the marketplace for what other people might want to have, see, or experience, and who understands how to deliver on these opportunities.

This second personality type is no less creative than the artist, inventor, or geek, but her creativity is of a different kind. Rather than seek novelty in a particular medium and find joy in overstepping its boundaries, she exercises originality in identifying people's possible wants and latent desires—desires that even those people may not have been fully aware of possessing, desires for products that do not yet exist. She is no less an expert than the geek, but her expertise, rather than involving a thing or a medium, focuses on others—business customers in a particular industry or sector of the economy, a set of clients, a cohort of young Internet users, likely voters—and she builds on that expertise by imagining new ways of satisfying and delighting them. She is no less absorbed in what she does than the geek inventor, but her absorption is in discovering what people want rather than in what a given medium can do.

This talent should not be confused with that of the conventional marketer or salesperson. These people have specific products to sell, and their job is to persuade customers to buy them. Their art—and it is an art (even a great con man possesses a certain artistry)—lies in knowing how to persuade, how to play upon the customers' emotional needs, how to turn a tangible product into something more by adding intangible qualities (such as glamour, sexual attractiveness, self-esteem, the esteem of others) that the customer desires for herself. In his smoothness, manipulativeness, and even his occasional failures, the salesman is something of an American icon—Sammy Glick, Willie Loman, the Madison Avenue advertising executive, the man or woman on the make.

But the person I'm now talking about—this second kind of creative innovator—has no particular product to sell. As has been noted, products increasingly can be built to order; services can be customized, software can be tailored to the needs of a particular business. Instead of persuading customers to buy a particular thing, her job is to imagine what they might want if it existed, and figure out how to create and deliver it.

My former student who's developing giant Internet games is also developing a feel for the kind of interactive cyber-experiences young people will find fun and exciting. She conducts "focus" groups and interviews hundreds of twentysomethings. She watches their behavior as they play various games. Now she's working with programmers to design ways players can invent their own games and attract other players from around the world to join them. Her artistry comes in asking the right questions, listening thoughtfully to the answers, watching for behavioral cues, and on these bases imagining what the customer will find most appealing or useful. In this sense, she works for the customer rather than on behalf of the seller of any specific product. She is the customer's agent, consultant, adviser, and voice.

Architect Thierry Despont designs mansions for the super-rich. He does not pretend to be one of the world's great architects; he is not a trendsetter or a visionary. His talent lies in discovering the personalities of his clients and giving three-dimensional form to their unique desires. "To be successful at my job," he says, "one must be very good at understanding not only the client's needs, but also the client's dreams and memories. One must know where the client comes from and what they desire. Part of the craft is learning to read people, to see things they are sure about, the things they are unsure about; the things they don't convey verbally, but express through their surroundings."[5]

In many respects, this second personality type resembles a counselor or even a psychotherapist, although she would never pretend to have their full set of skills or share entirely their motives. But she does share some of their abilities to elicit and intuit what people want or need. For want of a better term, and because it is important to emphasize the interpersonal nature of this work and distinguish it from that of the traditional sales or marketing role, let me call this second person a "shrink."

The geek draws on his endless fascination with a medium—a technology, a science, a visual art, a literary form, a system of symbols, with its own rules and internal logic. The shrink, by contrast, draws on her fascination with people—their aspirations and fears, their yearnings and needs, their unexamined assumptions. The shrink is empathic where the geek is analytic. The geek understands *it*—the possibilities for novelty within a given medium. The shrink understands *them*—what they could possibly want or need.

THE ENTREPRENEURIAL WHOLE

You may have noticed that just now, when I referred to geeks, I used the male pronoun, and for shrinks I used the female. Mainly, I simply wanted to avoid the awkward convention in these liberated times of saying "he or she" at every juncture. I didn't mean to presume that one gender predominates in either category. There surely are female geeks and male shrinks. But the choice of pronoun was not entirely accidental. Whether it's hardwired into our genes or conditioned by our upbringing, men do tend to be more focused on things, and women on relationships.

Every great entrepreneur is both geek and shrink. Entrepreneurial vision depends on combining the geek's insights into what's possible with the shrink's intuitions about what's desired. The entrepreneurial genius has near-perfect vision through both eyes. Thomas Alva Edison was a brilliant geek. He could see possibilities in electric currents that eluded most other inventors of the time. But he was also a brilliant shrink. He had a profound sense of what would delight the consuming public—reproducing music from a disk, or illuminating an area with a bright bulb. We now take these innovations for granted; in hindsight, it is easy to assume that people were clamoring for these innovations at the time, and that the market was already well established. But that was not the case. Think back a few years ago before you used e-mail, or the Internet, or cellular telephones, or even knew of the possible existence of such things. They were beyond your imagination, and they had not worked their way into your life. Now, although you may not like every aspect of them (you may even resent the fact that you need them), you are nevertheless dependent. And in all likelihood your children will take them for granted when they become adults, and perhaps even assume that the market for them was already well established before these innovations first appeared. Edison had no way of knowing for sure that there was a market for his inventions. He only imagined there would be. His genius lay in combining his technological insights with his marketing imagination.

Throughout history there have been other entrepreneurial geniuses who combined great scientific or artistic imagination with great marketing imagination. You may not think of them as marketers as well as artists, but their great artistry was combined with a powerful instinct for what would move the public. My list would include William Shakespeare, Isaac Newton, Benjamin Franklin, Claude Monet, and Henry Ford. History has not yet passed judgment on more recent candidates, but my bets are on the technological impresarios Bill Gates, founder of Microsoft, and Jim Clark, founder of Netscape and Silicon Graphics; producer and film director Steven Spielberg; the late fashion mogul Gianni Versace; the Argentine-born pianist Martha Argerich; the composer Leonard Bernstein; novelists Toni Morrison and Stephen King; and the great marketers Oprah Winfrey and Martha Stewart. Even if they don't rank up there with Shakespeare and Newton, all have an uncanny ability to invent things that people will want.

Few of us are brilliant geeks or shrinks, yet most of us are inclined in one direction or the other, gender notwithstanding. A highly simplified test: If you can labor alone on a problem for hours without being aware that time has passed, or if you take delight in solving puzzles, or enjoy "out of the box" or "lateral" thinking (by which I mean that you derive pleasure out of discovering a new way to accomplish a familiar task, and even greater joy in discovering new ways to do tasks you didn't know could be accomplished), you have the tendencies of a geek. If, on the other hand, you would rather spend the time discussing something with someone, or arguing with them (even if you lose the argument), or if you derive great satisfaction from advising and counseling others, or pleasing them, or negotiating with and striking deals with them, you have the inclinations, and perhaps even the talents, of a shrink.

Job recruiters who fail to note the differences between these two tendencies can make grave mistakes. I have hired brilliant geeks who I wrongly assumed at the time were talented shrinks. By the time I discovered my errors, I had a lot of mending to do with people who had been inadvertently ignored or insulted. Geeks can produce wonderful ideas and analyses, but they are not always gifted at interpersonal relations. I have also committed the opposite error. Shrinks, for their part, can "read" the subtlest of interpersonal cues, but are not always the most insightful when it comes to the substance of things. Great managers (among whom I do not count myself) intuitively know the difference, and place talented people where they can add the most value.

The charming 1996 movie *Big Night* depicted the combination exactly, if not in the extreme. Primo and Secondo, you may remember, are brothers who have emigrated to America to open an Italian restaurant. Primo is a gifted but moody and irascible chef who is determined not to squander his genius by making the standard dishes that customers always want and expect. Secondo is a smooth-talking front man who tries to keep the restaurant solvent and persuade its few patrons that they are getting what they desire. The central event of the film springs from an agreement between the brothers to have a special benefit dinner at the restaurant for which Primo will cook his masterpieces and Secondo will use his formidable marketing talents to draw a large crowd. The effort is doomed from the start because neither brother has listened to or learned from the other.

Geek and shrink—artist and agent, inventor and hustler, engineer and marketer, fashion designer and merchandiser, director and producer, provider of Internet content and of Internet traffic, politician and political consultant, talent and "suit," and so on—each of these couplets represents the two halves of the entrepreneurial whole. They exist symbiotically. They must learn from each other in order for innovation to occur. Without each other's contribution, the team would have no true entrepreneurial insight. The geek alone might create "cool" technologies, but they would have no economic value. They would not be informed by knowledge of what people want, and thus would risk being commercially irrelevant. The shrink alone might imagine ways of delighting customers, of responding to their deepest needs and yearnings, but her musings would be technologically irrelevant. They would not be shaped by knowledge of what was possible, and thus would risk being mindlessly conventional or wildly impractical.

Indeed, the questions "What might be possible?" and "What might consumers desire?" are becoming central to every enterprise. As the terms of competition shift from making and selling large numbers of identical things to innovating quickly and gaining a reputation for trustworthiness, geeks and shrinks are indispensable. Profits depend on knowledge of a certain medium (software, music, law, finance, physics, film, and so on) combined with knowledge of a certain market.

Buyers are paying more for innovation—the output of geeks and shrinks—and paying less for reproducing and distributing the creations. The cost of making a compact disc, transistor, or pain reliever is a few cents. Most of what consumers pay for is the cost of researching, designing, marketing, and advertising a steady stream of new items—the provinces of geeks and shrinks. A growing portion of the sticker price of a new car also goes to its design and marketing, along with the design and marketing of the software and computers used for controlling inventories, production, billing, payrolls, and distribution. The cost of manufacturing the book you're now reading was a relatively small portion of the price you paid for it. Most of your money went to the publisher, editor, jacket designer, merchandisers, marketers, and advertisers. Your author received a modest cut as well. And in cyberspace, it's all "content" and "traffic"—almost nobody there but geeks and shrinks.

FROM INFORMATION BROKERING
TO KNOWLEDGE BROKERING

You can see the same trend in professional services. A few years back, financial houses invested heavily in research and in information technologies. These generated up-to-the-minute data on stocks and bonds, and efficiently executed trades on behalf of clients. These days, clients can get almost the same data on their home computers, and can trade for themselves over the Internet. So what is Wall Street selling? Increasingly, advice. The advice draws on the same two realms of knowledge I've been stressing, of *it* and of *them*—knowledge of how financial markets are likely to perform in the future, and of what portfolios their individual clients are likely to want.

Wall Street "brokers" are being relabeled "financial consultants," but the change is more than in name only. I no longer need my broker to make trades, but I do need him to advise me about what I should do with my savings. And I count on his learning enough about me and my family, and knowing enough about finance, to give me good advice. The new stars of Wall Street are the research analysts who best combine technical knowledge of financial markets with specific knowledge about investors, enabling them to advise both issuers and institutions. They're selling a higher-powered version of the advice I'm getting from my own financial consultant.[6]

It's coming to be the same for all professionals who once traded in information—real-estate agents, mortgage lenders, insurance brokers, travel agents, media buyers, accountants, even doctors and lawyers who did routine diagnoses and offered standard "boilerplate" remedies. All had been *information* brokers who matched specific data about their clients, patients, or customers with a body of expert information available to people in their profession. Initially, computers enabled them to do the matching more efficiently: Real-estate agents consulted computerized multiple listings; lenders, databases on creditworthiness; insurance agents, tools for assessing risk and pricing various policies; travel agents, databases for flights and accommodations; and accountants, doctors, and lawyers, an expanded array of professional tools to deal with a variety of standard problems. But as their clients, patients, and customers gain access to the same expert information online, they no longer need information brokers.

These information brokers will have to do the equivalent of what stockbrokers have done, and shift to *knowledge* brokering—combining knowledge of what's possible with knowledge about what their clients might want or need. My family takes one vacation a year, for which I can easily make all the necessary reservations with a few clicks of a computer mouse. But over the years my travel agent has accumulated knowledge about a wide range of travel experiences, and also about us, and I rely on her to suggest where we might like to go and what we might like to do.

But even knowledge brokers won't be able to relax in their new roles. More and better customized advice will become available online, based on customer responses to online questionnaires. Soon, financial software will spew out advice about the proper allocation of assets between stocks and bonds, and categories of equity—depending on investors' responses to online questions about their financial circumstances, attitudes toward risk, age, and expected needs. Vacation-planning software will automatically generate advice about where to go and what to see—based on responses to online questions about family interests and previous successful vacations. Software containing advice from lawyers, financiers, engineers, architects, doctors, accountants, tax specialists, or financial planners will also be available online, in response to other online questionnaires. So what will professionals do next? Some will become the geeks and shrinks who design and market such knowledge-brokering software, and continuously improve upon it. Others will turn into specialists who attend to unique cases that the software doesn't address. Others will be advisers-cum-therapists to clients willing to pay extra for personal reassurance (more on this role later).

We will see something of the same shift, from information brokering to knowledge brokering, in retailing. Some people involved in retail sales will be replaced by the Internet (or, more specifically, by the geeks and shrinks who design and market Web pages and create the software for linking orders with inventories and billing, and by the people who ship and deliver). But there will still be a role for salespeople. Many customers will continue to seek personal assistance in deciding what they want or need. Some of this help will be provided over the Internet or on the telephone by people in customer service centers hundreds or thousands of miles away. Some of it—often, more expensive—will be provided in person. (On this, more later as well.)

MUTUAL LEARNING

Every great organization finds ways to combine the two types of creative worker—to cross-pollinate—so that the geeks understand enough about potential markets to direct their inventiveness toward where it is likely to be wanted, and so the shrinks understand enough about potential technologies and other mediums to direct their customers toward where they are most likely to be served. Movie studios must have their talented actors and directors, but also their producers who know how to put together a film that the public will want to see. Publishing houses combine talented writers with editors and publishers who understand how to market the written words. The best venture capitalists scout for both brilliant geeks and insightful shrinks, and know how to marry them within the same entrepreneurial enterprise. Fashion houses must have their designers and also their stylists who stay close to the market, discover what's going on in other design rooms, and work with fashion retailers and trend spotters to sense where the market is heading. And so on, throughout the economy.

Shrinks can find unexpected commercial applications for what the geek has devised. The drug minoxidil was originally developed for the purpose of lowering blood pressure. Although it proved effective against hypertension, it had one disconcerting side effect on women: It stimulated hair growth. Only then did shrinks, viewing it from a different perspective, see minoxidil's commercial possibilities for overcoming baldness. The innovative process often operates just this way. Breakthroughs come not only in scientific, technical, and artistic discovery, but in the discovery of how such insights can best be used.

Geeks, similarly, can discover new applications for widely available technologies by learning more about potential markets. Several years ago, hospitals needed better means of tracking patients as they moved through the health-care system. Too many patients were getting lost between HMOs, primary-care physicians, and specialists, and their records were incomplete. A geek familiar with software used by shippers to track packages as they moved through different modes of transportation figured that, with only slight modification, the same software could track patients. He then successfully customized it to the needs of specific hospitals and health-care providers.

The more geeks and shrinks can learn from each other, the more innovation will occur. But the typical large industrial-strength bureaucracy isolated geeks within reseach-and-development silos and isolated shrinks within sales and marketing departments. The result was occasional insights about technology and a set of insights about the needs of consumers, but little or no connection between the two, and very little real innovation. For many years, Xerox's famed Palo Alto Research Center was a seedbed of new ideas for the electronics industry. But Xerox itself never quite figured out how to use the ideas. Its corporate headquarters in Stamford, Connecticut, was fixated on the needs of current customers for duplicating and retrieving documents, and never understood the market potential for what its inventors in California were discovering. One of the very few innovations to make it from Palo Alto to Stamford was laser imaging—largely because an entrepreneur inside Xerox named Robert Adams happened to understand this emerging technology *and* its potential market well enough to connect them, and to champion the new product inside Xerox.

Mutual learning that leads to continuous innovation tends to be informal, unplanned, serendipitous. This is why the new economy is rewarding small entrepreneurial groups composed of geeks and shrinks, rather than big hierarchical bureaucracies—and why the best of such groups are organized loosely, often in open-style offices where they can see one another, or find each other within seconds. The casual attire you see in these new entrepreneurial businesses—open collars, blue jeans, and running shoes—isn't just for show. People tend to be at their most creative and spontaneous, and most willing to share casual thoughts and ideas, when they're feeling as comfortable as they are when they're with good friends.

Entrepreneurial regions of the country—places that spawn a disproportionately large number of innovative businesses—typically have pools of talented geeks and shrinks who constantly intermingle. Boston's high-tech corridor has benefited from proximity to both the technological insights of MIT and the marketing insights of Harvard Business School. Harvard's faculty is not reputed for its technological prowess, nor is MIT's for its marketing acumen, yet the students who emerge from both institutions and remain in the region subsequently learn from one another, and this mutual learning has helped fuel the regional boom.

Silicon Valley has similarly benefited from a concentration of geeks (many of them graduates of Stanford University, in Palo Alto) and also of venture capitalists with a keen sense of what it takes to make ideas commercially successful. The Valley's entrepreneurial roots go back to the late 1930s, when Fred Terman, an engineering professor at Stanford, persuaded two of his students, William Hewlett and David Packard, to form a company and got Stanford to transform some of its peach groves into a high-tech industrial park. But the eventual flowering depended on shrewd venture capitalists and marketers who turned this geek paradise into companies like Sun Microsystems, Cisco, Silicon Graphics, and Yahoo.

For seven decades, Hollywood has been a seedbed of artists who know how to utilize the film medium (screenwriters, actors, directors, costume designers, cinematographers) and also of marketing wizards who know how to take the public's pulse (agents, publicists, studio executives, producers)—the talent and the suits. On Wall Street, financial geeks come into direct contact with financial marketers, and the outcome is a stream of financial innovation.

These regions spawn innovation not because they have an abundance of either geeks or shrinks but because they have a concentration of both, in the right balance. If the balance tips one way or the other, the regions become less entrepreneurial, lose their "edge," and become either irrelevant or stale. Some would say Hollywood already has too many shrinks and not enough original artists to be capable of true innovation. Its output has become formulaic and predictable. Some allege that the New York literary "scene" has become unbalanced in the opposite direction—too ingrown and self-indulgent, too obsessed by its own cleverness and too indifferent to public taste, to set trends any longer in literary innovation. Israel is a major center of technological innovation—brimming with skilled engineers, technicians, and computer programmers, many of them emigrants from the former Soviet Union—but it still lacks the marketing savvy to be entrepreneurial on its own. Israel's geeks rely on global firms with shrinks who know what will sell.

A CAUTIONARY NOTE ON INTEGRITY AND MARKETABILITY

Nothing I have said should be taken to suggest that invention or artistry requires commercial popularity in order for it to be great, beautiful, or otherwise worthy. Software can still be "cool" even if no one outside the world of geekdom appreciates it. A film can merit an Oscar even if its box office take is disappointing, a novel deserve a National Book Award even if few readers enjoy it. The customer is not *always* right. In fact, an excessive reliance on pleasing consumers may rob creativity of its very soul.

There are two distinct vantage points from which a piece of work may be evaluated: according to the aesthetics of its medium, or according to its popularity in the market. Film critics, book critics, those who pass judgment on new software or any other new invention may be using either measure. "This is a wonderful film" may mean that its talented creators have pushed the art of filmmaking to a new level of taste, subtlety, and beauty, even if it's a dud at the box office; or it may mean that the public is likely to find the film to be enormously enjoyable, even though it's drivel.

That these distinctions are rarely made explicit causes no small mischief. As the economy grows more fiercely competitive, commercial evaluation ("Two thumbs up!") can all but silence aesthetic criticism. Consumers face so many choices that they place ever-greater value on advice about what they will enjoy or find satisfying. There's correspondingly less interest in aesthetic criticism—what consumers should or would like, were their tastes more finely honed.

And yet society needs both. Consumers surely are helped by reviews alerting them to software or films or any other inventions they're likely to enjoy; and it is perfectly reasonable for geeks and other creators to know how they can best delight the public. But there is also value in educating the public about aesthetic standards inherent in a medium, quite apart from the public's likely enjoyment. And in a culture obsessed by what sells, inventors and artists can benefit from aesthetic criticism. Otherwise, society runs the danger of losing that which provokes, angers, ennobles, challenges, or otherwise forces people to face truths from which they would rather escape.

Several decades ago, before competition began to intensify, there were arbiters of taste—art critics, reviewers, essayists, educators, and graybeards—within the professions who continually passed judgment on the quality of work being done. Some were stuffy and self-important, and their pieties reflected conventional doctrines and tired formalisms. Others, however, were daring and insightful. All presided over a continuing discussion about standards, which reminded society about the difference between the good and the popular.

But in a world of intensifying competition in which consumers can get exactly what they want—where software can even analyze their past purchases and advise them on what else they will enjoy or find interesting—such standard-bearers seem increasingly irrelevant. The only legitimate measure of worth seems to be what is desired, and the best indication of that is what sells. All else is deemed arbitrary. Yet when it is all marketing, there is less space for professional or artistic integrity.

Jason Epstein, who joined Random House as an editor in the late 1950s, writes that he and his colleagues at that time thought of themselves as "caretakers of a tradition, like London tailors or collectors of Chinese porcelain," rather than as businessmen. "It was always a pleasure when one of our books became a best-seller, but what counted more was a book that promised to become a permanent part of the culture."[7] Intensifying competition, propelled by the new power of buyers, is forcing every publisher to worry more about the bottom line. When all writers, actors, and musicians work for global media and communications conglomerates locked in intense competition, who will dare flout convention and create something startling or disturbing? When every geek works for relentlessly commercial enterprises, who will do the basic research that has no immediate or apparent commercial value?

The danger is acute for professionals who once were sheltered from the demands of the marketplace and who have a special responsibility to reveal truths in ways that may be unpopular or unfashionable. Their livelihoods now increasingly depend on their popularity. Journalists are now under increasing compulsion to write or broadcast whatever sells, regardless of how incendiary or inaccurate. New technologies permit almost instant feedback. Online magazines know how many people have clicked on each article they offer, within each issue; so do their advertisers and investors. As the ability to measure market responses grows ever more sophisticated, pressure grows to give buyers exactly what they want.

The nonprofit world provides scarcely more shelter to do or say what's provocative but unpopular. A friend, a program director of a nonprofit foundation, tells me that she is pressured to steer grants in directions that corporate funders think advantageous for public relations, and away from anything that might be considered controversial or embarrassing. Not a few university professors have been known to target the topics of their research—although, one hopes, not their findings—to the interests of organizations with money to back research projects. Museum directors want "blockbuster" shows that will lure the crowds and please the patrons—which almost always means yet another round of Impressionists or antiquities.

It's of course possible that the exquisite tailoring of products to unique tastes made possible by new technologies will offer talented geeks and shrinks new outlets for their more eccentric efforts. They'll be able to connect with equally eccentric buyers without having to worry about acceptance by a mass market. If that's the case, then integrity need not be overly compromised by marketability, because there's almost always going to be *some* market, even if a tiny one. At least one among 1,500 television channels will offer a niche for richly provocative TV; at least one small online publisher will distribute intriguing books for which very little readership exists. And yet, it must be asked whether these little slivers of artistic defiance will exert any influence on a culture pandering more efficiently than ever to what's popular, or whether they will merely function as remote and harmless escape valves for the ever more conveniently ignored.

The greatest threat to freedom of speech in many modern societies comes not from overt controls by oppressive regimes but from a more fiercely competitive market in which buyers can so easily switch to whatever they find more satisfying. Such a marketplace dictates with increasing ferocity what will be written, broadcast, and researched. The public, deluged with what delights it and protected from what may cause it discomfort, is thus armored against what it may need to know.

THE DEMAND FOR creative workers—for geeks and shrinks, as I have called them—will continue to grow because they are the masters of innovation, and innovation lies at the heart of the new economy. These workers can quickly create products that are better or cheaper than what came before. They're competing with other groups of geeks and shrinks who are racing to create even better and cheaper products, and do so even faster. As this competition intensifies, it's fueling even greater demand for the services of such creative workers. These jobs, therefore, are likely to pay increasingly well. They also are likely to be intellectually or artistically engaging, emotionally absorbing, personally satisfying, and sometimes boundlessly frustrating. They are almost certain to claim a lot of time, even outside formal business hours. The working mind of the creative geek or shrink rarely shuts off completely.

CHAPTER FOUR

The Obsolescence of Loyalty

I NNOVATIVE GEEKS and shrinks are in greater demand, but anyone who does anything for pay that's repetitive or routine—which can be done more cheaply by a machine or computer software or someone elsewhere around the world—is likely to be losing economic ground. This is because of the intensifying pressure on all enterprises to trim costs, and their increasing capacity to do so through technologies with global reach. Most of these people will remain employed, but fewer of them will engage in routine production. Many will be providing personal attention, which computers cannot do because it requires a human touch, and foreign workers cannot do from abroad because it involves direct contact with those receiving it.*

The problem for most people who aren't doing particularly well isn't that they lack a job. If they inhabit the United States, they're likely to be employed if they want to be. Their larger problem is that they

---

* Since 1950, the U.S. Bureau of the Census has been dividing workers into "Major Occupational Groups," such as "managerial and professional specialty," "technical, sales, and administrative support," "service occupations," "operator, fabricator, and laborer," and "transportation and material moving." But these categories have very little bearing on the new work. In *The Work of Nations* (1991), I reclassified workers into three more relevant groups: "symbolic analysts," "routine production workers," and "in-person service workers." Among the remainder were government employees, farmers, miners, and other extractors of natural resources. Assessing the job data at the start of the twenty-first century, I would assign the highest-paid 25 percent to the category of "creative worker," which, as I suggested in the preceding chapter, seems a more accurate description of what they do and will be doing in the future; about 20 percent to routine production; and slightly more than 30 percent to in-person services. Again, government employees and others make up the remainder.

don't earn much. In Europe and Japan and much of the rest of the world, where wage rates are still less flexible than they are in America, workers who are not in much demand are either unemployed and living on welfare (as in Europe) or employed in "make-work" jobs and living off the good graces of companies willing to pay them more than the market value of their services (as in Japan). Yet the salad days of generous unemployment benefits and of corporate benevolence are coming to an end even in European countries and Japan. These other nations are gradually falling in line with the American system. Global investors and consumers are insisting on it.

Even profitable American companies have been "downsizing," "rightsizing," "reengineering," "decruiting," "deselecting," or whatever is the currently fashionable euphemism for firing. At the same time they're bidding more for talented geeks and shrinks, they're also cutting the jobs or the wages of routine workers, eliminating or reducing their health benefits, trimming their pension contributions, and subcontracting work to other firms with lower wages and benefits. Increasingly, they're relying on Web-based business-to-business auctions to find best buys among suppliers, who in turn must cut *their* costs in order to stay competitive. The nonprofit sector is going through a similar squeeze. Hospitals, museums, and even charities are slashing costs in ways that would have been thought brutal even in the private sector three decades ago. Universities are paring back the ranks of tenured professors and relying more on academic nomads on yearly contracts with low wages and no benefits. They're turning over much of their maintenance, dining, custodial, and other routine services to for-profit vendors who can do all of it more cheaply.

Nor are companies any longer especially loyal to their hometowns. This is because fewer of them *have* hometowns. Gone are the days when large firms could be relied on to be the major employers and benefactors where they were headquartered—Kodak in Rochester, New York; Procter & Gamble in Cincinnati; Coca-Cola in Atlanta; Levi Strauss in San Francisco. All are downsizing, outsourcing, and dispersing.[1] Typically, worldwide corporate headquarters are now found in well-manicured office parks conveniently located near international airports; factories and laboratories are everywhere around the globe; suppliers and partners are nowhere in particular, and they continuously change. When the Dodgers left Brooklyn in the 1950s, people wept. How *could* they? Now teams routinely leave one town for another offering a newer arena with more skyboxes. Fans still refer to "their" home teams, but the pronoun's meaning has become cloudy. The Florida Marlins, lacking a hometown even in their name, won the 1997 World Series with a transitory group of players cobbled together by an owner who had bought most of them the previous winter, and who shortly after the victory threatened to unload the stars and sell the team if Miami didn't build him a new stadium.

It's tempting to conclude from all this that enterprises are becoming colder-hearted, and executives more ruthless—and to blame it on an ethic of unbridled greed that seems to have taken hold in recent years and appears to be increasing. But this conclusion would be inaccurate. The underlying cause isn't a change in the American character. It is to be found in the increasing ease by which buyers and investors can get better deals, and the competitive pressure this imposes on all enterprises. As the pressure intensifies, institutional bonds are loosening.

Years ago, when choice was far more limited and switching more difficult, consumers and investors tended to stay put. As a result, institutional bonds were stronger. The tameness of competition allowed for an implicit social compact. Employees worked steadily and reliably, in return for which employers provided them with steady work as long as the enterprise was profitable. Local retailers and service businesses, facing only limited competition in their neighborhoods, did likewise. Universities, receiving a steady stream of students and donations, granted tenure to a large portion of their professoriat. Hospitals, enjoying predictable numbers of patients and steady budgets, steadily enlarged their medical and nursing staffs. The wages of almost everyone drifted upward.

The executive suite of the large-scale American enterprise at midcentury was a quietly distinguished place of mahogany and glass, pile carpeting and oriental rugs, in which men went about their work with no particular urgency. The stability that characterized large-scale production bestowed a quiescence and certitude upon those who were in charge. With investors and consumers securely in place, the chief executive at midcentury could be magnanimous toward all. "The job of management," benevolently declared Frank Abrams, chairman of Standard Oil of New Jersey, in a 1951 address that was typical of the era, "is to maintain an equitable and working balance among the claims of the various directly interested groups . . . stockholders, employees, customers, and the public at large." The large organization, from this perspective, was a quasi-public enterprise with responsibilities toward everyone. And those who headed them were gaining professional status, Abrams opined, because "they see in their work the basic responsibilities [to the public] that other professional men have long recognized in theirs."[2]

Such magnanimity also afforded men like Abrams a wide latitude to do whatever they wished with their companies' revenues, balancing claims as they saw fit. One claim notably missing from Abrams's list but often honored above all others was the claim of executives themselves for comfortable lives, not unduly impinged upon by any of the other claimants. The midcentury executive served on a multitude of corporate and nonprofit boards, pursued several rounds of golf each week, entertained lavishly, engaged in highly visible acts of charity, sometimes dabbled in public affairs. University presidents and foundation heads led similarly unperturbed lives.*

At the start of the twenty-first century, top executives are sounding a sharply different note. No longer are companies responsible to employees, communities, and the public at large. They view their sole duty as maximizing the value of their investors' shares—which they accomplish by furiously cutting costs and adding value. Roberto C. Goizueta, former CEO of Coca-Cola, stated the new logic with particular clarity. "Businesses are created to meet economic needs," he said. When they "try to become all things to all people, they fail.... We have one job: to generate a fair return for our owners.... We must remain focused on our core duty: creating value over time."[3] Presidents of universities, hospitals, museums, and major charities are now similarly obsessed with building their endowments and assuring adequate revenues.

---

* The wide latitude accorded midcentury executives had already been the subject of considerable commentary for several decades. In 1932, Adolf A. Berle and Gardiner C. Means, lawyer and economics professor respectively, wrote *The Modern Corporation and Private Property*, a highly influential book which revealed that top executives operated corporations "in their own interests, and . . . divert[ed] a portion of the asset fund to their own uses." But to overcome this plutocracy, Berle and Means did not suggest that shareholders become more powerful. They recommended instead that the powers of all groups affected by the corporation be enhanced. "Neither the claims of ownership nor those of control can stand against the paramount interests of the community," they wrote. "It remains only for the claims of the community to be put forward with clarity and voice." Executives should become a "purely neutral technocracy, balancing a variety of claims by various groups in the community and assigning each a portion of the income stream on the basis of public policy rather than private cupidity" (New York: Macmillan, 1932), pp. 300, 312.

THE NEW LOGIC OF DISLOYALTY

Who's to blame for America's increasingly singular focus on earnings? Indirectly, and in large measure, I am, and you probably are too. It's not that we've intentionally willed any of this to occur. Rather, the new logic of disloyalty is the unintended by-product of the increasing ease with which all of us can get better deals. The new logic of disloyalty, in other words, begins at home. Take a close look at the big corporations that have been doing most of the cutting and slashing, and you'll see why.

Start with a share of stock, which is literally a share of future profits. Stock prices at any moment reflect the best guess of large numbers of investors, sifting through all available information, as to the current value of those future profit streams. Share prices are not perfect predictors; investors may be irrationally exuberant or overly pessimistic. But over the slightly longer term, a company's share price is the best predictor available about a company's future profitability, and thus its current value. In this way, the share price acts like an early-warning system: If top executives make decisions that most company investors think will reduce future profits, investors will sell their shares, and share prices will drop. If they drop too low, the company will have a harder time raising the money it needs to innovate for the future. Investors simply won't trust current managers to use the money well. A low share price invites efforts to oust current executives and replace them with those who'll do better.

Investors have become steadily more powerful in this role because of their increasing willingness and ability to switch to better deals. It started in 1974, without fanfare or even much notice, when the International Nickel Company bought up enough shares in the Electric Storage Battery Company to give International Nickel control, and promptly ousted Electric Storage's executives. Before International Nickel did this dirty deed, Wall Street had viewed such aggression as unseemly, if not unethical. But a precedent had been set. Soon, what seemed audacious was commonplace. There were twelve hostile takeovers of companies valued at $1 billion or more during the remainder of the 1970s. During the 1980s, there were more than 150.

"Raiders," as they came to be known around corporate suites with awe and trepidation, saw opportunities for large returns by acquiring companies and slashing costs. You might say these aggressors saw possibilities that had escaped notice by comfortable executives accustomed to the tame old world of stable oligopolies. Or you might say the raiders were willing to be more ruthless by borrowing to the hilt in order to mount their raids (wielding high-risk "junk" bonds to do "leveraged buyouts"), squeezing suppliers, fighting unions, slashing wages, and subcontracting to lower-cost producers all over the world. Both descriptions would be equally accurate. The result was higher profits, which meant higher share prices. Several of the warriors and junk-bond kings who were condemned in the 1980s for their ruthlessness are today lionized for making American companies more "competitive." It's a fair point, although their strategies hardly always work as planned. When the prices of junk bonds plummeted in the late 1980s, savings-and-loan companies that had been eager to purchase them when their prices were higher went famously bust, and American taxpayers ended up footing a very large bill. RJR Nabisco, the largest of the leveraged buyouts of the 1980s, was unceremoniously dismembered in 1999.

The mere possibility of a hostile takeover has altered the behavior of corporate chieftains as well as investors. Investors—including the pension funds and mutual funds where most of us now park whatever savings we have—demand and expect more. These institutions have grown large because they can so efficiently choose and switch investments on our behalf. And they're willing to grant eye-popping rewards to executives who act aggressively to cut costs and gain larger profits, and thus lift share prices. Increasingly, executive "compensation packages" are linked to share prices through generous stock options and rich bonuses if targets are met or exceeded. My colleagues and I in the Clinton administration inadvertently contributed to this trend. Arriving in Washington in 1993 with the new President's pledge that no company should be able to deduct from its corporate income taxes executive compensation in excess of $1 million, we advised that the deduction be allowed if the extra inducement was linked to "performance"—that is, an increase in the company's share price. Stock options and bonuses thereafter exploded. Raising the share price became paramount, whatever that required. In 1980, the typical chief executive of a large American company took home about forty times the annual earnings of a typical worker; in 1990, the ratio rose to about eighty-five times. Between 1990 and the end of the century, total executive compensation rose from an average of $1.8 million to an average $12 million—an increase of more than 600 percent, resulting in compensation packages that averaged 419 times the earnings of a typical production worker.[4]

Executives who fail to raise their stock prices, on the other hand, are apt to lose their jobs.[5] Between 1990 and 2000, high-priced heads rolled at IBM, AT&T, Sears, General Motors, Xerox, Coca-Cola, Aetna, and other blue-chip American corporations. Such decapitations often occur quickly, bloodlessly, sometimes after a tenure of only a few months. In the wake of results that disappointed Wall Street and sent stock prices tumbling in the first quarter of 1999, the board of Compaq Computer immediately ousted its chief executive. "[S]ome of our competitors have done a better job positioning themselves" for the Internet, Compaq's board chairman explained to the *New York Times*.[6] Translation: We had to get another chief executive who would move faster to slash costs and shift to new technologies—and show dramatically to Wall Street that we were back on track.

Traditional corporate boards were filled with handpicked cronies of the chief executive. But under the banner of "good corporate governance," pension funds, mutual funds, and other institutional investors have demanded that boards be more independent. If they don't oust a poorly performing chief executive, investors may sack the entire board. This happened in May 1998, when the giant pension fund that manages the retirement savings of most college professors, including mine, ousted the nine-member board of Furr's/Bishop's, Inc., a company that runs a chain of cafeterias in the South and Midwest. One of the ousted board members described the coup as "astonishing."[7]

Each of the steps I've described was "astonishing" the first time it happened—the first hostile takeover, the first use of junk bonds for a leveraged buyout, the first corporate executive to receive tens of millions of dollars in stock options in one year, the first major chief executive to be overtly fired by a board, the first entire board to be ousted—because each violated then-prevailing norms of stability and predictability in economic relationships. But each changed the rules thereafter by extracting more value for investors and forcing top executives to focus ever more exclusively on the price their company's shares fetch on the stock market.

THE CONSEQUENCES

Nothing focuses the mind of a chief executive, or of anyone else for that matter, like the prospect of vast wealth and the possibility of being sacked. The increasing single-mindedness of top executives on increasing their share prices by cutting costs and improving their products is reverberating throughout the economy. The good news: American corporations have become more productive, and their goods and services dramatically better. The not-so-good news: All jobs and earnings have become less secure, and wages and benefits of routine production workers have eroded. [8]

Employees have always been laid off during economic downturns, but the old practice had been to rehire them when demand picked up again. That didn't happen in the wake of the 1991–92 recession. As corporate investments in information technology soared, layoffs continued at a high pace during the economic boom of the 1990s, even as the national rate of unemployment dropped. After executive heads rolled at IBM and Xerox, both companies slashed payrolls. One financial analyst characterized Xerox's late-1990s bloodletting as "an heroic thing"; another noted "a real paradigm shift here, from an engineering-driven company to one that really knows how to rip out infrastructure to get costs down." [9] Shortly after its new CEO took over in January 2000, Coca-Cola, which had long been known by Atlantans for its generous benefits and secure jobs, announced it would cut half of its Atlanta-based workforce. "The world in which we operate has changed dramatically," explained the new chief, "and we must change to succeed." [10]

Most of the people laid off from their jobs in recent years have found new ones fairly easily because the economy has continued to grow robustly. At this writing, the labor market is tighter than it has been in more than thirty years. In this environment, people who are fired have many other job opportunities. What they lose is a sense of economic security.

Large companies are ripping out entire bureaucracies—using computer software to streamline all billing, procurement, and inventory; shifting customer services to the Internet; renting space and equipment instead of buying them; and relying on Internet auctions to subcontract almost everything to the lowest reliable bidder. Forget the old pyramid-shaped organization. If the current trend continues, tomorrow's enterprise will be little more than a chain of contracts, with an auction at each link designed to get the best deal for each business customer along the way. For example, Weyerhauser's door plant in Marshfield, Wisconsin, used to consider Columbia Forest Products Company among its best suppliers of veneers—until Weyerhauser discovered over the Internet that several of Columbia's rivals could do it cheaper and better. Weyerhauser showed Columbia the data and gave it six months to improve or Weyerhauser would buy its veneers elsewhere. Columbia got the message, and squeezed its costs and improved its quality to match or exceed its rivals—making Weyerhauser more competitive as well.[11]

Some transformations have been particularly abrupt. In the nineties, the 230-year-old *Encyclopaedia Britannica* reduced its famous door-to-door sales force from 2,300 to zero. The reason was simple: Why would anyone buy a thirty-two-volume encyclopedia costing $1,250 when most of the information could be found on the Internet? In 1999, the company released its entire opus—extending from "a-ak" (an ancient East Asian music) to "Zywiec" (a town in Poland)—on the Web.

Entire industries have imploded. As recently as 1980, when producing a single ton of steel required ten hours of human labor, America had 400,000 steelworkers. Two decades later, a "mini-mill" could produce a ton of steel in two hours, and less than 150,000 steelworkers remained. The value of the entire American steel industry was by then half the stock market value of a single Internet company, Amazon.com.

With greater alacrity, companies are moving or subcontracting to lower-cost foreign nations, especially in Southeast Asia and Latin America. One of General Electric CEO John F. Welch's favorite phrases is "squeeze the lemon," which GE has been doing by pushing its suppliers to move their operations to Mexico.[12] More than a million Mexicans now work in "Maquiladoras," trading zones along the U.S. border, up from 400,000 in 1990. Within a few years, hundreds of thousands of Indian and Chinese technicians, programmers, and software engineers will be working for American corporations over the Internet, directly from their own computers in Asia. By 2000, about 50,000 Indians were already doing the "back office" work of global corporations headquartered elsewhere: entering and retrieving Internet data, transcribing records, handling customer-service calls, and doing online accounting.

Companies are fighting more brazenly against unions, replacing strikers and firing workers who lead organizing efforts. The latter practice has been illegal since the 1930s and, until recently, rather uncommon. In 1950, there was one such illegal dismissal for every twenty union elections; by the 1990s, the National Labor Relations Board found illegal dismissals in one out of every three union elections.[13] Union membership has plummeted from 30 percent of all private-sector workers in 1973 to 9.6 percent in 2000.

Where is the impetus for all this coming from? Here's where we come full circle and arrive back home, to mine and probably to yours. Among the most vociferous investors demanding such bold cost-cutting moves are large charitable foundations, the retirement funds of university teachers, and even union pension funds. People like you and me who invest our savings in these entities are unlikely to be fully aware of this, but competition for our savings acts as a kind of flywheel for everything else. That's how, in my own small way, I've forced some of these things to happen. I'm not directly aware of doing so. But if a portfolio manager in charge of my teachers' retirement fund doesn't get the best possible return on my savings, I'll switch funds. I can switch more easily now than ever before. He knows that, and acts accordingly.

You and I are also, unwittingly, pushing for all of this in our role as consumers. We're not aware that we're demanding wage cuts and fighting unions, but that's often the effect we have when we choose the cheapest product or service. Companies can't pass on to us and to other consumers wage increases in the form of higher prices as easily as they could in the old industrial economy (with its accompanying oligopolies, regulations, and trade barriers). We have more choices now, and don't have to pay the higher wages embedded in what we buy. We can choose cheaper products made wholly or partially by people around the world who receive lower wages than Americans, or offered by nonunionized workers in the United States, or produced by automated machine tools and robots. You and I and other consumers may not *want* to bust unions or exert downward pressure on the wages of people doing routine operations, but by exercising our wider choices and greater ease of switching to better deals, this is what we're doing. We're making the nonunionized sectors of the economy grow faster than the unionized sectors, and indirectly encouraging companies to fight unions more ardently than they did in the era of oligopolies and large-scale production.[14]

Some of us might change our ways as consumers and investors if we had better information about the consequences of our choices. We could, for example, "look for the union label." We might demand assurance from a seller that a particular product wasn't made by a six-year-old child working all day, seven days a week, in Southeast Asia. We could confine our investments to "socially responsible" mutual funds that invest solely in companies that behave in ways we consider acceptable. We might choose to take all these steps and many others even if, as a result, we had to pay slightly more or get a somewhat lower return on our investment. (In fact, some "socially responsible" investment funds have been outperforming regular mutual funds in recent years.) We might simply think the sacrifice worth it. If the social consequence of choosing a particular product or investment was thought especially heinous, we might even join with other citizens and seek to pass legislation making it illegal for *anyone* to do so. After all, we don't allow child labor in the United States, for example, and we don't trade with or invest in rogue states around the world, even if such restrictions may bar us from some good deals. There's no constitutional right to the best or cheapest product or the highest return on an investment. But any such limitation on choice is likely to cost us *something.* The question, again, is whether the sacrifice is worth it.

WHAT YOU AND I ARE DOING ABROAD

Even in cultures where traditional bonds between companies, employees, and communities have been strong—in much of continental Europe, Japan, and Southeast Asia—they're coming apart because global investors (like me, and probably you) are, in effect, demanding it. Foreign-based companies need American capital, and American investors are eager to diversify their portfolios around the globe. During the 1990s, American holdings of foreign stocks soared from 6 percent of total U.S. equity investments to almost 10 percent.[15]

America's large institutional investors are quietly in the lead. Klaus Pohle, chief financial officer of the German drugmaker Shering AG, told a Berlin audience recently how he makes decisions: "I go to Boston and visit Mrs. Firestone [a portfolio manager at Fidelity Investments]. She tells me what to do."[16] When in 1998 Alcatel, a mostly French-owned telecommunications company, announced that its annual profit would be less than had been forecast, its share price dropped 55 percent.

It bounced back six months later, in no small part because of extensive cost-cutting, including the loss of some 12,000 jobs—prompting French President Jacques Chirac to explain, in his 1999 Bastille Day address, what triggered the sequence of events: "California retirees suddenly decided to sell Alcatel," he noted testily, referring to California's giant public-employees' retirement fund.

California's public retirees—tens of thousands of gentle, elderly people who spent their careers working for the state and are thus improbably cast as rabid promoters of free-market capitalism—have their savings in a giant pension fund that is busily severing bonds between companies, employees, and communities around the world. When the fund recently complained that a German utility company, RWE, gave the cities it served too much control over its board and thus diminished the value of RWE shares owned by California public retirees, the utility argued that the share structure established an important bond between it and its customers. But when the fund, evidently unimpressed, then threatened to dump its RWE shares, the company promptly scrapped its system of city representation.[17]

Don't blame American investors entirely. European investors are following closely behind, similarly moving their savings to where they can earn the best return. These investors are also prodding European companies down the American road—mounting unfriendly takeovers, firing executives who fail to maximize share prices, and moving operations to lower-wage nations. High labor costs in Germany have spurred German firms to move to Asia and even South Carolina, where BMW has set up shop. Sweden's telecommunications giant (and biggest employer) Ericsson moved its world headquarters out of high-cost Sweden to lower-cost London. In 1999, the new president of Daimler-Chrysler, a transatlantic hybrid, boldly declared that his most important objective was "maximizing shareholder value," and duly closed some German plants and switched to Asian suppliers. Soon thereafter, Edouard Michelin, the scion of the French tire manufacturer, did the unthinkable—announcing plans to shed 7,500 jobs in Europe over three years, even though Michelin's profits had just risen 20 percent during the preceding six months. Talented European executives, meanwhile, are being lured to American companies that offer far better pay. "If the politicians don't act quickly," warned Jean-René Fourtou, chairman of Rhône-Poulenc SA, a French chemicals and pharmaceuticals giant, "companies will leave Europe. . . . [S]tep by step they will move investments outside of Europe."[18]

Japanese companies are also becoming more dependent on global investors who pay attention to credit ratings and returns on investment. So even the Japanese are starting to do what seemed impossible just a few years ago: cutting payrolls, subcontracting to lower-cost producers in Southeast Asia, and ending the practice of "lifetime employment." At the close of 1999, Nissan announced cuts of 21,000 jobs, mostly in Japan. NEC and Sony announced layoffs of 15,000 and 17,000, respectively.[19]

Do not assume that this trend is inevitable everywhere. Any society might still choose to maintain old jobs, keep venerable companies rooted within traditional communities, or prevent global capital from moving as quickly or being as demanding as it has become. But such a society would pay a price. Its pace of innovation would be slower than in less bonded societies. And its people would no longer have as ready access to better products or to global capital. I do not want to portray this choice too starkly; there are many gradations between preserving the old and embracing the new with abandon. Nor, at this juncture, do I want to get ahead of myself. I will return to this basic issue later.

WHEN LOYALTY PAYS

Some will object that I've failed to account for the positive effects of institutional loyalty on the bottom line. Surely, being nice to employees and suppliers can pay off. There's ample evidence that employees who feel well treated are willing to work harder and better. Employee turnover can be expensive. Sometimes a union can give such efficient voice to employee concerns and ideas that it enhances productivity. Suppliers that are treated as partners rather than as vendors from whom every last ounce of cost-saving is squeezed are often more willing to share customer data and invest in new ways to improve efficiency along the entire supply chain. Overt displays of good "corporate citizenship" can burnish a public image and thus help sales. And not a few "socially responsible" investment funds enjoy high returns to shareholders, precisely because certain kinds of social responsibility pay off.

Whatever financial rewards accrue to being nice do not, however, imply *separate* obligations toward employees, suppliers, or communities over and above the necessity of maximizing returns to investors (or, if a privately held company, of generating enough revenue to be able to reinvest and stay competitive; if a nonprofit, of maximizing revenues in order to better accomplish whatever the nonprofit is set up to do). To the extent that being nice to others furthers these more basic goals, being nice makes good business sense, but *only* to this extent. When more money can be made by severing these other relationships, the bonds will be cut. Even Levi Strauss, a clothing manufacturer with a sterling reputation for social responsibility (it kept most of its idle workers on the payroll during the Depression), was, by century's end, severing bonds with its communities and employees, closing most of its North American plants and firing nearly half of its workforce while subcontracting production to foreign factories with lower labor costs. To be sure, the company did the severing nicely, providing its former employees generous severance payments and helping them train for new jobs. But in the end Levi Strauss had no choice but to cut the bonds. Its competitors had already done so, and their lower costs gave them an advantage that threatened Levi's future.

In the new economy, there will be no random acts of kindness to employees, suppliers, or communities separate from their positive impact on the bottom line. If being "socially responsible" helps the bottom line by eliciting good will from employees, suppliers, or the public at large, then such actions make sound business sense, and the new competitive logic dictates that executives pursue them. If, however, being "socially responsible" detracts from the bottom line—handicapping the enterprise by drawing resources away from, or otherwise preventing, production that's better, faster, and cheaper than rivals'—then it creates the risk that consumers and shareholders will switch to a better deal. By the new logic, executives then pursue such actions at their peril.

THE ABNORMALITY OF LOYALTY

The unexpected, or even repellent, repeated often enough, eventually becomes acceptable; the acceptable, replicated widely, becomes the norm. Commercial behavior once thought to be a betrayal of trust is now common practice. When, at the start of 1996, AT&T announced it would fire tens of thousands of workers and award its chief executive a fat bonus, the press roundly excoriated the corporation. After a few other big companies followed suit, a Republican presidential candidate condemned the perfidy of big business, and a prominent national newsweekly carried on its cover the photographs of several chief executives under the headline "Corporate Killers." By the end of the decade, firings were continuing on about the same scale, even though companies were more profitable than they had been during the mid-nineties and executive compensation was considerably higher. Yet by then the blame, and the shame, had disappeared. Such practices had become a routine aspect of American business.

A generation before, being fired from one's job suggested a moral failure—a personal defect, a profound flaw. An employee might be temporarily laid off during an economic downturn but not permanently fired. It wouldn't be rational for an employer to fire someone who was doing an adequate job. Firing signaled that the person had failed to do the job expected of him, or was no longer capable of doing it. A firing thus entailed a profound loss of self-respect. Great tragedies centered on such events. When young Howard fires Willie Loman in Arthur Miller's 1949 play *Death of a Salesman,* it's because Willie can no longer make the grade. Willie was once a great salesman but is no longer useful, and this knowledge breaks him. "You can't eat an orange and throw the peel away," Willie roars. "A man is not a piece of fruit."

Willie's plight is still poignant, but the play seems strangely dated. Someone who is fired from a job may still feel angry or humiliated, but he is no longer presumed to be flawed. People are fired all the time for reasons having nothing to do with their failure to achieve. John Scully, the former CEO of Apple Computer, saw this as a California phenomenon, but by century's end he was describing almost all of America: "When someone is fired or leaves on the East Coast, it's a real trauma in their lives. When they are fired or leave here, it doesn't mean much. They just go off and do something else."[20]

The old economy rewarded stable, predictable relationships—among customers, investors, companies, suppliers, employees, and communities—because large-scale production depended on stability and predictability. Any deviation undermined efficiency. Thus all participants came to rely on permanence. But the emerging economy is altering expectations. Commercial relationships are no longer assumed to last. People figure that everyone with whom they deal will switch to a better alternative should one become available, as will they.

As disloyalty is "normalized," loyalty itself comes under suspicion. Remain too long with one company or in one job, and your behavior must be explained. Perhaps your immobility is due to your spouse or family, but it also may be due to some failing on your part—a lack of options (no other opportunity has beckoned) or a notable lack of ambition. A company or organization that keeps its same executives and employees for too long invites similar scrutiny. Maybe it is just quaintly old-fashioned. But it may harbor deeper problems—it's too stodgy to keep up with the times, too hidebound, stale, lacking in new blood and vision. A community that retains the same residents decade after decade is sometimes presumed to be insular and ingrown, obviously lacking in vitality.

LOYALTY TO WHAT?

In the years ahead, it will be unclear, in any event, what the entity *is* that might summon loyalty, or be loyal in return. The very meaning of a company or university or any other institution is growing less coherent. All institutions are flattening into networks of entrepreneurial groups, temporary projects, electronic communities and coalitions, linked to various brands and portals. In this emerging cyber-landscape, it will be odd to speak of institutional loyalty because there will be fewer clear boundaries around any institution.

Organizations used to be recognizable: They were shaped like pyramids, with top executives, layers of middle-level managers and staff, and a larger number of people doing relatively simple and repetitive tasks at the bottom. You were either in—a member, resident, partner, or employee—or on the outside. Now bureaucratic controls are no longer necessary for coordinating large numbers of people. People can coordinate themselves through the Internet. Broad constellations of designers, suppliers, marketers, financial specialists, contractors, and shippers can function *as if* they were a single enterprise, then form a different constellation tomorrow. So who's in? Who's out? In a few years, a "company" will be best defined by who has access to what data, and gets what portion of a particular stream of revenues, over what period of time.

A glimpse of the future: The Monorail Corporation owns no factories, warehouses, or any other tangible asset. It operates from a single floor it leases in an office building in Atlanta. A few designers on contract to Monorail devised a personal computer that could fit into a standard box shipped by Federal Express. To place orders for it, customers call a 1-800 number connected to FedEx's Logistics Service, which passes the orders on to a contract manufacturer that assembles it from various parts coming from around the world. FedEx then ships the computer to the customer and sends the invoice to the Sun Trust Bank in Atlanta, whose factoring department handles billing and credit approvals, remits a prearranged portion to everyone who played a part along the way (including a small commission to Monorail), and assumes the cost and risk of collecting from the customer. A customer who needs help at any point can call "Monorail's" 1-800 service center, which is actually staffed and run by Sykes Enterprises, a call-center outsourcing company based in Tampa, Florida. As a result of this network, Monorail can offer among the lowest-priced PCs available anywhere. It can also increase its sales almost effortlessly, simply by expanding its network of suppliers.[21]

But Monorail, by this account, is not what it seems. It's not really much of anything except a good idea, a handful of people in Atlanta, and a bunch of contracts. By the time you read this, Monorail may not even exist any longer. Can Monorail be "loyal" to anyone? Can anyone be loyal to Monorail?

RESPONSIBILITY TO WHOM?

Through the Internet, responsibilities for who does what and who gets what in return can be distributed through a wide cluster of temporary contracts. But such contracts can't take into account all possible problems. Example: For about ten days starting on August 7, 1999, a number of small businesses that depended on the Internet to link them to their customers lost Internet service—a near-death experience. Who was responsible? Follow the trail: Their Internet service providers had relied on DataXchange, a Washington, D.C.–based company that had bought large chunks of Internet access wholesale and then sold it to them in pieces. DataXchange had bought its largest chunk from MCI World-Com. On August 7, MCI WorldCom's high-speed network went down. Why? MCI WorldCom's network used software from Lucent Technologies (once the research arm of AT&T); on August 7 that software developed a glitch that MCI engineers couldn't fix. And why not? Because the software had been developed several years before by a different group of engineers working for an outfit called Cascade Communications. Cascade was subsequently acquired by Ascent Communications, which Lucent acquired along with the software in early 1999 for $20 billion. That's how the software got into Lucent's system, and hence into MCI WorldCom's data network.

Strip away all the corporate names, and you get a truer picture of what happened—like clicking on "reveal codes" in your computer program and discovering the underlying instructions. All we now see is a bunch of people who contracted with one another for specific services. Those who contributed services several years ago by writing the original software are now working on other projects. The problem is, they're the only ones who know enough about the software to be able to fix the glitch quickly, and they are no longer available. They didn't come with the software that went from Cascade to Ascent and then on to Lucent in early 1999. Their intelligence is crucial, but it wasn't part of the intellectual property that changed hands.

When the "glue" that holds an enterprise together is little more than a bunch of temporary contracts, who's responsible for making sure that the system as a whole works as planned? It's one thing if a lot of small businesses lose money because nobody can fix a software glitch, but the subcontracting of responsibility can sometimes cause graver problems. When a small company in Indonesia employs young children to weave its fabrics ten hours a day for six days a week in unsanitary conditions, and then sells the fabric to a Taiwanese company, which cuts and sews it into garments that, in turn, are sent to a jobber in California who supplies Wal-Mart—is Wal-Mart responsible for how the children are treated? How can it be, if it has no practical way of knowing? But how can it *not* be, if a significant percentage of the American public finds child labor morally offensive? When a few employees of a now-defunct aircraft maintenance company improperly packed oxygen generators that were then delivered to its client, an airline, sparking a fire in a plane's cargo hold and causing it to crash in the Everglades, who is morally responsible?*

---

* Legal responsibility for the 1996 ValuJet crash was established, but without practical effect: In 1999, a federal jury convicted SabreTech, Inc., the now-defunct maintenance company, of nine felony charges related to its mishandling of the oxygen canisters which led to the crash. A for-

The Obsolescence of Loyalty

COMMERCIAL LOYALTY has not disappeared entirely. You may still feel loyalty toward your employer and your employer may feel it toward you. But the trend is undeniably against such sentiments, and the reason should be clear. Every consumer and every investor can switch to something better with increasing ease and speed—which means that everyone along the supply chain must be changeable as well, in order to be better, faster, and cheaper. Consumers and investors like you and me are taking advantage of technologies—most recently, the Internet, e-commerce, and fancy software—that allow greater flexibility at all junctures. Under the combined pressure, enterprises are becoming collections of people bound to one another by little more than temporary convenience.

The result is boundless innovation and unprecedented dynamism. But it's also a set of economic relationships so transient as to render ambiguous who owes what obligations to whom—and who will be there for whom tomorrow. My students view the world they are entering in far more temporary terms than my generation saw it. They don't plan to spend more than a few years in any job. They don't anticipate any loyalty from any organization or institution, and rarely from another person—and they don't expect to be loyal in return. To them, a commercial relationship is fleeting. They assume they'll have to take full responsibility for navigating their careers; they cannot entrust that responsibility to anyone else.

---

mer SabreTech mechanic and a maintenance supervisor were acquitted on all charges. After the verdict, SabreTech's attorney said the company was a corporate shell with virtually no assets. In 1997, ValuJet merged with another airline.

87

CHAPTER FIVE

The End of Employment
As We Knew It

Work is of two kinds: First, altering the position of matter at or near the earth's surface relative to other such matter; second, telling other people to do so.
— Bertrand Russell, *In Praise of Idleness and Other Essays*

K EEP FOLLOWING the logic: Technology is speeding and broadening access to terrific deals. Buyers and investors can switch to something better with ever-increasing ease. In order to survive in this new era of fiercer competition, sellers have to innovate continuously and do so faster than their rivals. The best way is through small entrepreneurial groups linked to trusted brands. At their core are talented geeks and shrinks, in ever-greater demand. The enterprise must also continuously cut costs, leasing almost everything it needs, finding the lowest-cost suppliers, pushing down wages of routine workers, and flattening all hierarchies into fast-changing contractual networks.

It's not like this everywhere, at least not yet. Most people still work for, and within, organizations. But the logic of the new economy is changing the employment relationship. Fewer working people are "employees," as that term was used through most of the twentieth century—and in the future there will be fewer still. The working citizens of other nations are treading the same path away from steady employment, although several steps behind.

What's in store for you and your children? You won't be an utterly free agent selling your individual services in the open market to the highest bidder, nor will you be an "organization" man or woman. Instead, you're likely to become a member of an entrepreneurial group whose profits vary yearly or even monthly, your share depending on your contribution. Or you'll be part of a professional-services firm, for whose clients you do projects and for which you receive a share of overall earnings. Or you'll work for a talent agency or temp firm that sends you to work on specific projects for a limited time and takes a percentage of your earnings in return. Even Silicon Valley is sprouting agencies that rent out top programmers for $200 or more an hour.[1]

Regardless of your precise relationship to the people who buy your services, the organization that stands between you and them is thinning out. Even if you're *called* a full-time employee, you're becoming less of an employee of an organization than you are a seller of your services to particular customers and clients, under the organization's brand name. Accordingly, your income will depend on how much these buyers are willing to pay for your services, and the reputation of the brand that attracts them to you.

In some respects, we're coming full circle to an earlier stage in economic history in which people contracted to do specific tasks. The whole idea of a *steady* job is rather new, historically speaking—and, as it turns out, short-lived. It flourished in the United States and other industrialized nations for a century and a half, during the industrial era of large-scale production. And it's now coming to an end.

THE ORIGIN OF EMPLOYMENT

A brief pause for some history. Before the dawn of large-scale production in the latter half of the nineteenth century, few people were permanently employed at a fixed wage. Most work occurred on family or tenant farms or in small family-run shops, or it was done by craftsmen, artisans, and tradesmen. In the old South, most of the tasks of planting and harvesting large tracts of tobacco, rice, and indigo fell to people who did work permanently for someone else but were not free: indentured whites and black slaves. In none of these cases were earnings "steady." Income depended on the vagaries of weather, pestilence, disease, and warfare. It required unflinching effort, often hard on muscles and joints. Nor was there a sharp divide between work life and home life, between paid work and unpaid. Women and children worked alongside men, and home production was a central feature of a family's economic well-being. This is all still the case today for the majority of humankind around the world.

When industrial production first made its appearance in America, the very idea of working permanently for someone else was thought degrading, if not a threat to individual liberty. Typical was the view of the political pamphleteer Orestes Brownson, a fierce Jacksonian Democrat, who wrote in an 1840 tract that "wages are a cunning device of the devil for the benefit of tender consciences who would retain all the advantages of the slave system without the expense, trouble, and odium of being slave holders."[2] Wage work was morally acceptable only as a step toward economic independence—a transient condition that, to the minds of many Northerners, distinguished it from slavery. Abraham Lincoln offered himself up as an example—beginning as a hired laborer splitting rails, then learning the law and earning his own living. "They insist that their slaves are far better off than Northern freemen," Lincoln scoffed at Southerners who defended the slave system. "What a mistaken view do these men have of Northern laborers! They think that men are always to remain laborers here—but there is no such class. The man who labored for another last year, this year labors for himself, and next year he will hire others to labor for him."[3]

Owners of the small mills and factories that had sprouted around New England and the mid-Atlantic states contracted directly with skilled craftsmen and paid them according to what they produced. The craftsmen's knowledge of, and control over, most manufacturing tasks gave them significant bargaining power in this arrangement. But as large-scale production spread after the Civil War, factory owners began replacing skilled craftsmen with machines, and hired unskilled laborers—many of them new immigrants—to run them at fixed wages. The craftsmen responded by joining together in America's first large union, the Knights of Labor, whose goal was to "abolish the wage system."[4]

The first major clash occurred in 1892 at Andrew Carnegie's Homestead Works, near Pittsburgh. When the craftsmen refused to accept lower pay, they were locked out of the mill, but they refused to allow unskilled laborers in. The standoff lasted several months, until nonunion workers were ushered into the mill under the protection of the Pennsylvania state militia, and the union surrendered. For several years thereafter, state and federal governments, backed by business interests, continued to weigh in on the side of owners. In 1894, Chicago and much of the Midwest were immobilized by striking rail workers protesting the treatment of workers by the Pullman Car Company. In quick succession, a federal court enjoined the strikers, President Grover Cleveland deployed federal troops at key railway junctions, martial law was declared in Chicago, and the leaders of the strike were jailed.

The Knights went down to defeat, and wage work became the norm. Between 1870 and 1910, while the American population more than doubled, the number of wage workers in industrial labor more than quadrupled, from 3.5 million to 14.2 million.[5] And the number employed within any given factory soared. The New England mills of the mid-nineteenth century had employed no more than a few hundred people; the first Ford Motor plant in 1915 employed 15,000.

Drawing from the ranks of coal miners, cigar makers, printers, iron and steel workers, and garment sewers, a new union appeared—the American Federation of Labor—that accepted the inevitability of wage work. Samuel Gompers, the AFL's first president, conceded that "we are operating under the wage system, and so long as that lasts it is our purpose to secure a continually larger share for labor."[6] To Gompers, industrial concentration was "a logical and inevitable feature of our modern system of industry."[7]

Progressives like Woodrow Wilson still pined for a simpler time when "men were everywhere captains of industry, not employees, not looking to a distant city to find out what they might do, but looking about among their neighbors,"[8] but reluctantly accepted that the new economy required wage work. The question that preoccupied Progressives was how to reconcile wage work with the American values of individualism and freedom, while at the same time protecting workers from its more unsavory aspects. The answer they devised was to set broad limits on business, within laws establishing maximum hours, minimum pay, compensation for injuries, and minimal requirements for safety and sanitation.

The limits were not established without a struggle. There were those who wanted to argue that wage work represented just another kind of freedom. In the 1905 case of *Lochner v. New York,* the Supreme Court decided that New York's maximum ten-hour day for bakery workers was nothing less than an "illegal interference with the rights of individuals, both employers and employees, to make contracts regarding labor upon which terms they may think best." New York had no business "limiting the hours in which grown and intelligent men may labor to earn their living."[9] Only three years later, in *Muller v. Oregon,* the Court reached a very different decision, upholding Oregon's ten-hour day for women because, the Court reasoned, "healthy mothers are essential to vigorous offspring, [and] the physical well-being of women becomes an object of public interest and care in order to preserve the strength and vigor of the race." Women differed from men not only "in structure of body," but also in "the self-reliance which enables [men] to assert full rights."[10] In point of fact, of course, neither male nor female wage workers were free to negotiate terms of employment in the new system of large-scale production. Neither had any bargaining leverage.

After a prolonged legal and political struggle, labor protections were finally extended to the nation's entire workforce, along with the right to bargain collectively. Social Security and unemployment insurance were added as well, protecting workers against the risks of job loss during downturns in the business cycle, the death of a working husband and father, permanent disability, and inadequate savings in old age for retirement. The most unique aspect of the American system of social protection (in contrast with those being adopted in other industrializing nations) was that it was available only to people in permanent wage work—precisely the circumstance that had been rejected less than a century before. All benefits depended on being (or having been, or been married to) a full-time employee. Notably excluded were casual workers, part-timers, independent contractors, the self-employed, and the chronically unemployed. Even welfare as originally conceived was intended only for the widows of working men. Franklin D. Roosevelt's Committee on Economic Security, headed by my formidable predecessor Labor Secretary Frances Perkins, reported that the purpose of Aid to Dependent Children (as it was then called) was to free widows with young children from "the wage earning role" so they could keep their children from "falling into social misfortune," and "more affirmatively to rear them into citizens capable of contributing to society."[11] In other words, in the new industrial order, it was assumed that all men should be wage earners; women with young children should not be working.

One final but often overlooked aspect of America's twentieth-century system of social insurance bears mention, because it also depended on full-time employment. This was the tax-favored fringe benefit, such as company-provided health insurance and a company pension. Most people still think of these as private rather than public benefits, but they ballooned in the 1940s, and unions pressed for them, because employees didn't have to pay taxes on employer-provided health insurance and could defer taxes on employer-provided pensions until retirement. These benefits were thus the economic equivalent of direct government payouts, since the forgone taxes left equivalent-sized holes in the government's budget. And the holes steadily widened: By the mid-1980s, at the peak of their scope and generosity, the revenue losses to the Treasury from such tax-favored employee benefits were larger than expenses on all federal programs for the poor. The tax subsidy for employee health plans roughly equaled what was spent directly on health care for the poor through Medicaid, and revenue losses from tax-advantaged pension contributions totaled more than twice the total cost of cash aid for the poor.[12]

THE RULES OF EMPLOYMENT

By midcentury, the transformation was complete. More than a third of all working Americans belonged to a union, and agreements between management and labor set wage and benefit levels throughout industry. Labor, management, and government together ushered into the middle class a large phalanx of blue-collar workers and stabilized the middle-class status of an expanding group of white-collar employees. The careers of these latter "organization men" (to use the felicitous phrase of sociologist William H. Whyte, Jr.'s best-seller of the era)[13] came to be as ordered and predictable as those of their blue-collar counterparts. So common as to be taken for granted, the implicit rules of employment at midcentury still frame much of our understanding, although they have almost nothing to do with the emerging reality of work in the twenty-first century. For example:

Steady work with predictably rising pay. The typical employee spent almost his entire working life within the same enterprise. This was true not only of blue-collar workers; middle-level managers often joined their companies fresh out of college and remained with them until retirement. Two-thirds of senior executives surveyed in 1952 had been with the same company for more than twenty years.[14] The young white-collar men interviewed by Whyte gave voice to the accepted view: *"Be loyal to the company and the company will be loyal to you,"* they told him (emphasis in the original). "[T]he average young man cherishes the idea that his relationship with The Organization is to be for keeps," wrote Whyte. Mutual loyalty could be counted on because, it was thought, "the goals of the individual and the goals of the organization will work out to be one and the same."[15]

Take-home pay depended more on the number of years with the organization than on individual effort. Union contracts stipulated seniority; white-collar workers moved up pay ladders. Such predictability not only helped the large-scale organization plan its production; it also helped families plan their futures. One's pay "grade" started at a modest level, when household expenses at that early point in life rarely required more. The grade level gradually rose with experience and maturity, allowing employees to take out home loans and car loans with confidence that they could be repaid. As paychecks grew, "starter" homes and cars could be traded up, and children could be raised. At age sixty-five, after forty or more years with a company, the typical full-time employee retired with a gold watch or pin and a company pension providing a modest fixed sum thereafter. Social Security and personal savings provided the rest. Retirees could then expect another five or six years of card games with old friends and visits from the grandchildren before dying with the satisfaction of having put in a full working life.

Limited effort. Factory work was still hard on muscles and joints, but by the midpoint of the twentieth century it was no longer dangerous, for the most part. And the effort it required of blue-collar workers was carefully circumscribed by work rules and job classifications. The white-collar worker of midcentury took the job seriously but rarely obsessed. "[T]here are few subjects upon which [young men] will discourse more emphatically," noted Whyte, "than the folly of elders who have a single-minded devotion to work."[16] The employee sold the organization his time, not his soul. Young Tom Rath, the hero of Sloan Wilson's best-selling novel of the 1950s, *The Man in the Gray Flannel Suit,* typified the prevailing norm. Tom turns down a challenging job, explaining to his boss, "I'm just not the kind of guy who can work evenings and weekends and all the rest of it forever. . . . I'm not the kind of person who can get all wrapped up in a job—I can't get myself convinced that my work is the most important thing in the world." The benevolent boss understands. "There are plenty of good jobs where it's not necessary for a man to put in an unusual amount of work," he says, kindly. "Now, it's just a matter of finding the right spot for you." [17]

By law, blue-collar workers were owed time-and-a-half for any more than forty hours of work each week. White-collar salary workers were also expected to put in no more than a fixed amount of work time, beginning and ending strictly on schedule. In the pre-employment era, people had been paid for completing particular tasks; the large-scale enterprise, by contrast, paid people for putting in predictable time. It has been suggested that even the way people *thought* about time shifted with industrialization, from "task time"—the number of minutes or hours necessary to finish a particular task—to "clock time," as measured in uniform intervals. [18] Large economies of scale could be achieved only if jobs were coordinated like clockwork. Frederick Winslow Taylor, the management theorist, pioneered "time and motion" studies to discover the most efficient means of doing a particular set of repetitive movements within a certain fixed interval of time.

Efficiency came at the price of tedium for some. The organization was, in this respect, like a large version of the machines at its core. All the pieces had to fit together, unobtrusively. The organization ran by rules. Factory workers were not paid to think. Henry Ford once complained that when he hired a pair of hands, he also got a human being. Where no rules were available, there were rules for setting new rules. If the vast organizational machine was to attain maximum efficiency, all behavior had to be fully anticipated. Blue-collar workers adhered to job classifications and work rules; white-collars followed standard operating procedure. "What should a person do," a midlevel executive asked Norman Vincent Peale, America's most popular armchair therapist of the 1950s, "who is unhappy and bored in his job after twenty years but who earns a nice salary and hasn't the nerve to leave?" Seeking a different job was out of the question, Peale counseled; even altering the current one was too ambitious an undertaking. Peale advised accepting one's fate: "[W]ake up mentally and strive for some understanding of what [you] can accomplish in [your] present position." [19]

All of the above allowed for a strict border between paid work and the rest of one's life. By midcentury, work and home were different places. Home was often in the suburbs, a commute away from office or factory. Most blue-collar men could afford the accouterments of middle-class life without relying on a second wage earner. Some middle-class women worked outside the home nonetheless, within the few professions (such as teaching) open to them; poor women continued to clean houses and cook for pay. But most women remained in their homes, waxing, polishing, and cleaning them until they shone as brightly as they did in the advertisements, and rearing children with the kind of supreme attentiveness guaranteed to produce a self-indulgent generation of postwar boomers.

This allocation of responsibility was widely accepted, although it created new problems. "At first she is slightly resentful" of her husband's life on the job, a magazine for salesmen solemnly warned. "In time she may become openly jealous." Here was a particularly dangerous juncture: "Unless brought under control, [the jealousy] can end up in irreparable damage to the salesman's worth to his employer." The solution was for housewives to join the League of Women Voters, the Parent-Teacher Association, or even the school board, and thus feel "worthwhile." A corollary danger arose "if the husband [was] moving up rapidly" in the corporation, thus creating "a wedge between husband and wife, for while he is getting post-graduate finishing through travel and exposure to successful older men, her tastes are often frozen at their former level by lack of any activity but child rearing."[20] The remedy was for her to throw herself into voluntary suburban activity with even greater gusto.

Wage compression, and the expansion of the middle class. The large-scale organization compressed wages, raising them for workers at the bottom and limiting them at the top. Unions prevented wages from dropping too low, and the organization had no need to bestow lavish compensation on top executives since most of them rose through the ranks and would not be poached by another firm. The constraint was also social: It would be thought unseemly for top executives to earn large multiples of the earnings of people in the middle ranges or at the bottom.

Apart from the occasional promotion, the large-scale organization did not differentiate among employees who had put in the same number of years on the job. All midlevel executives of equal tenure were paid about the same, as were university professors of the same rank and experience, hospital administrators, journalists working for large daily newspapers, and civil servants. In short, one's status and income were bureaucratically determined. "[B]usiness is coming more and more to assume the shape of the government civil service," noted a sociological text of the 1950s. Employees' incomes "depend upon the rules of bureaucratic entry and promotion. . . . Income is determined by functional role in the bureaucracy." It was not surprising therefore that "[t]he trend of income distribution has been toward a reduction in inequality. Owners have been receiving a smaller share relative to employees; professionals and clerks have been losing some of their advantages over operatives and laborers."[21]

At midcentury, almost half of all American families fell comfortably within the middle class (then defined as family units receiving from $4,000 to $7,500 after taxes, in 1953 dollars). Notably, most of these middle-class families were headed not by professionals or business executives but by skilled and semiskilled factory workers, clerks, salesmen, and wholesale and retail workers, who managed the flows of product through the great pyramids of large-scale production. A majority received health and pension benefits through work.

To be successful was to be respected in one's community, to earn a decent living and be promoted up the corporate ladder, to own a home in the suburbs and have a stable family, and to be well liked and widely admired. These aspirations were not unrealistic for a large and growing percentage of Americans.

Yet America of the 1950s still harbored vast inequalities. The very poor remained almost invisible. Discrimination was deeply entrenched. Blacks were overtly relegated to second-class citizenship and inferior jobs. Few women dared aspire to professions other than teaching or nursing. It would be decades before such barriers began to fall.

POST-EMPLOYMENT

By the turn of the twenty-first century, these tacit rules of employment had all but vanished. The new logic detailed in preceding chapters demonstrates that they have become increasingly irrelevant to working life. Less than one in ten private-sector workers belongs to a union;

the white-collar "organization man" is a vanishing species. While most people still rely on wages or salaries, the old employment contract is quickly eroding. To wit:

The end of steady work. Steady work—a predictable level of pay from year to year—has disappeared for all but a handful of working people (among the rare holdouts, tenured professors who write about employment). Buyers' widening choices and easier switches have made it almost impossible for any organization to guarantee a consistent stream of income to anyone working within it. To stay competitive in this volatile environment, organizations have to turn all fixed costs (especially payrolls, which are among their largest) into variable costs that rise and fall according to the choices buyers make. As a result, earnings have become less and less predictable. Evidence of *job* instability is less conclusive, but this is largely a matter of semantics. A job that's formally classified as "permanent" or "full-time," but whose pay varies considerably from month to month or even from year to year, is not, as a practical matter, a job one can rely on.[22]

The new precariousness is manifest in many ways. Nearly everyone is now on "soft money," in the sense that their earnings vary with contracts, grants, or sales from one period to the next. Much has been said about the rising tide of temporary workers, part-timers, freelancers, e-lancers, independent contractors, and free agents—variously estimated to constitute a tenth to a third of the civilian labor force.[23] But the portion of employees uncertain about how much they'll earn from year to year or even from month to month is far bigger than even the largest estimate. Increasingly, the take-home pay of full-time employees depends on sales commissions, individual bonuses, work-team bonuses, profit-sharing, billable hours, stock options, and other indicia of performance—all of which can as easily drop as grow.[24] An increasing number of workers also move from project to project within their companies, or for clients. If there's no project for them to work on, or if no project manager wants their services, they're unceremoniously "beached," and their pay declines accordingly. They may continue to be listed as full-time employees, but as a practical matter they are barely on the payroll.

Small businesses of less than twenty-five employees are creating most new jobs, but the incomes of their full-time employees are also unpredictable, because small businesses disappear at a much higher rate than larger ones; job tenure in small businesses averages 4.4 years, in contrast to 8.5 years at firms with 1,000 or more employees.[25] In addition, many large companies are discovering they can make more money turning full-time employees into full-time licensees or franchisees, thereby shifting market risks onto them while increasing their incentive to work hard. Before 1979, taxicab leasing was illegal in New York City. Drivers were employed by large fleets of cabs, sharing with the company a percentage of each day's receipts. Many companies offered health insurance and retirement plans. But the taxi companies found it more profitable to lease the cabs to the drivers, and pressed for a change in the law. By the late 1990s, most drivers were independent operators, paying taxi companies $90 to $135 for a twelve-hour rental, with no health or pension coverage. They could earn more money than before if they hustled, but might end up with less. Perhaps not incidentally, taxicab accidents were on the rise.[26]

Benefits have become as precarious as earnings. In 1980, more than 70 percent of workers received some form of health benefit from their employers. By the late 1990s, the percentage had slipped to about 60 percent. And even when employees have some coverage, it has become less generous, requiring them to take on higher co-payments, deductibles, and premiums.[27]

Employment in the nonprofit sector of the economy offers no greater security. Donors, foundations, and grant-making agencies that once routinely renewed their contributions are now almost as fickle as consumers and investors. A growing portion of university payrolls depends on grants and funded research from outside the university. And as support has become less predictable, universities have had to rely more on contract workers whose jobs and pay vary accordingly. In 1970, only 22 percent of university faculty were part-timers. By the end of the 1990s, the proportion had risen to more than 40 percent, not including a rising tide of graduate-student teachers.[28] All told, slightly more than half of university teachers are itinerants, moving through the groves of academe like migrant farmworkers.

The necessity of continuous effort. Earnings now depend less on formal rank or seniority, and more on an employee's value to customers. It's not unusual for a twenty-three-year-old geek with a hot skill to be earning several times more than a "senior manager" three levels up.[29] In America's most competitive industries—harbingers of times to come—the half-life of talented people continues to shorten. The stars of Wall Street, Silicon Valley, and Hollywood are coming to resemble professional athletes who can count on no more than ten to fifteen years before losing their competitive edge. Twentysomething software engineers are in great demand; when they're over forty, they're over the hill. Surveys show that six years after graduating with a degree in computer science, 60 percent are working as software programmers; after twenty years, only 19 percent are still at it. This largely explains why high entry salaries and generous signing bonuses are still not enough to entice greater numbers of undergraduates into the field. They know how quickly they'll become obsolete.[30]

An inverse relationship between creativity and age has long been established, although most of us with graying heads would rather avoid the subject. The field of mathematics is built almost entirely on the creative breakthroughs of young mathematics whizzes; great musical compositions typically come from young composers; great research, from young scientists; great poetry, from younger muses. What older people lack in creativity, they make up for in experience, wisdom, and judgment—attributes that continue to be valued, although not to the same degree as creativity. As a consequence, more older and middle-aged workers are experiencing flat or declining earnings, and middle-aged people who lose their jobs have difficulty finding new ones, even when the overall rate of unemployment is low.[31]

There's no coasting, no cruising altitude. Work requires continuing effort. Home is no longer a haven from paid work; the border between the two is vanishing. Most women with young children now have paying jobs. And regardless of the official hours of employment, many men and women must be "on call" at all hours. The physical distinction between the place of paid work and the home is blurring; almost a third of the workforce works out of their homes at least part of the day. And wherever they are, cell phones, beepers, e-mail, and faxes keep them connected to customers and clients. Or they're in the air, traveling to and from one project or client to another. Sometimes they travel so much, they have no settled place of work but only temporary "hot desks" in a variety of locales.

Eight-hour days and forty-hour workweeks are becoming obsolete. Working hours now extend in all directions. The emerging economy runs twenty-four hours, seven days a week. This is partly because spouses or partners both work during the day and need the remaining hours to shop, run errands, and eat out—requiring other paid workers to be there for them at those odd hours. And it's also due to an increasingly globalized marketplace that never sleeps. Global companies, worldwide stock markets, and clients suffering insomnia demand around-the-clock attention.

Widening inequality. Firms no longer compress the wages of people who work within them. To the contrary, firms are competing furiously to attract and keep valuable performers—rewarding them with high wages, signing bonuses, stock options, year-end bonuses, memberships in health spas, and on-premises exercise rooms with hot tubs—while at the same time slashing the wages and benefits of routine workers. A similar divergence is occurring in nonprofits, although not quite as extreme. Professors of finance are earning far more than professors of English on the same faculties. The chief executives of giant foundations are earning many multiples of lowly staffers.

As enterprises morph into contractual networks, such disparities are widening. Workers are summoning what they're "worth" in the market. As noted, the demand for talented innovators is outrunning the supply. At the same time, routine production work can be done more cheaply by digital machines or by workers elsewhere around the world. Surely, some routine workers could learn the skills needed to become innovative geeks and shrinks, but the widening earnings gap suggests that not enough are doing so to keep up with the demand or to outrun the burgeoning supply of low-cost replacements.

Data on inequality are not free from controversy, but the trend is unassailable. By the end of the 1990s, according to the U.S. Census Bureau's Current Population Survey,[32] family incomes in the United States were diverging more widely than they had at any time since the 1920s, before the upheavals of the Depression, the New Deal, and World War II. From the late 1940s until the eighties, the top fifth's share of total family income had remained remarkably steady, claiming about 40 percent. The large middle three-fifths of families received close to 54 percent of total income. The poorest fifth got what remained. Then in the early 1980s the gap began to widen, and widened further in the nineties. The top fifth's share began rising, reaching almost half of all income by the end of the century, while the share going to the middle three-fifths dropped to 48.6 percent, and the share going to the bottom fifth shrank. Even *within* the top fifth, income and wealth shifted to the top. While the share of family income claimed by the top 5 percent had also been stable for most of the postwar era, at about 15 percent of the total, this portion, too, began rising in the eighties, reaching almost 25 percent by century's end. And the top 1 percent soared from 11 percent of total income in 1990 to nearly 18 percent in 1999.[33]

Since the early nineties, the incomes of people at or near the top have grown twice as fast as those of people in the middle. Despite the decade's boom, the median income has barely increased.[34] And although stocks have become far more widely held, most of the boom in the booming stock market of the nineties also went to the top. According to computations based on Federal Reserve data, about 85 percent of the value of the stock-market gains during the decade went to the wealthiest 10 percent of families; 40 percent, to the top 1 percent.[35] These widening gaps in income and wealth paralleled a widening benefits gap. Health coverage for workers in the bottom fifth of the income scale dropped more precipitously than for any other group—from about 41 percent covered in 1980 to 32 percent by the late 1990s. Employer-provided pensions diverged as well. The top 5 percent of households with incomes above $100,000 received almost a quarter of all pension tax benefits.[36]

These changes have large consequences. The rich and the middle class are now living in parallel universes, and the poor are almost invisible to both. By the end of the century, the richest 1 percent of American families, comprising 2.7 million people, had as many dollars to spend, after they had paid all taxes, as the bottom 100 million. And they owned most of America. (Bill Gates's net worth alone equaled the total net worth of the bottom 50 percent of American families.)

Some argue that inequality is not nearly the problem it seems. They point out that, starting in 1996, real incomes of workers at the bottom of the ladder stopped declining and actually began to rise.[37] True enough, but this welcome reversal was due almost entirely to an unusually low rate of unemployment—so low that bottom-rung workers could easily find one or more jobs, and put in many more hours than before. But we can't count on the economy continuing to remain robust forever; it seems doubtful that the business cycle has been permanently repealed. And even though their incomes rose, they still became poorer *relative to* the top 5 percent, whose incomes rose at a faster rate. Others point out that measures of inequality are mere snapshots of incomes at one point in time, and fail to account for the movement of people out of the bottom into higher levels of income. True, but research shows that most people who start out at or near the bottom end up there.[38] Others argue that poor people are still better off than they were several decades ago, before inexpensive long-distance telephone service, drugs to control hypertension, and other advances.

These perspectives contain important truths, but they don't contradict the blunt fact of widening inequality. Controlling for the ups and downs of the business cycle, the entire spread of wages and benefits has elongated: Workers at the top earn vastly more than top workers used to earn, those at the bottom earn relatively less than workers at the bottom used to earn, and workers at every point in between are wider apart than before. The same trend toward widening disparities can be observed in most other advanced economies, although it is not yet as pronounced as in the United States.

America is splitting because the old bureaucratic organizations are disappearing, along with their wage scales. Increasingly, people are being paid whatever they're "worth" on the market. During the Roaring Nineties, the average yearly compensation of Silicon Valley's one hundred highest-paid executives nearly quadrupled, to more than $7 million a year (about $2,800 an hour, assuming a fifty-hour workweek). Add in stock options, and the figure was far higher. Why were they worth so much? Because consumers wanted their inventions, and investors wanted a piece of the action even though profits were still far in the future for many of these enterprises. During the same interval, the wages of the bottom quarter of workers in the Valley—doing everything from assembling computer parts in their homes to caring for the children of software engineers—dropped 20 percent, to just over $9 an hour.[39] Why were they worth so little? Because they could so easily be replaced. In King County, Washington (comprising Seattle and Redmond, the home of Microsoft), 23,500 software workers each earned an average of $287,700 in 1999, including share options. The median household income of everyone else in the county was $34,300.[40] Why so large a large gap? Because the software workers' services were in high demand in the world; most other residents of the area provided retail, restaurant, hotel, hospital, and transportation services, which were not.

Comedian Jerry Seinfeld received $22 million for the last season (1997–98) of his widely popular television show. The NBC network apparently thought he was worth it. During each episode, NBC pulled in $1 million per minute of advertising. Advertisers figured many of us were watching and would buy their products as a result. We were, and we did. NBC also relies on an increasing number of freelancers—studio technicians, makeup artists, and "stringers"—to whom it pays the lowest wages it can, lower than its old union wage rate. Other broadcasters are doing the same, including the cable channels that are eating away at network-TV audiences, making it all the more imperative that NBC take these cost-cutting steps if it's going to do well by its parent, GE, and by GE's investors—among them, my teachers' retirement fund. The laundry worker down my street earned $13,500 in 1999, she tells me. Even though the American economy was booming, the brute fact was that the laundry where she worked could easily find someone to replace her if she demanded a penny more. And, in truth, I didn't want to pay any more than necessary to have my laundry done, although I didn't admit that to her.

FULL CIRCLE?

It's not coincidental that the old ideals of personal responsibility and freedom of contract heard in the years before industrialization are being heard once again. Legal protections against employers seem increasingly irrelevant where the employer-employee relationship is coming undone. The forty-hour workweek is meaningless to a taxi driver who leases his cab and medallion, or to a day trader who sits at his computer and gambles on stock prices. Both put in as many hours as they wish; it's up to them. The right to bargain collectively makes little difference to them, either—or to growing numbers of people who work in small businesses and move from project to project, or who style themselves as free agents or professionals. With whom, exactly, would they bargain?

Laws ensuring a minimum level of workplace safety don't reach the one-third of workers who work from their homes at least part of the day. An "ergonomic" standard intended to guard against repetitive-strain injury doesn't protect me, now sitting at my home computer, writing this book. (For one brief day in January of 2000, the Labor Department extended rules governing workplace safety to work done at home, until the absurdity of the order became so apparent that the department quickly and unceremoniously withdrew it.) For that matter, I'm not particularly helped either by the Family and Medical Leave Act, which guarantees workers the right to leave work in the event of a family or medical emergency. Should there be an emergency in my house, I'll turn off the computer and rush downstairs. If the condition is troublesome but not critical, I may have a heated debate with myself about whether to leave work, and for how long, but I don't need to involve anyone else in that debate.

A mandatory minimum wage made sense when large-scale enterprises established prevailing wage rates and when most people were permanently employed. But in the post-employment world it's easier to argue, or to perceive, that people are paid what they're worth in the market. They determine their incomes on the basis of their skills, talents, and willingness to work hard. On this view, if they can't find someone willing to pay them more, it's their own fault. Similarly, unemployment insurance seemed reasonable when dips in the business cycle could hurt millions of innocent employees. But in the post-employment era, people without jobs seem more responsible for their situation: If they can't find a job, maybe it's because they're charging too much for their services. Maybe they should charge less, or get additional skills, or market themselves more effectively.

In the era of employment it seemed fitting that employers were the chief conduits for health insurance and private pensions, and contributed to Social Security. Employers had a legitimate interest in their employees' health security, and their employees had a stake in one another's productivity. But in the post-employment era, when people move from project to project and job to job, it seems reasonable that individuals take more responsibility for their own health care and retirement savings.

Yet there are some important differences between the pre- and post-employment eras that suggest it can't all be a matter of personal responsibility. In the pre-employment era, markets were mostly local and sellers faced little competition, so they had some power to set prices. They could also rely on their communities to come to their aid if they fell on hard times or needed help raising a barn or digging a new well. Communities, in that sense, provided an early form of social insurance. In the post-employment era, by contrast, most working people face the full gale force of a highly volatile market in which customers and investors can switch to better deals all over the world. And, increasingly, working people are on their own. Social insurance is eroding.

Even informal neighbor-to-neighbor social insurance is waning; many people barely know their neighbors.

REPRISE: THE NEW WORK

To summarize, about three decades ago the American economy began to shift out of stable large-scale production toward continuous innovation. The shift has been accelerating since then. Technology has been the driving force. New technologies of communication, transportation, and information, culminating recently in the Internet and so-called e-commerce, have dramatically widened customer choice and made it easier for all customers (including business customers) to shop for, and switch to, better deals. Wider choices and easier switching have intensified competition at all levels—forcing every seller to innovate like mad, cutting costs and adding new value.

In the old industrial economy, profits came from economies of scale—long runs of more or less identical products. Now, profits come from quickness to innovate and attract (and keep) customers. Before, the winners were big corporate bureaucracies. Now, the winners are small, highly flexible groups that devise great ideas, and trustworthy brands that market them effectively.

These changes have come faster to the United States than elsewhere, partly because America was the first to develop many of the underlying communication, transportation, and information technologies on which the changes are based, and partly because the American economy started out less regulated than the others, so capital and labor could move more quickly. Other societies are now showing signs of following in America's steps.

We're reaping significant benefits. The American economy has grown much larger, and more dynamic. In recent years, productivity has soared. The economy is capable of putting a much larger portion of its population to work, and keeping unemployment low, without risking wage inflation. A far wider array of goods and services is available, and it's much easier for customers to get terrific deals. In terms of our material quality of life—what we get for our money—most of us are better off than ever before. There's a lively debate about whether Americans at or near the bottom of the income ladder are better off than they were, say, in 1970. Relative to what they could afford to buy before, they are in many ways; relative to what most people in American society can now afford, they're more deprived.

Regardless of how you come out on this last question, it's important to remember that we're not just consumers. Most of us spend most of our days working for a living. We also exist within webs of personal relationships comprising families, friends, and communities. With the shift toward a more dynamic and innovative economy have come changes in how work is organized and rewarded, and these changes are altering our personal lives. We couldn't reap the benefits of the new economy without also experiencing these changes. They're two sides of the same newly minted coin.

As technology gives all buyers more choice and easier ability to switch, it makes all sellers less secure. The dynamism and innovation that rewards buyers also subjects sellers to less certainty, more volatility, higher highs and lower lows. Almost all earnings are becoming more volatile, and less predictable.

The new era raises the stakes in other ways. Talented and ambitious people have vast opportunities. They can make much more money relative to the median wage than could talented and ambitious people in the industrial era. And many find their work far more stimulating than the mind-numbing bureaucratic jobs of that time. Yet it is also the case that more jobs require unremitting effort, and all workers are subject to greater risks of sharp drops in earnings. Disparities in income and wealth have widened considerably. Not for a century has America endured, or tolerated, this degree of inequality.

What is the true meaning of success under these more extreme conditions? And how do we make adequate room for ourselves, our families, and our communities without some defense against the harsher realities? It is to these questions we now turn.

PART TWO

THE
NEW LIFE

CHAPTER SIX

The Lure of Hard Work

W HAT DO PEOPLE DO when their earnings are less predictable, their jobs less secure, and their incomes potentially higher or lower than before? They work harder. Not only do they put in more hours on the job; they also work more intensively.

By official estimates, the average American is working longer hours, although there's some dispute over exactly how many more hours, and some researchers don't even agree that Americans *are* working longer hours. Each spring the Census undertakes a large-scale survey of some 50,000 households, asking, among other things, how many weeks people worked for pay during the previous year and how many hours they usually worked per week. This isn't a perfect measure, because some people forget how hard they worked and other people exaggerate—they may feel as though they worked longer than they actually did, or if they didn't work very much, they might be reluctant to admit it. The vanishing boundary line between paid work and the rest of life causes additional difficulties. Where does work end? Nonetheless, this survey is the best measure we have, and because the same question is asked every year, it at least provides a rough indicator of whether work time is increasing or decreasing over time.

According to this gauge, hours of paid work are climbing. The average adult working American now puts in almost 2,000 hours a year for pay. That's the equivalent of about two weeks more than he—or, especially, she—put in two decades ago. In 1999, the average middle-income married couple with children worked a combined 3,918 hours—about seven weeks more than a decade before.[1]

Americans are now working longer for pay than even the notoriously industrious Japanese, who are currently putting in about as many hours as Americans did in 1980. According to a recent report of the United Nations' International Labor Organization, while Americans have been working more, most adults in other advanced economies have been working less. Up until the late 1980s, the average adult American worked about the same number of hours as the average adult European. Now the typical working American puts in 350 more hours a year than the typical European. In France, the number of hours of paid work has dropped from 1,810 in the eighties to 1,656 in the late nineties.[2] (As their economies follow the path blazed by America, there's reason to expect that the Europeans and Japanese will start working harder, too.)

Much of the trend in America can be accounted for by a dramatic shift by American women—especially mothers—from household work into paid work, or from part-time paid work into full-time paid work. Social changes of this magnitude don't often happen so quickly. You may be old enough to have lived through all of this and yet still not have appreciated just how big the shift has been. In 1969, according to Census data, 38 percent of married mothers between the ages of twenty and fifty-five worked for pay. Now almost 70 percent do.[3]

The trend toward more paid work in America isn't entirely due to women. Men in professional or managerial jobs are also working longer hours. Since the mid-1980s, the proportion of professionals and managers who work at least fifty hours a week has grown by more than a third. The only people who might be working fewer hours for pay are men whose education went no further than high school, largely because they're often the first to lose their jobs when businesses lay off workers or when the economy slows.

A PROBLEM?

Simply because most of us are putting in many more hours of paid work than we used to doesn't mean we're worse off. Fewer hours are needed to prepare meals these days, thanks to microwave ovens, preprocessed dinners, and ubiquitous fast-food restaurants; there are more options for child care than there used to be (if you can afford it); and the Internet is cutting back on shopping time. There's a lively debate among researchers about exactly how much time we're putting in on the job relative to "free" time for other pursuits.[4] Some contend that we actually have more free time than we used to. John Robinson, a professor of sociology at the University of Maryland, and Geoffrey Godbey, a professor of what's called "leisure studies" at Penn State, examined detailed time diaries kept by a sampling of people between 1965 and 1985—the people in the study kept track of everything they did during the day, including not only paid work but also unpaid household tasks—and found that free time increased over the two decades.[5] The professors' sample was small, and the kind of people with enough time on their hands to diligently keep track of how they spend their time may not exactly represent the average American. Moreover, the professors acknowledge that at least since 1985 most Americans seem to have less free time than they did. Nonetheless, Robinson and Godbey offer a valuable insight: When assessing just how much of a bind we're in, we need to take account of *unpaid* as well as paid work.

In fact, if you add paid and unpaid work together, it seems doubtful that there was ever a golden age in which more than a handful of wealthy people had a lot of free time on their hands. Most adult women and men have always worked hard. Farmwork was (and still is, for the tiny percent of Americans who continue to do it) among the hardest work, on backs and limbs. Generations of shopkeepers and their spouses put in very long hours. My parents ran a small clothing shop in upstate New York, which demanded their full attention six days a week and most evenings. Figure in the housework, and I don't remember them with any free time at all.

Writer Alice Walker offers this description of her mother's work in the early part of the twentieth century:

> She made all the clothes we wore, even my brothers' overalls. She made all the towels and sheets we used. She spent the summers canning vegetables and fruits. She spent the winter evenings making quilts enough to cover our beds.
>
> During the "working" day, she labored beside—not behind—my father in the fields. Her day began before sunup, and did not end until late at night. There was never a moment for her to sit down, undisturbed, to unravel her own private thoughts; never a time free

from interruption—by work or the noisy inquiries of her many children.[6]

Having a lot of work to do isn't necessarily bad. Work can give order and meaning to one's life. It can also provide a sense of self-worth and dignity. Working hard is, after all, a core tenet of the moral consciousness of the West, a cornerstone of the Protestant ethic. In this view, there's virtue in hard work. "Free time" means idleness, which, even if not inviting sin, surely corrodes character. Much of the debate over ending welfare in the United States has rested upon these beliefs and values, but you hear them in all sorts of places.

Recently I came across an interview with a person named Milton Garland who, at the age of 102, was America's oldest known wage-earner. Garland had worked for the same firm—the Frick Company of Waynesboro, Pennsylvania—for seventy-eight years, since joining it in 1920. Frick does not, apparently, lay off its workers at the same rate as most American companies. The interview occurred at Washington's National Press Club, which is headquartered in a building whose refrigeration equipment Garland helped install in the late 1920s. "I love the work I am doing," Garland said, referring to his current twenty-hour-a-week job coordinating Frick's international patents and training young workers. "My advice," he added, "is to go into something and stay with it until you like it. You can't like it until you obtain expertise in that work. And once you are an expert, it's a pleasure." Asked where would he be had he retired thirty-seven years before, when he reached the age of sixty-five, Garland snapped, "In my grave."[7]

You may consider certain tasks drudgery while other people find the same tasks richly rewarding. I hate to garden. To me, picking weeds for hours on end is the kind of activity that belongs in one of Dante's outer rings of hell. You'd have to pay me a large sum of money to do it. But I have a good friend for whom gardening is a delight. He does it whenever he has a spare moment. He even does it on vacation. Some people find taking care of other people to be deeply satisfying. Caring for children, the elderly, the sick, or the disabled can give rich meaning to the life of the caregiver—either when caring for one's own children or close relatives, or when volunteering to take care of strangers in need. But other people find caretaking to be hard labor. Women may feel morally bound to do it in any event, and may not even want to admit to themselves how much they dislike it (society puts most of the moral burden on women to do caring work, both paid and unpaid).

Sometimes the same activity can be perceived as being pleasant or unpleasant depending on its context, or how it's described at the outset. Psychology professors Sophia Snow and Ellen Langer divided a sample of adults from the Boston area into two groups. They asked both groups to do the same tasks. Among the tasks were sorting a set of Gary Larson cartoons into whatever categories the groups chose (funny / not-so-funny, cartoons about men or about women, or anything else) and also changing one or two words in each cartoon to alter the meanings. For one group, the experimenters referred to these tasks as a "game." For the other, the experimenters referred to the tasks as "work." Afterward, the people in both groups were asked questions about their experience, including how much they enjoyed the tasks and how much their minds wandered while doing them. It turned out that more people in the "game" group than the "work" group reported that they enjoyed the tasks, and "game" group members reported that their minds wandered less when doing them.[8]

My former student who's creating Internet games for thousands of simultaneous players seems to love her work, and not just because she expects to make a lot of money from it. She's actually having fun. She likes the people she works with. She loves the crazy, hip, frenzied world of the Internet start-up. So what if she rarely gets home before 10 p.m. after having put in at least twelve hours, and doesn't have time on weekends to do much of anything except her washing and her bills? She doesn't seem to mind.

It's not unusual for professional women to find paid work outside the home more fulfilling than unpaid work inside the home. Sociologist Arlie Hochschild interviewed and observed the behavior of 130 employees of a particular company (she didn't reveal its name).[9] She found that many of the women employees preferred to spend time at the company rather than at home. They felt that home imposed more difficult demands on them (sullen teens, needy babies, dirty dishes, unappreciative spouses). They often felt more competent and appreciated at work than at home. Their friendships with co-workers were stronger than with people outside work; their "parenting" of subordinates at work was better and more satisfying than their real parenting at home. They even found co-workers to be more helpful in coping with traumas, such as the death of a parent, than was their family or their religious congregation (many men felt the same way). Hochschild is a careful researcher, but her findings probably can't be generalized to the entire workforce. The company in which she did her interviews and observations treated its employees unusually well. Yet it is surely the case that unpaid work at home is sometimes felt to be difficult and unrewarding, relative to paid work outside the home.

Work can be a "calling," in the sense that it expresses some deeply personal commitment, or draws upon a talent or source of energy that would exist regardless of how much the job pays. I have met a number of doctors who still view their practice primarily as a public service, a labor of love and duty. So too with many teachers, social workers, and—yes—even politicians. I have not yet found an investment banker who feels this way, but there must be one or two out there.

Tasks undertaken because of their inherent fascination can motivate harder and more passionate work than jobs performed solely for money. "In the last year I have worked more strenuously than ever before in my life and a few weeks ago I finally solved the problem," Albert Einstein wrote to his cousin Elsa, when working on the mathematical underpinnings of what was to be his general theory of relativity. "Now I have to give myself some peace or I shall go *kaput* right away."[10]

Many authors, artists, philosophers, and actors do their work for no reason other than the deep satisfaction they find in it, or a deep compulsion to do it. Often they take another job to pay the bills. This is not a new phenomenon. *Know your bone,* advised the nineteenth-century writer and philosopher Henry David Thoreau. "Pursue, keep up with, circle round and round your life. . . . Know your own bone: gnaw at it, bury it, unearth it, and gnaw at it still."[11] When Thoreau needed money and wasn't gnawing on his bone, he surveyed land. T. S. Eliot was a bank clerk; Nathaniel Hawthorne, a clerk in the Salem customhouse he immortalized in *The Scarlet Letter;* Wallace Stevens and Charles Ives sold insurance. William Faulkner claimed to have written *As I Lay Dying* in time left over from twelve-hour days as a manual laborer. From 1866 to 1885, Herman Melville was an outdoor inspector for the New York customhouse; Walt Whitman was a copyist in the U.S. Army paymaster's office in Washington, D.C.; Matthew Arnold, a school inspector. Alexis de Tocqueville, the great French sociologist who came to understand more about this nation than anyone before and perhaps since, was a government clerk in France. Benedict Spinoza, the great seventeenth-century philosopher, earned his keep by grinding and polishing lenses. Einstein wrote a paper setting forth his theory of relativity when he was a twenty-six-year-old examiner in a patent office. William Carlos Williams was a physician. And Stanley Bojarski (whom you may not have heard of because he has not yet made his name) works by day as a legal assistant in the sedate, buttoned-down law offices of Dewey Ballantine, in midtown Manhattan, and by night as a comic female impersonator in a gay-themed musical revue called *Howard Crabtree's When Pigs Fly*. There is a long tradition of American actors and aspiring actors—especially the latter—waiting tables, painting apartments, and driving cabs. After retiring from working in my father's shop, my mother turned to painting lovely pastel portraits and landscapes, and sells enough of them to pay for her art supplies and have a small kitty left over.

YES, A PROBLEM

So what's the problem? Just this: The amount of paid work in most people's lives is increasing dramatically. And it's not just formal work hours that are expanding, as measured by official surveys. The very character of paid work is becoming far more intrusive on the rest of our lives. Much of it is becoming more emotionally or intellectually taxing. It preoccupies more of our waking hours, and sometimes even reaches deep into our sleep. It also intrudes more unexpectedly, and makes more unpredictable demands.

There's something insistent about home faxes, voice mails, e-mails, beepers, cell phones, and car phones. They must be responded to. Or you have to use them to contact someone else if you gain some piece of knowledge that the other person is likely to value and *expects* you to share at once. After all, the sole purpose of these gadgets is to locate us when we're doing something else. They put us, literally, on call. They break into our lives like burglars. They lay claim even to those small units of time and space that used to be entirely private, like when we're behind the wheel of a car, in an airplane, or walking from place to place. Even the possibility that they might intrude requires that a tiny piece of our brain remain ready to respond to the intrusion when it comes, like a sentry on continuous alert. Presumably we'd be less efficient at our jobs if we didn't have these gadgets, but they overrun more and more of our personal territory. In a few years, each of us is likely to have a universal connection attached to a wristband through which, at any time of day or night, certain people (whom we've designated in advance) will be able to find us and speak with us, perhaps even see our faces as we see theirs. We'll be at liberty to shut off the device, of course, and it will also be our decision to whom we give such unbridled power to intrude. But imagine the pressure to keep the device turned on at least eighteen hours, and to extend the list of potential intruders to include not only loved ones but also those who seem (and consider themselves) important to our working lives.

Commuting time has lengthened. Time away from home on business has increased, too. According to the Travel Industry Association of America, Americans took 42.9 million business trips in 1996 (the most recent data available), a 21 percent increase from just five years before. Another survey, this by the Family and Work Institute, reveals that one out of five working people now regularly takes an overnight business trip (the survey did not define "regularly," but it can safely be assumed to be at least once a month).[12] Add to this the ever more frequent and ubiquitous corporate conferences, retreats, seminars, and meetings at remote locations—totaling 805,000 corporate overnight "events" in fiscal year 1998, compared with 580,000 in 1996, according to Meeting Planners International.[13]

There is no way to measure the preoccupation and emotional energy demanded by this new work, but it is certainly greater than before. The percentage of Americans who say they "always feel rushed" jumped by more than half between the mid-1960s and the mid-1990s, and significantly more Americans also said they "work very hard most of the time" and "frequently stayed late at work."[14] Home computers are now "work stations," even for people who have separate offices outside the home. Work is trundled back and forth from home to office not in bulky briefcases stuffed with papers and reports but in little diskettes and weightless e-mail attachments. A quarter of all regular Internet users say they're now working more hours at home but no fewer hours at the office.[15]

Markets are open all the time and gadgets are potentially connected all the time, so there is no good excuse *not* to work except for intervals when one has made a clear and principled decision not to, in order to do something else. But the threshold for deciding to do something else keeps rising as work keeps getting more accessible. Architects Frank Lupo and Daniel Rowen recently designed a Manhattan apartment for two young Wall Street currency traders. The abode comes with six strategically placed video monitors so that the agile couple can keep track of world markets twenty-four hours a day from any vantage point in their new home, including the bathroom.[16]

As paid work pushes on the rest of life, other things, inevitably, are compressed, or pushed out. Substantial public attention has been focused on the dwindling time parents give to their children. According to the White House Council of Economic Advisers, American parents now spend, on average, twenty-two fewer hours each week with their children than did parents thirty years ago. (But this doesn't necessarily mean that each child is losing twenty-two hours of attention, because adult Americans are having fewer children to begin with. In fact, there's evidence that mothers in 1998 were spending about as many waking hours with their kids as did mothers in 1965, while sleeping less.[17] The point is that adults are devoting fewer hours to children in general.) Other aspects of life are being pushed out as well—friends, spouses and partners, voluntary work in the community, housework, one's "calling," tasks that are enjoyable as well as those that aren't, unpaid activities that are deeply fulfilling as well as those that are regarded as mere duties.

Because of the press of paid work, everything else has to be more regimented: children bustled from activity to activity according to ever more precise schedules; weekend calendars crammed with errands, events, drop-bys, fleeting meetings; upcoming vacations planned far in advance with contingency plans in case something goes awry. And all the while, there are continuing preoccupations—work yet undone, clients not yet pursued, deadlines looming—that distract attention from the rest of life even when you're trying to live it, like noisy traffic just outside the living room window.

Paid work is crowding out the rest of life even if—especially if—it is interesting or rewarding, as I discovered when I was in the President's cabinet. If you have managed to find the time and energy to read this book to this point, you are not yet in dire straits. Still, the pressure is mounting. Why is that?

PROPPING UP FAMILY INCOMES

The first and most obvious reason that Americans are working harder is to prop up family incomes. Many women began streaming into the workforce in the late seventies and eighties as their husbands' paychecks began to flatten or decline. As noted, the midcentury system of large-scale production, with its fleets of routine workers linked to steady jobs with ever-rising wages, has been disappearing. It ushered blue-collar America into the middle class. Its replacement—innovative production of anything, from anywhere, at the lowest price and best quality—is ushering blue-collar America out. In 1979, a thirty-year-old man with no more than a high-school diploma earned an average of $32,000 if he worked full time (in today's dollars). Today, his thirty-year-old counterpart earns about $5,000 less. To fill the gap, more women have gone into paid work, or work longer.[18]

Something else has also happened. An increasing number of people—mostly women—have become single parents. Thirty years ago, fewer than 15 percent of all families were headed by a single parent. Today the figure is more than 30 percent.[19] This trend is often cited as another reason that women have moved into paid work. They have more responsibilities now. But the actual direction of cause and effect may be the reverse. Arguably, more women have left their male spouses or partners (or decided not to marry them in the first place) precisely because the women now have jobs and men have been losing ground economically. Why take on the additional "home work" of supporting a man, who might also be abusive or unappreciative, when his earnings are dropping and you can earn money on your own? More on this later.

MAKING HAY

The need to supplement male earnings, however, can't be the sole reason that people are devoting more time and energy to paid work, because upper-income people have been working harder as well. What else has stimulated the extra effort? As noted, almost everyone's earnings are now less predictable. You may be earning good money today, but the flow might slow down tomorrow, and the spigot be turned off next week. You simply don't know. In the old economy of steady jobs, you were reasonably assured of receiving the same wage in the future, adjusted upward for inflation. This confidence allowed you to buy cars on credit, and take out a home mortgage. Now you don't know how much you'll be earning, yet you still need to buy a car on credit, you still need a home mortgage, and you also have a credit card or two, or ten. And then there are all the monthly bills that come with normal living—gas, electricity, telephone. So how do you reconcile your unpredictable earnings with your predictable bills?

Here's an aspect of the new work that's rarely mentioned but affects almost everyone—rich, poor, and middle—and forces people to work harder *today* than they otherwise need to in order to pay *tomorrow's* bills. Unable to predict future earnings, people tend to work as hard as they can when jobs with decent pay are readily available to them. They also fall into debt. But this only adds to the pressure on them to accept any opportunity today that may not be there tomorrow. In other words, they make hay while the sun shines.[20]

Even in the old economy, blue-collar workers had an incentive to put in "overtime" when it became available because they never knew how long an economic upswing would continue to provide overtime work. But during the boom years of the 1990s, hourly wage earners put in much more overtime than they did during typical expansions. Some of this was involuntary. Companies haven't wanted to bring on additional workers, and under American labor law they can demand that hourly employees work overtime. But more workers also volunteered for overtime even when their companies didn't insist. They did so because America's dwindling number of blue-collar workers know how precarious their paychecks are. They want to take advantage of any extra work hours that might come along—not just because the extra hours may not be there in the future but because the jobs themselves may not be.[21] The company might "downsize" and move operations abroad at any time, or it might merge with a company in another state and move there. Workers' monthly household bills will continue, regardless.

Even professional and managerial workers are busy making hay in sunny weather. Data from the Bureau of Labor Statistics show that the proportion of them who put in more than fifty hours a week has risen by more than a third since 1985.[22] And they're working harder than people in most other occupations. Nearly 40 percent of male college graduates and 20 percent of female graduates are working more than fifty hours a week—quadruple the proportion of people with less than a high-school degree.[23]

What's going on? Remember that even though many of these workers are considered "full-time employees," a growing number depend on commissions, billable hours, performance bonuses, and continuing grants and projects for their incomes. They have no way of knowing for sure how much they'll earn six months from now, or even next month. As their companies or nonprofit enterprises busily turn all "fixed" costs—like steady payrolls—into "variable" costs in order to become more agile, the enterprises in effect shift to their employees the economic risks of an uncertain market. But these employees face "fixed" costs of their own, like mortgage payments and electricity bills. In consequence, even higher-wage workers are likely to go full-out when the work is available—accumulating more commissions, billable hours, bonuses, grants, and projects—against the time when there may be less.

A friend, a new father who works for a consulting firm in New York, is putting in fourteen-hour days and seventy-hour weeks. He says he'd rather not be working so hard, especially now that he has a child. No one in the firm has asked him to put in so many hours. In fact, the firm is trying to cultivate a "family friendly" image in order to recruit other talented young people. The problem is, he says, that it's a small firm, and demand for its services goes up and down. My friend figures he should put in all the hours he can as long as the work keeps coming.

In the emerging economy, as I have emphasized, consumers have almost boundless choice, and they can switch in an instant. So if you, as a seller, are "hot" right now, you're likely to want to take maximum advantage of it. Andy Warhol once famously declared that in the future everyone will have fifteen minutes of fame. It's now more likely to be thirty seconds. In the growing portion of the economy that depends on attracting attention—on being in the "buzz," being hip or cool, or riding some wave of public fascination—the pressure is on to make the most of it when you get it. These people, too, will work longer and harder than they might otherwise want to work, in order to make hay while the sun shines more brightly on them than it ever did before or may ever again.

KEEPING UP TO SPEED

A third aspect of the emerging economy compelling harder work is the necessity of staying even with, or beating out, the competition. Again, recall the contrast: The midcentury system was premised on stability and tame competition, with minimal innovation. The new, emerging system is premised on instability and fierce competition, with maximum innovation. These days, there's no coasting. Competitors are eager to break into your market.

"This is not about business hours. It's about *waking* hours," says Todd Wagner, thirty-seven, co-founder and CEO of Broadcast.com, a Web company based in Dallas, Texas. Wagner's new idea was to broadcast live programming over the Web—"streaming media" programming, it's called. But Wagner and Broadcast.com had to move fast if they were to make a mark and capture consumers, and the race is still on. There are thousands of potential rivals, each trying to run faster with the same or a similar idea. Wagner's days start before the sun rises, and rarely end before midnight—meeting with investors, trading ideas with technical people, checking in with marketing and advertising staff, considering consumer ideas and complaints. "You try to do as much as you can for as long as you can stay awake," he says. Mark Cuban, cofounder and president of the company, asks, rhetorically, "What price do you have to pay to win? That price is the 'sprint.' You have to build your business faster than anyone else. The 'sprint' doesn't have a finish line. There's never a point where you can say, 'We've made it.'"[24]

Wagner and Cuban were profiled in a cheery monthly magazine whose very name typifies the new economy, *Fast Company*. I've written for *Fast Company*, and I knew its two editors, Alan Webber and Bill Taylor, many years before they founded it. I remember talking with them about their vision for the magazine before it became a reality. They had a good idea—to target primarily executives of small, fast-growing companies, entrepreneurs, and young people with jobs in information-technology start-ups. Now the magazine is a big success, but there's no relaxing for Alan and Bill. Neither of them ever struck me as laid-back, but I don't think it an exaggeration to describe both these days as frenetic. All sorts of rivals and potential rivals now see what Alan and Bill have accomplished and are aiming to do the same thing, even better, online or off. "I was naive," Alan told me over coffee recently. "I thought once we had the magazine up and running, and hit our targets, we could relax. But now we have to work even harder to stay ahead of the pack."

Competition is intensifying at all points along the supply chain—meaning that people at all these points have to work harder to retain their customers. Recall that companies are morphing into many different nodes of expertise, connected by webs of contracts and subcontracts, linked together by the Internet. Many of the contractors and subcontractors in this system are continuously bidding for work against other contractors and subcontractors—inside electronic auctions that measure price, quality, and (as one aspect of quality) speed of delivery. Every "node" in the system—every company, every group—is under intense pressure to keep its customers by outbidding its rivals and getting the next contract.

It's not unusual for a company to bid on a project by promising to deliver something that will be a stretch for them. Say they agree to do it a bit more cheaply than they did it before, or to meet specifications that are somewhat more advanced than what they've produced before, or to deliver it more quickly. Maybe they promise a software project in forty-five days when the last project took them sixty. In making the bid, they have not dissembled—they don't dare. Their reputation (their most important asset) depends on their coming through, as they promised. But they also know that the only way to keep their customers is by staying ahead of their rivals—and they can only stay ahead by continuously stretching their capacities. They must continuously invent new ways of doing it better, faster, cheaper.

What does this mean for people on the project? They have to work harder. The deadline they faced last time around was difficult enough for them to meet; the new one is even more of a challenge. They now have to figure out ways to cut costs and improve performance more effectively than before, which was hard enough then. This requires extra hours of tinkering, experimenting, pushing themselves to the limits. There are late nights, early mornings—and as the deadline looms, even longer days. When they have a spare moment for family or friends, they may find their minds drifting to the project. They may even dream about it.

"Keeping up to speed" pressure comes in more disguised forms. Say you consider taking a month's vacation but decide against it because there's too much risk that your customer may need you in the interim, and you don't want to run even the slightest chance of losing the customer to a rival. (Sometimes the rival may be sitting in the next cubicle.) Or you think about cutting back on the number of hours you put in, but you decide not to because you don't want to be thought of as someone who's out of the loop, who's "second string." If you're not there, you may miss a critical meeting. Or you won't learn about some new piece of software that changes the entire competitive environment. Or you'll miss out on a new client.

The problem, in short, is that very often there are only two tracks, fast or slow. The emerging economy doesn't offer many gradations in between. Hourly and salaried workers are still with us, of course, but more of their pay turns on how hard and how well they work. For professionals, managers, and geeks and shrinks of all kinds, keeping up to speed is now a necessity. Markets and technologies are changing so rapidly that you need to be totally involved in order to keep up. If you're on a slow track, you fall further and further behind. You may have a difficult time ever getting back on the fast track. In many quick-moving fields, opting to work part-time is often seen as an automatic career-breaker. This is why relatively few professionals take advantage of options to take longer vacations, cut back on work time, utilize family-leave policies, or go off on "sabbatical"—even in so-called family-friendly companies. If you opt out even a little, you may be opting out for good.[25]

MAKING MORE MONEY

There's a final aspect of the new economy that compels people to work harder. I'm referring to the disparities in income and wealth that have widened during the last several decades. It's easy to see why people feel compelled to work harder if they (or their spouse or partner) have lost ground relative to where they think they should be. But the kind of compulsion I'm now talking about affects people toward the top of the widening spectrum—people who stand to make a great deal *more* money in the new economy than someone just like them could have earned in the old one. You'd think they might work less, because they're earning so much they can afford to. Think again.

Even women whose husbands' wages have been rising since the 1970s have streamed into paid work, and they now work as hard as, if not harder than, women who went to work because their spouses' wages were flat or dropping. Look at married couples in which the husband has a college degree: Even though *his* pay has been rising buoyantly since 1970, *she* has been working harder, with the result that their combined increase in hours of paid work a year has been almost *twice* that of couples where the husband has no more than a high-school diploma.[26] And if she has a college degree, she's likely to be working harder still. In 1970, less than 40 percent of women college grads married to male college grads were in the workforce. Now, even though their husbands' pay is far higher, nearly three-quarters of these women are earning a paycheck, including a higher percentage with young children.[27] (No mystery, therefore, why disparities are widening in *family* incomes even faster than in individual incomes.)

Why are women who don't have to go into paid work working so hard? Because they have more opportunities today not only for work that's interesting and fulfilling, but also for work that pays far more than it used to. Women's career ambitions have risen in tandem: In 1968, nearly 40 percent of women entering college said they were aiming to become schoolteachers. Just six years later, as higher-paying professions began to open their gates to women, only 10 percent of women who were entering college wanted to teach school, and the rate has remained about the same since then.[28] You can see the same pattern among single parents. Those whose formal education ended with high school are working about 16 percent more than they did three decades ago; if they graduated from college (and are earning considerably more than the first group), they're working 20 percent more.[29]

It stands to reason. As the income ladder lengthens, people on the upper rungs can earn far more than ever before. So a choice by them to work *less* entails a correspondingly greater financial sacrifice. Suppose you're offered a job that pays twice what you're now earning, but it requires that you give up two nights a week with your family. If you decide against taking the job, you're sacrificing a great deal of money for the sake of those two family evenings. Even if you and your family don't desperately need those extra dollars, the huge hike in pay would allow you and them to live far more comfortably and securely. Those two evenings with the family are now more "costly" to you, in the sense of money forgone.

A year or so ago one of my sons was running a big cross-country race. I was determined not to miss it. After all, I had left my job in Washington to spend more time with the boys, and nothing was going to keep me away from that race. Then I got a phone call from someone asking if I'd help work on a project in another city. The timing couldn't have been worse. The project was to begin the same morning as the race, and it couldn't wait. If I missed the start of it, I might as well not join up. The sum being offered in payment was generous. These kinds of offers are rare. Until I received the call, I was happily looking forward to the race. Now I was in a quandary. There was no way I could both see the race and do the project. I ended up turning down the project and going to the race, and I'm glad I did. But I wish I could tell you I had no regrets. Not a few times that Saturday I thought about what it was "costing" me to go to my son's race. Before the offer, the cost was zero. Now it seemed a considerable sum.

My choice was hard enough, but what if the dollar stakes keep rising? In a sense, this is what has happened at the top rungs of the economic ladder. Say a family considers cutting back on work—the husband thinks about taking a different job that allows him more time to see his kids; the wife ponders working part-time in order to pursue volunteer work in the community. They figure that their cutback would result in their family income dropping from midway in the top 5 percent of all incomes to midway in the top 20 percent. Two decades ago, when the income ladder was shorter and all its rungs were closer together, that decision would have cost the family 29 percent of their family income. That's a big sacrifice, but not nearly as large as the one they would have to make if they cut back as much today, when that drop means an income loss of about 44 percent.[30] A family that might have accepted a 29 percent drop might draw the line well before they reached a 44 percent drop, and decide that the sacrifice just isn't worth it. Since all the rungs on the new, longer economic ladder are wider apart than they were on the old ladder, any step downward takes them a longer way down than before.

Wider inequality also means, by the same token, that every step *up* the ladder takes you that much higher than before, so every additional hour of effort counts much more. This helps explain why recent college graduates tend to work harder than college grads did decades ago. It also helps explain why far more college freshmen today say they're interested in being "well off financially" than did so three decades ago.

Every year since the late sixties, a random sample of college freshmen have been asked to choose their most important personal objectives from among several alternatives, including "to be very well off financially" and "to develop a meaningful philosophy of life." In 1968, only 41 percent listed being "very well off financially" as very important. Over time, that goal has grown in importance. By 1998, fully 74 percent of college freshmen listed it as very important. Developing a meaningful philosophy of life, on the other hand, moved in the opposite direction. In 1968, 75 percent chose it, but it steadily dropped until, by 1998, it was selected by less than 41 percent.[31]

Today's college students are not necessarily more materialistic than former generations of students. Other surveys, in fact, show record numbers of students volunteering to help in their communities. What's changed is their future economic stakes. The income ladder now extends much higher, and every step up it is connected to much bigger gains than before. So the monetary penalty for seeking a "meaningful philosophy of life" over being "well off financially" has grown. When college freshmen thought about their priorities three decades ago, the best-paid 10 percent of male workers (I'll use men because women's opportunities were then so limited) earned only about 70 percent more than the man in the middle of the wage ladder. Today, a college freshman contemplating the future would see men in the highest-paid 10 percent earning well over twice what the man in the middle makes. Meanwhile, the distance between the top 1 percent and the middle has expanded fivefold.

Likewise, if today's college students seem much more interested than previous generations in preprofessional courses (economics and business management now top the list of majors at most universities) and in making connections that may help them land the right job after college, it's not necessarily because the students are greedier than those who came before them. It's because their actions today have much weightier consequences for their future incomes. With the gap widening, even a relatively small step in an upward direction is a bigger deal, as is the failure to take it. For the same reason, if today's parents seem more obsessed with their children getting into the "right" school or university, it's because the stakes have risen. These institutions are seen as pathways to high-paying jobs, and high pay has grown, relative to the median wage, much higher than it used to be.

When I graduated from college in 1968, someone who aimed to

become a college teacher rather than a top corporate lawyer or investment banker sacrificed some income, but assumed that the psychic rewards of college teaching would make up for the financial loss. As the third millennium commences, the pay gap between college teachers and top corporate lawyers or investment bankers has widened into a chasm. One of my former students who recently joined a New York law firm *began* at an annual salary plus signing bonuses that totaled far more than the yearly salary of the tenured fifty-three-year-old professor to whom he had bade farewell only weeks before. Had the aging professor faced similar temptations upon finishing college in 1968, he would like to think that the psychic rewards of teaching would have given him the fortitude to resist, but, to be candid, he can't be sure.

If a young college graduate is interested in teaching in a public school rather than becoming a top lawyer or investment banker or dot-com impresario, the current structure of rewards tests his or her dedication as never before. In 1999, the average salary of a public-school teacher was $39,347. This was but a fraction of the *bonus* received by many twenty- and thirtysomethings on Wall Street that same year.

WIDENING INEQUALITY, then, spurs hard work, both because people near the bottom have to work harder than before to have a decent level of income, and because people near the top have to make a bigger sacrifice than before if they *don't* work hard. This seems to be the pattern in other nations as well. Looking at data from different countries, Professors Linda Bell of Haverford College and Richard B. Freeman of Harvard found that how hard people work is related to the extent of income disparities. Where the disparities are wide, such as in the United States, people put in more hours of paid work each year than do people in countries where the disparities are narrower, such as Germany.[32]

Bell and Freeman's finding is confirmed by a survey that asked workers from different nations to choose which of the following three statements best described their feeling about their job: (1) "I work only as hard as I have to," (2) "I work hard but not so much that it interferes with the rest of my life," or (3) "I make a point of doing the best work I can *even if it interferes with the rest of my life*" (italics added). In the United States, where income disparities are widest, more than 60 percent agreed with the third statement. In Germany, where disparities are among the smallest, only 37 percent chose the third statement. In Britain, where income disparities aren't as wide as in the United States but are much wider than in Germany, 55 percent chose the third.[33]

WORKING HARD AND LIVING WELL

As I noted in the introduction, the British economist John Maynard Keynes, writing during the Depression, predicted that in 2030 England would be far better off economically and its people would work far less.[34] Most likely he will be right about the former, but not about the latter.

This is not to argue that we *couldn't* simplify our lives a great deal. The current fashionable word for it is "downshifting." I know a number of downshifters who seem perfectly happy with their new downshifted lives. I downshifted out of a fifteen-hour-a-day job in Washington to a nine-hour-a-day job near Boston, and couldn't be more pleased. The purpose of this chapter isn't to argue about what people could do or should do. It's to explain why most people haven't, and probably won't, as long as things are organized the way they are.

Downshifters are in the distinct minority. I've come across a number of polls in the last few years in which most Americans say they want to work hard for pay. Similar polls, from longer ago, show less proclivity for hard work—suggesting that Americans' preferences have shifted. A researcher looking at the long hours American families now work, as compared to decades ago, might conclude that this must be the case. But surely what most Americans say and how they act depend on the circumstance they find themselves in. Americans want to work hard *given* that their future incomes are less predictable than they used to be, that competition is more intense, and that income disparities are wider. Were paid work organized and rewarded differently, they might "want" to work less.

In the most recent international survey of attitudes toward work for which data are available, only 8 percent of Americans said they would prefer fewer hours of work and less earnings. But 38 percent of Germans said they'd prefer fewer hours and less earnings, as did 30 percent of Japanese, and 30 percent of British respondents.[35] It is of course possible that these differences are attributable to a unique genetic endowment that makes Americans into workaholics, or to a cultural commitment to work and to consumption that is overwhelmingly greater here than elsewhere, but I doubt either hypothesis. If you've followed the logic of this chapter, the easiest explanation is found in the differences in how work is organized and rewarded.

Americans are not working harder because they "want" to in some deeply psychological sense, but because they're directly up against a dynamic market. We can rise very high in it, or fall very low; we have no way of knowing how high or low we'll go, or of predicting what opportunities will come along, and when; we know only that we have to push ourselves very hard to take advantage of all of them. Europeans, Asians, and everyone else on the planet are becoming part of the same system. In time, they, too, will probably "want" to work harder.

The deeper questions are not asked on standard surveys, because they're probably too difficult to put into them, and the answers would be too difficult to decipher: Do we want to live and work according to these new incentives? What's the price we're willing to pay for prosperity?

CHAPTER SEVEN

The Sale of the Self

WITH YOUR INCOME UNPREDICTABLE, and facing the possibility of earning a whole lot or a very little, you have every incentive to work hard. But how do you make your hard work pay off? After all, you're unlikely to be promoted up through the ranks of a large organization any longer, because most organizations are flattening into networks of alliances and contracts. So who exactly gives you a promotion? You. Increasingly in the new economy, the only way up is to promote yourself.

At midcentury, the self-promoter was shunned because he threatened social stability. The "organization man" aimed to fit in. His greatest aspiration, wrote William H. Whyte, Jr., was to be "obtrusive in no particular, excessive in no zeal . . . the man in the middle."[1] The eagerness with which he conformed to the organization's demands appalled social commentators of the era, who had recently witnessed the horrors of totalitarianism. "[T]here has been an enormous ideological shift favoring submission to the group," warned sociologist David Riesman in 1950. "The peer group becomes the measure of all things; the individual has no defenses the group cannot batter down."[2] The challenge, these social critics thought, was to keep hold of individuality. "[T]he peace of mind offered by the organization remains a surrender, and no less so for being offered in benevolence," concluded Whyte, urging his readers to *"fight* The Organization."[3]

When few individuals could succeed outside a large organization, the admonition to fight it may have invited heroism but not promotions. Careers started at the organizational bottom, where you "paid your dues." After displaying sufficient diligence and appropriate obsequiousness, the organization steadily conferred upon you more responsibility. From then on, you owed your career to the organization. Its success was your success.

Now you owe your career to yourself. Financial success depends on how well you sell *you*. Selling yourself can be a full-time job.

WHY PERSONAL CONNECTIONS
MATTER EVEN MORE

The sale of the self begins with the right connections. Connections mattered in the old economy, too. "It's who you know and the smile on your face. It's contacts, Ben, contacts!" the salesman Willie Loman tells his brother.[4] But the gradual disappearance of organizational ladders has made connections even more important, both for people seeking to sell themselves and for potential buyers seeking to hire.

If you lack a college degree, you'll have trouble selling yourself, but even if you do have one the sale's just beginning.[5] A degree doesn't mean as much as it once did. In 1960, only 8 percent of adult Americans had a four-year college degree; now it's 25 percent, and rising quickly. Two-thirds of high-school seniors are continuing their education beyond high school. More than half of America's newly employed young people now have at least a two-year college degree, and almost a third have a four-year degree. The trend toward more years of education is appropriate in an advanced economy. Learning skills enable a person to identify and pursue good ideas. But as the numbers of degree-holders mount, the mere possession of a college degree is less useful as a selling tool.

A degree from a prestigious university is helpful, but not as much as many ambitious parents assume. As has been noted, the emerging economy confers its highest rewards on talented geeks and shrinks— people who are creative and original, and who possess insights into what others might want. Prospective employers know that young people with an abundance of these attributes don't always migrate to the most prestigious universities. Nor do these qualities readily reveal themselves on university transcripts, or lend themselves to easy quantification. A recruiter for a major investment bank told me he no longer

bothers to interview straight-A students from the Ivies because he figures they're the sort who have spent their whole lives jumping obedi-
ently through every hoop placed before them and are too intent on
pleasing others. He wants young people who are out to beat the system—who are innovative and aggressive. He says he's had the best luck
with athletes from middle-sized universities who major in math and
have B+ averages, but he's trying many other combinations, too. In the
emerging economy, financial success turns more on motivation and
creativity than on elite credentials.[6]

Here the truth can be told. The real value of a college education to
one's job prospects has less to do with what is learned than with who is
met. The parents of one's classmates, and the friends of their parents,
provide connections to summer jobs and first jobs, then later to clients
and business customers. Loyal alumni offer further leads. The more
prestigious the university, the more valuable such connections are
likely to be. To the extent that an Ivy League education has superior
value, that value has less to do with the grandeur of its libraries
or the cleverness of its professoriat than with the superiority of its
connections.[7]

Businesses looking to hire are placing greater reliance on referrals
from people they trust, for the same reason that trustworthy brand-
portals are becoming more important to buyers who are drowning in
information and need guidance as to what's good. Even in a tight labor
market, the sheer volume of résumés in circulation at any moment is
beyond the power of employers to process. Entire galaxies in cyberspace will soon be taken up with Internet job boards deploying millions
of electronic résumés, from young people entering the job market as
well as others who want better jobs. Several of my students already
have mastered the art of filling résumés with "scannable" keywords
guaranteed to be picked up by every digital résumé-management system in the civilized world. They're also "blast-faxing" their credentials
to thousands of additional employers, and combing Internet databases
for more addresses. One student told me proudly that she'd sent more
than 5,000 "personalized" résumés, each highlighting aspects of her
education and experience most likely to be attractive to a particular
target.

Most new hiring is by smaller enterprises that can't possibly afford
to screen hundreds of thousands of "personalized" electronic résumés,
and are looking for qualities that elude simple measurements. These

enterprises can't afford many mistakes in hiring, because they know their "human capital" is their most important asset, and they have only a limited number of hires. So increasingly, they rely on the recommendations of knowledgeable friends and associates.

Think of junk mail, a larger pile of which seems to arrive in my mailbox every day. The only envelopes I now open (apart from bills and checks) are addressed to me by hand, and I'll get to them right away if I recognize the name in the return address. Similarly with my e-mail, which has expanded to the point where I have to delete most messages without reading them; the only ones I'm sure to read come from people I know. And my wife and I just put a contraption on our telephone that alerts us to where the call is coming from before we answer it. Here too, a familiar name will do the trick. Personal job referrals are like letters, e-mails, and phone calls from familiar names in this era of communication overload. They're convenient filters.

TRADING ON CONNECTIONS

Although the best connection is someone who knows the person who's doing the hiring and can put in a good word directly, thus placing the hirer only "two degrees of separation" away, three degrees of separation might also suffice, sometimes even four. Recently I came across an Internet company called sixdegrees.com. You enter the names of all friends and acquaintances, and the software charts a personal pathway to anyone else you might want to meet. If you want to get a message to Alan Greenspan, the chairman of the Federal Reserve Board and the most powerful man in America, this software tells you that your friend Herman knows a person named Muriel who knows Lester who knows Penelope who knows Charles, who is a good acquaintance of Alan. So it's theoretically possible for you to enlist Herman to ask Muriel, and so on, all the way to Charles asking Alan if he'd take your call, or at least send you a smiling photograph. Sixdegrees.com may not work this well every time, but it does capture, in exaggerated form, how the new system works.

The idea that we're all connected to within six degrees goes back to experiments conducted by Yale social psychologist Stanley Milgram in the 1960s. Milgram's device was a kind of chain letter, sent randomly to 160 people living in Omaha, Nebraska, and containing the name of a stockbroker who worked in Boston. Milgram asked each recipient to send the packet to a friend or acquaintance who they thought would get it closer to the stockbroker. As the packet meandered across America, each recipient along the way sent the packet on to someone who they, in turn, thought would bring it closer to the stockbroker. In the end, most packets reached the stockbroker in five or six steps.[8] Hence the term "six degrees of separation."

But not all connections are equal, as anyone engaged in personal sales quickly discovers. In Milgram's experiment, certain people along the way were far better connected than others. Half the packets delivered to the stockbroker came by way of just three people. The lesson for anyone looking to make a personal sale is to find highly connected people with fat Rolodexes.[9]

A few years ago, a woman named Marcia Lewin used a political connection to help secure a job for her daughter. Lewin contacted her friend Walter Kaye, a retired insurance executive from New York, who was a major donor to the Democratic Party, having enriched its coffers by between $300,000 and $350,000. Not incidentally, Kaye was a friend of Hillary Rodham Clinton, the First Lady.[10] With the help of Kaye, Marcia's daughter Monica got a job as a White House intern, and the rest, sad to say, is history.

One of the major economic values of college internships comes in the connections they offer. So, too, with professional associations, conferences, conventions, World Economic Forums, and Renaissance Weekends. Throughout the economy, there has been a boom in such Rolodex-enhancing events. The convention industry, among the fastest-growing service sectors in America, lives off them. Any self-respecting city has built or is now building a convention center designed to be a connection center.

Ten percent of the undergraduates at Beijing University are now members of the Communist Party, up from 5 percent in 1991, and applications continue to surge. Upwardly mobile Chinese students have not grown noticeably more enthusiastic about communist doctrine, but they have become more interested in access to exciting and potentially lucrative jobs in China's marketizing economy. The Communist Party has become China's preeminent job network. One young party member in her thirties explained to a reporter for the *New York Times* that being an "outstanding worker" did not in itself guarantee a good job; it was also necessary to stand out. "And [the party] is the only thing you can join to get any recognition."[11]

POLITICAL CONNECTIONS

Political connections are not much different from any other kind, although they often have more dire consequences for our democracy. Their economic value can be measured fairly precisely on K Street in Washington, D.C., in the increasing earnings of well-connected lobbyists and the flows of campaign contributions. As with other connections, competition for access to powerful Washington ears has intensified in recent years as a result of advances in communication, transportation, and information technologies, which now inundate the offices of the powerful with faxes, phone messages, e-mails, and even live constituents. People who can break through the clamor and actually whisper into the powerful ears are thus in greater demand, and their rewards are rising precipitously.

Former members of Congress can reach powerful ears by virtue of their past associations. At last count, 128 former members of Congress are paid lobbyists. Some began lobbying after being defeated for reelection, but an increasing number have left Congress voluntarily in order to trade on their connections. According to one survey, more than one out of five former members who left Congress in the 1990s has turned to lobbying, up from a much smaller fraction of congressional retirees before.[12] Congressional aides also trade on their connections on increasingly profitable terms, which partly explains why the average length of tenure of high-ranking aides has been dropping. Even relatives of members and former members are busily trading on their valuable names.[13] Rather than viewing this as yet another symptom of moral decay in our nation's capital, we could more accurately see it as the consequence of intensifying competition for access. The potential income a member of Congress, or aide or relative, sacrifices in *not* becoming a lobbyist makes the decision to pursue an alternative line of work exceedingly expensive.

Someone with a great deal of money can gain direct access to the powerful. Political corruption in modern America rarely takes the form of outright bribes, or even campaign contributions expressly linked to particular votes. It is more subtle. Money does corrupt politics, and the current system stinks, but to think about it in terms of purchasing specific policies or pieces of legislation misses the real corruption.

Here's how it works. A wealthy individual receives an invitation to have coffee with the President or, say, the chairman of a congressional committee. The invitation may have come about without any effort on the part of the wealthy individual, or the wealthy individual may have solicited it. In either case, the real value of the event to the individual is that it confirms the impression to others that he is capable of commanding the attention of a President or another powerful person in Washington. The photograph memorializing the coffee chat, complete with signature, hangs by no means discreetly on the person's office wall. The personal thank-you note to the wealthy individual that arrived from the politician is slyly shared with others. Word spreads of a subsequent invitation to golf.

What this does for the wealthy individual is incalculable. Suddenly he has become someone with access to a powerful ear—become a person, it is presumed, with connections, a person of influence. Such a reputation is valuable to him socially, financially, and in all the dimly lit areas in between. It gives the people with whom he does business the sense that he can deliver on whatever he proposes. After all, if he commands the attention of a President or a leader of Congress, he must be capable of opening any door below that exalted level and, by extension, of getting his way. It doesn't matter if this inference is incorrect. The appearance of power means that from now on his clients, customers, suppliers, creditors, investors, and contractors will be that much more willing to cut a deal.

In return, the politician may or may not get a campaign contribution directly from the wealthy individual. But as far as the politician is concerned, that donation is not the point of the transaction. Through the wealthy individual the politician gains access to a network of wealthy people: the individual's friends, business partners, and colleagues, and members of his club or board. These new contacts may have previously harbored misgivings about the politician's values or objectives. They may have heard unflattering rumors. But now the wealthy individual's relationship to the politician reassures them: the photograph, the handwritten notes, the golf, the coffees. "If our colleague likes and trusts this guy," they say to themselves, "perhaps we should be more open-minded." The wealthy individual introduces them to the politician when the occasion arises. The politician is not a bad fellow, they conclude. And then come their own invitations to breakfast, dinners, golf. Members of the network are reassured, charmed, seduced. In time, the new acquaintances will give money, and also ask that others do so. The connections are made.

No policy has been altered, no bill or vote willfully changed. But inevitably, as the politician enters into the endless round of coffees, meals, and receptions among the networks of the wealthy, his view of the world is reframed. The seduction has been mutual. The access that the politician provides the wealthy and the access that the politician thereby gains to the ever-expanding network of money reinforce each other. Increasingly, the politician hears the same kinds of suggestions, the same voicing of concerns and priorities. The wealthy do not speak in one voice, to be sure, but they share a broad common perspective. The politician hears only indirectly and abstractly from the less comfortable members of society. They are not at the coffees and the dinners. They do not play golf with him. They do not tell him directly and repeatedly, in casual banter or through personal stories, between sips of coffee, how they view the world. They do not speak continuously into the politician's ear about their concerns. The politician learns of their concerns from the pollsters, but he is not immersed in them the way he is in the culture of the comfortable. In this way, access to the network of the wealthy does not buy a politician's mind; instead, it nibbles constantly, sweetly, at his ear.

At regular intervals, the United States piously accuses certain nations of being in the thrall of "crony capitalism," where, despite advances toward free markets, prominent people continue to bestow important economic favors on friends and associates. But perhaps we are also susceptible to the charge. The increasing importance of personal connections here, as elsewhere, puts people who are inside the web of powerful connections at a distinct advantage.

THE DISCONNECTED

In many respects, the new economy is an equal-opportunity employer. With talented geeks and shrinks in short supply, no organization can afford to discriminate on any basis other than ability. Racial, ethnic, or gender bias was a luxury affordable only to managers with broad discretion to do as they pleased. Fierce competition is forcing them to do what pleases their customers and investors instead. As a result, significant numbers of well-educated blacks and Hispanics have moved into the American middle class, and some into the upper reaches. Women are ascending professional and managerial ranks as well. Look at the most nimble entrepreneurial groups, and you're likely to find a diverse mix; peer into the top tiers of companies in the fastest-moving segments of the economy, and you're sure to see a far wider variety of human beings than you'll find in the executive suites of old large-scale bureaucracies.

Nonetheless, minorities and women continue to be underrepresented among corporate chieftains, law and consulting partnerships, fund managers, tenured professors, and the top ranks of foundations, hospitals, and other nonprofits. The "glass ceiling" is thick and double-glazed. For blacks and Hispanics, this is partly due to the overlapping residue of race and poverty; young people of color still tend to grow up in poor neighborhoods with single parents and lousy schools. For women, it's partly due to their desire to have families and thereby move to the slow track or off the track entirely. But another reason for the relative scarcity of minorities and women in high places is the growing importance of connections. Relative to white men, minorities and women still lack them.

The "old boy" network is being replaced by an "attest for" network in which the best jobs go to people whom others already in the network know and can vouch for. Poor youngsters who barely finish high school have no set of friends, parents' friends, or friends' parents who can murmur nice things about them to people in high places, and thereby open doors to jobs and clients. Women seeking top positions have no readily available pool of women on boards of directors, trustees, and tenured faculties who can personally attest to their competence and thereby overcome the skepticism of some men in high places. Internet connections don't compensate for these deficiencies. If anything, as I have argued, the new ease of communication actually increases people's reliance on referrals and recommendations from people they know, on whom they rely to filter the cascade of incoming messages. And the people who make the referrals and do the deals are still, overwhelmingly, white and male. Among the most important purposes of "affirmative action" in the new economy is to broaden these informal networks to include the socially disconnected.

MAKING A NAME

Connections are a start. They give you a foothold, an interview, a first job, access to a powerful ear. But to make a name for yourself in the emerging economy, you need a means of continuously attracting new business your way. Success depends on linking up with a name that already has the power to draw business, and using it as a springboard to develop your own. It is directly analogous to the symbiotic relationship between small niche businesses and big brands that we examined in Chapter 2.

It's a common misconception that easy entry into the market through the Internet reduces the need to make a name—that superior products or services will automatically attract customers. If the prolific horror novelist Stephen King can distribute a best-seller over the Web, then why not you? Just pull your old unpublished novel out of the dresser drawer, put it online, and sell millions of copies direct. Don't fool yourself. Even if quite respectable, your novel will be lost amid the noise and clutter. Here, as elsewhere in the new economy, buyers need guidance.

Musician Todd Rundgren has his own Internet site where you can download a sampling of his latest creations—electric-guitar pyrotechnics and synthesized percussion, overlaid with rap and blues medleys that emerge and then disappear into a sonic soup—and if you like them, subscribe to receive Todd's music as it emerges directly from his studio throughout the year. In this way, Rundgren circumvents the record companies and all the people who advertise and market company labels. "[I]f I were to go to a record label and ask for a deal, they would make a guess as to how many people would buy the record and give me an advance based on that number, in effect lending me some fraction of the money that my fans would eventually (2 or 3 years later) pony up," Rundgren writes on his Web site,[14] summarizing the old industrial model of selling music. "It occurred to me that with the aid of some modern advances, I could go directly to my audience, ask them if they would commit to buying my music, and then deliver it to them as it is produced."

You may have a lovely singing voice or a great band, and you can now post your music at any number of "MP3" sites on the Internet. But don't count on attracting many fans simply by doing so. There are too

many other voices and bands there already, and the numbers are growing daily. To attract a following, you'll have to promote yourself. Rundgren didn't start his career on the Internet, and his innovative music
hasn't attracted many fans there directly. Before he launched himself
into cyberspace he had already built a following. Rundgren was heavily
marketed. Advertisers and promoters for the record labels for which
Rundgren worked had drawn attention to his music, as had the promoters of his tours. In his new online incarnation, Rundgren has, in
effect, moved this marketing "in-house" and altered its techniques. Presumably he's hired people to design and upgrade his Web page, write
the software, publicize and promote him, and manage the Rundgren
brand overall. In short, the Internet has not reduced the need for marketing; it has merely given people other means of promoting themselves.

Rundgren's passage from record label to personal brand is mirrored
elsewhere in the emerging economy, and not only on the Internet.
About as far as you can get from synthesized percussion is the hushed
New York investment house of Morgan Stanley Dean Witter, a distinguished brand with an impressive roster of blue-chip clients. Inside
Morgan Stanley are many people busily making their names, including
Mary Meeker, who advises both institutional investors about where to
place their Internet bets and Internet start-ups about how and when to
offer their shares of stock to the public. As I write this, Meeker is considered hot. At age forty, she's the top-ranked Internet analyst on Wall
Street. *Barron's* calls her the "Queen of the Net." On a typical day she
gets about fifty voice-mail messages, roughly one hundred e-mails, and
up to a dozen requests for press interviews or public appearances. She
has a bevy of secretaries and assistants. She travels at warp speed. Internet companies are desperate for her advice, as are investors.

This didn't happen because Morgan Stanley recognized Meeker as
being clever and insightful and promoted her up through the ranks, as
would have been the case in the old economy. Meeker was clever and
insightful, all right, but she promoted herself. After graduating from
DePauw University with a double major in business and psychology,
she worked at Merrill Lynch for two years, and then received a Master
of Business Administration degree from Cornell. In 1986, she joined
the New York investment firm of Salomon Brothers, where she
became a junior research analyst covering the personal-computer
industry. After three and a half years there, Meeker moved to Cowen &

Company, another New York investment house, as a PC analyst, and then, in early 1991, she was hired by Morgan Stanley, which wanted to build up its PC expertise. In December 1993, Morgan Stanley managed a stock offering for an Internet service called America Online. Even though it was losing money and its shares were selling for about 95 cents each, Meeker recommended it to investors. America Online's shares are now trading for about $175 each. By the time you read these words, they may be trading for far more, or far less. No matter. America Online's meteoric rise after 1993 helped fuel Meeker's meteoric rise.[15] In the mid-1990s, she and an associate wrote a voluminous paper entitled "The Internet Report," which described the Internet revolution and sparked a heated debate within the computer industry, many of whose companies were still skeptical about the Internet's commercial potential. She followed it up with two further reports, both of which were widely read. She became an Internet "thought leader."

Meeker's compensation in 1999 was reported to be in the range of $15 million, surpassing that of many of the suspender-clad bankers at the firm. Many of the "dot-coms" have lost their initial luster, but Meeker still has hers. She doesn't need the Morgan Stanley brand to attract business to *her* as much as Morgan Stanley needs the Mary Meeker brand to attract business to *it*. In 1999, Morgan Stanley earned some $100 million in fees underwriting Internet initial public offerings, many of which came to the firm because Meeker was there. "We don't compete against Morgan Stanley," says the head of technology investment banking at a rival firm. "We compete against Mary Meeker."[16] It is in Morgan Stanley's interest to pay Meeker the value of her brand to the enterprise. Presumably she'll remain with Morgan unless or until another investment house believes her brand will be even more valuable to it and makes her an offer she can't refuse.

Individuals now blaze their own career paths by making their reputations in their fields, not in their organizations. Decades ago, most journalists toiled in anonymity. Pick up a magazine from the fifties or sixties and you'll rarely find a byline. The brand was the journal's, not the journalist's. But in recent years there's been a marked shift. Although *Time* has scarcely changed its format over the past quarter century—each week, about eighty-five pages; a major cover story, twenty or so articles, shorter news briefs, sidebars, and an essay—in one respect the magazine has changed significantly. It has been giving steadily greater prominence to its writers and reporters. In the 1970s, no names were associated with any of its articles. In the early eighties, about half its articles ended with the names of writers and reporters, in boldface type; by 1988, the names of essay authors were displayed prominently just under the title; in 1990, *Time* began listing lead authors under the titles of about half its articles; and by the mid-nineties it was listing them at the top of every article. Now it even features a page of biographies and photos of columnists and contributors.

The shift toward individual credit throughout journalism is not due to any upsurge in the public's curiosity about who is writing what. It's because journalists are now selling themselves. They have less job security but also greater opportunity to make it big. Many move in rapid succession from one publication to another as they build their reputations. Among the highest achievements for a print journalist is to be invited to appear on television, and thence to be a "regular" guest. Magazines and newspapers, continuously seeking talented people, are willing to accommodate their growing desire for visibility. Besides, a celebrity journalist on staff can help sell the magazine.

It is much the same in computer software, where individual credits are appearing more often at the start of programs and even on the packaging; and in law firms, investment banks, and other professional partnerships, which increasingly advertise the names and accomplishments of their major partners. All are moving toward what's been standard practice in the movie industry for many years, where the size and positioning of credits has been among the most contentious issues in contract negotiations. Hollywood has long been inhabited by talented people who are forever building their names.

In politics, today's up-and-comers are more interested in building their personal brands than in building their parties. Increasingly, they're targeting their own donors, developing their own images independent of their parties, seeking personal credit for legislative accomplishment, and creating their own personal buzz. In the old system, a Jesse Ventura would have had to toil for years in the vineyards of party politics before becoming governor of Minnesota. Instead, he built his name as a wrestler known for fighting with a pink boa under the klieg lights of the World Wrestling Federation and then as a radio talk-show host. Pat Buchanan, a perennial candidate for president, belongs to no particular party. His brand identity is as a pugnacious TV pundit. For a short while in 1999, the press gave respectful attention to the possible presidential candidacies of Hollywood star Warren Beatty, entertainment mogul Oprah Winfrey, and New York real-estate tycoon Donald Trump. None got far, but the mere fact that anyone with name recognition can now run for President of the United States suggests how far we've come toward a system of self-marketing politics. American politics is also going the way of Hollywood. "This whole relationship between Hollywood and Washington is as natural as marriage," says Norman Lear, the television producer. "We're basically in the same business. We're coveting the audience's attention."[17]

PUTTING YOURSELF IN PLAY

Years ago, most people didn't know what they were "worth" on the open market because there wasn't much of an open market for their services. They were part of an organization, and they tended to remain inside it. For them to solicit offers from rival enterprises would have been as unseemly as for rival enterprises to try to lure them away. But increasingly, people know what they're worth on the market because they're "in play," as are their colleagues. Specialized Internet chat boards (like "Greedy Associates," for young lawyers) keep them apprised of the going rates. They let it be known they're looking for new opportunities, and rival groups bid for them with abandon.

A rising star typically solicits an offer from a rival firm that is considerably more generous than the star's current compensation, and then dangles the offer in front of a senior executive. "I really don't want to leave here," the star says sorrowfully. "This is a great place to work, and you've been damn good to me." And then, innocently: "What do you think I should do about *this?*" The message is clear: Match the bid or better it, or I'm gone.

Some enterprises depend on rival bids in order to establish appropriate pay levels. When an acquaintance who is a computer engineer recently sought a raise, the head of the software house where he works asked him to get a bid from a rival software house, and the executive would match it. The executive explained that there was no better way to determine the engineer's market value than to test it in the market.

Not long ago, it was reported that the president of Brown University, after only eighteen months on the job, received a salary offer from Vanderbilt University roughly three times larger than the $300,000 a year Brown was paying him. It used to be an unwritten rule that Ivy

League presidents remained at their posts for a decade or more. Apparently, that is no longer the case. The still-new Brown president told the Brown trustees about the offer from Vanderbilt, and then departed for the more lucrative position, leaving in his wake a lot of hurt feelings as well as a powerful lesson for thousands of Brown undergraduates about money and loyalty in the new economy. The Vanderbilt trustee who recruited him said she didn't see what all the fuss was about. She runs a large wholesale book business. "People take people from my company all the time," she said.[18]

"Headhunters" maintain stables of prospective candidates for potential spots even if the candidates are now happily employed elsewhere. "Eventually they'll want to try something else," one headhunter explained to me, referring to the people in his stables, "and eventually something will open up that will be perfect for them. We want to establish long-term relationships in advance, with both sides—people who are hot prospects, and hot groups that are likely to need them."[19]

It's been this way in professional baseball for years, ever since free agency. Ball clubs have valuable franchises in their brands. Up-and-coming players develop their own brand names. I used to take my son Adam to see Red Sox games in Fenway Park. His favorite player was a big hulk of a first baseman named Mo Vaughn. Mo could hit balls out of the park with greater ease and regularity than anybody else on the team, and when Mo came up to the plate, Adam silently prayed that the pitcher wouldn't walk him. As Mo's star rose, he attracted more fans to Fenway Park; and as he did so, his compensation package kept rising. A few years ago, Mo wanted more than the Sox were willing to pay him. He rejected their offer of about $64 million over five years. "It's been a great time here," he told his disappointed fans on his way to a somewhat more lucrative contract with the Anaheim Angels. "I hold no grudges in the situation. I want to thank my teammates. Best wishes to the Boston Red Sox and *their* fans." The italics are mine, because I wanted to emphasize the shift in the pronoun. The two brands—the Red Sox brand and the Mo Vaughn brand—were now going their separate ways. As Mo explained, "I'm not moving, I'm just going somewhere else to work."[20]

One important consequence of the bids and counterbids is to widen the gap between the highest-paid and lowest-paid members of any team or group—reflecting their relative drawing power. You can see the phenomenon in law firms and other professional partnerships, where rainmakers who pull in clients now take home pay packages that are multiples of those received by lowly partners who simply do careful professional work. This is because the "rainmakers" aren't just selling the firm; they're selling themselves. They pull in clients because of their carefully cultivated reputations and connections. Years ago, that wouldn't have mattered; all partners received approximately the same compensation because they were partners, and they expected to remain with one another for most of their professional lives. But in the new economy, valuable rainmakers can go anywhere. Naturally, they expect compensation to reflect the value of their personal brand. If they don't receive it, they'll go to another firm that will treat them more generously—and bring their personal brand (and a bevy of clients) along with them.

About the last place you'd expect to see this bidding game is among the tenured professoriat of America's great universities. It used to be that tenured faculty within such rarefied environs stayed put for decades, unto death, occasionally even beyond death—delivering the same lectures to generations of students within the same lecture halls, writing variations on the same papers (read and commented upon by the same circle of colleagues), attending the same annual academic conferences. It was assumed that these institutions were sufficiently prestigious that the mere honor of being associated with them satisfied most ambition. The late C. P. Snow, author and philosopher, once said that Cambridge dons were not distinguished men, but merely men who conferred distinction upon one another.

And yet, even in these musty climes, there are rumblings of a new order. In the fall of 1998, Columbia University agreed to pay Robert J. Barro nearly $300,000 a year if he would leave his tenured position at Harvard and join Columbia's economics department. To put this sum in perspective, it was at the time roughly twice the top salary paid to arts and sciences faculty at Harvard, Columbia, and other elite universities. According to the *New York Times*,[21] Columbia also agreed to give Barro three spacious offices (office space inside a typically cramped university building is coveted almost as much as parking space outside) and a sizeable research allowance, as well as the opportunity to recruit a number of promising younger economists. This was not all. Columbia would also place Barro's son in an exclusive Manhattan private school, give Barro's wife a $55,000-a-year university post, and install the entire Barro family in a 2,300-square-foot university-owned apartment on Riverside Drive, which Columbia would renovate and rent to him at half the estimated market rate.

I do not know Barro, but I am sure he is very able. His theoretical work has had considerable influence in the economics profession, and he was distinguished before he came to Harvard. The offer that Columbia University made to Barro is significant not so much for what it signals about him, or about Columbia, as for what it suggests about the new market in personal brands even within the most hallowed of academic sanctuaries. Heretofore, there was no question but that the brands "Columbia University" and "Harvard University" were far more significant attractions than were the names of any individual members of their respective faculties. Both universities had built their faculties slowly, nurturing their star doctoral students, culling their postgraduates, and only occasionally, painstakingly, selecting a few rising young stars from elsewhere. And despite the inevitable deadwood that accumulates in tenured ranks, both universities continue to house many great and lively minds whose reputations have deservedly grown over time.

But even Harvard and Columbia are transmuting into fast-moving networks whose continuing ability to attract talented people—both teachers and students—depends on the talented people they already have been able to attract. They need to maintain virtuous cycles in which the reputation of their brand enhances the personal reputations of their faculties and students, who in turn enhance the reputation of the university brand and in that way attract more illustrious faculty and students. With talent now on the move, such a virtuous sequence cannot be taken for granted. Greatness can be bought wholesale. An entire department can be poached if the package of pay and perquisite is sufficiently generous.

Columbia was willing to pay Barro an extraordinary sum by university standards because it thought his reputation in the field of economics would burnish Columbia's reputation and accelerate just this sort of virtuous cycle. In fact, through Barro, Columbia could create an even more lustrous economics department, wholesale. In one of his rounds of negotiation with Columbia, Barro submitted a list of ten to twelve rising economics stars whom he wanted Columbia to snare as part of the deal. Presumably, many of them would be attracted to Columbia both by Barro's presence and by the presence of the other young stars in the package. Rather than painstakingly build its department person by person, Columbia would buy a whole piece of it. "[I]f it's successful, it will change the way people think about the build-or-buy decision," a University of Chicago economist commented about the package deal. "Money will talk and blitz campaigns will work."

Before making its initial bid, Columbia measured the worth of Barro's drawing power by consulting other stars in the economics firmament. A Columbia dean sought the advice of Milton Friedman, an eminent conservative economist. "Milton was very positive," the dean told the *Times*. "He said, 'Barro's young. He's got visibility. People are drawn to him.'" One Columbia economist described the deal in terms of costs and benefits. "We're capturing a lot of the surplus that Robert will generate," he said.

The raid shook Harvard to the core. Was it just possible that the Harvard brand was no longer sufficient, in and of itself, to guarantee that the school's more illustrious faculty would stay put? The dean of the faculty, who until then had bragged that he had never been forced to match an offer from another university, invited Barro to what was described as a "long, wine-drenched dinner" to present Harvard's counteroffer—involving a new research center and more. Whatever was put on the table apparently worked, because in the end Barro decided to stay put. Yet it was a close call for Harvard, which the dean apparently does not want to repeat. He is reportedly building a "war chest" to fend off future raids.

The Barro case is also interesting for the subtle tension it reveals between the two brands for which Barro was working: the Harvard brand and the Barro brand. For much of his career, Barro's research and writing had contributed to developing the Barro brand while simultaneously burnishing Harvard's reputation. By working for Barro, he had also been working for Harvard.

But not even Harvard can survive by relying solely on individual entrepreneurs. It also needs people who invest in the institution as a whole. Suppose you are a young Harvard assistant professor, having witnessed Barro's near defection to Columbia. Harvard clearly wants you to do research and writing. But it also wants you to do many other things that will uniquely help Harvard but not build your own reputation in the field. It wants you to teach students, advise them, make speeches to alumni groups, and serve on faculty committees. How much of your time and energy are you likely to devote to these institutional activities, as opposed to building your own brand? Probably as little as you can get away with. You know that the odds are against your remaining at Harvard for your career. You can now see quite clearly the considerable rewards of building your own brand as diligently as you can.

The new economy offers entrepreneurial professors ever more opportunity to profit from their brand names. Soon well-known professors will be able to sell their personal brands over the Internet—through their very own lectures and courses. Instead of teaching 100 students a year, each of whom pays him, indirectly through their tuitions, roughly $1,000, he can reach 100,000 students around the world. If each of them nets him $10 for his labors, he'll earn a million dollars. (The legal question of who owns the courses and the brand—the star professor or the brand-name university at which he nominally teaches—is sure to become a lively one.)

The point is generalizable across all institutions: As talented people become more mobile and the market grows more competitive, the incentives are on the side of investing in one's personal brand rather than devoting time and energy to the organization. Apart from the group whose mission is sufficiently compelling as to command the passions of its members, their first priority will be to sell themselves.

The Barro saga is interesting for another reason. After Barro had so conspicuously determined his "worth," professors all over America were able to compare their own levels of compensation with what he was offered and estimate their own relative "worth." Such a revelation may have made many who were otherwise quite comfortable feel a measure of discontent. In the old economy, remember, you earned about the same as anyone else occupying a position with the same seniority in the same industry. Salary wasn't something to be discussed, in any event. But in the emerging economy, replete with bids and counterbids, your compensation level is likely to be different from that of your colleagues, and yours and theirs are both more likely to be widely known—suggesting your and their relative "worth." Few pieces of information can cause more distress and instigate more rancor.

Mo Vaughn could have lived a fairly comfortable life on the $64 million that the Boston Red Sox were willing to pay him. Count in taxes and the cost of living in Los Angeles, and the Angels' $72 million offer wasn't much better. But the New York Mets had offered Mike Piazza $91 million in 1998, and the Red Sox paid Pedro Martinez $75 million. Mo probably figured he was worth at least as much as Pedro. The Sox's $64 million final offer told him they didn't think he was. And that difference of opinion about Mo's relative worth may have been just enough to send him packing.

A good friend on my faculty recently decided to move to another university that offered him a better deal. He had been a valued colleague, and hardly the sort of person who cares about how much money he earns as such. I asked him why he was leaving. He looked at me for a long instant before answering. "I just don't feel valued here," he said.

I didn't understand at first. My friend had been given a number of awards, was the chairman of a major department, everyone who knew him appreciated his scholarship and his service to the university community, and his students were enthusiastic about his classes. Why didn't he feel valued? He explained that his current salary was not particularly high relative to many other professors at the university, and that the other university had "pulled out all the stops" to get him.

I asked him, "If you didn't know the level of anyone's salary here, or at any other university—and practically no one else knew, either— would you still feel undervalued?" He thought for a moment. "I suppose that would be different," he said.

It would be different because my friend would then have looked for other cues about his "worth"—cues more subtle and supple than his salary and perquisites relative to others on campus, and relative to the higher salary and perquisites he was being offered by the other university. But there's something particularly stark about the numerals in a paycheck relative to the numerals in other paychecks, especially when they are all so public. I don't think my friend cared a hoot about the relative earnings in terms of how much the dollars would buy. He was sensitive, rather, to what the dollars meant about his worth in his chosen profession. It was a signal of how much value was attached to his work in his community. My friend simply wanted to go to a place that valued him more.

WHY WINNERS DON'T TAKE ALL

One newly popular theory about why certain people like Robert Barro earn so much more than everyone else is that within the national or global marketplace only a few people gain big visibility and credibility—and they "take it all."[22] At first blush, the theory sounds plausible.

There are only a certain number of openings in the freshman classes of Ivy League universities and only a limited number of slots on the best-seller list. But in a dynamic economy, there are actually few such "zero-sum" situations. Typically arrayed behind each big brand name are a number of people with smaller names, some of considerable talent and salesmanship. As the big names do better with the help of these smaller names, the reputations of the smaller ones begin to grow. And because the smaller ones are in the business of marketing themselves rather than the organization, they can exact larger payments reflecting their new worth, or else leave for better deals elsewhere.

In his annual letter to shareholders in the spring of 1999, Disney chairman Michael Eisner gushed about *SportsNight,* a new comedy series on Disney's ABC Television. "It is fantastic," Eisner wrote. "It is one of the building blocks we are putting together to eventually make ABC Number One."[23] Assume for the moment that Eisner's enthusiasm for *SportsNight* was merited. The question is, whose "worth" is boosted by a television hit like this?

It turned out that Disney didn't own *SportsNight.* It was the brain-child of a production house run by the movie producers Ron Howard and Brian Glazer and longtime Hollywood agent Tony Krantz. The trio have been responsible for several TV hits, not only on ABC but also on its rivals NBC and Fox Broadcasting. Howard, Glazer, and Krantz are "hot." If *SportsNight* was a hit, advertisers would pay Disney a lot of money in order to lay claim to thirty seconds of commercial time when it was aired on ABC. But all those extra dollars wouldn't flow to Disney. If Disney wanted to continue to receive *SportsNight* programs from Howard, Glazer, and Krantz, it would have to pay them a portion of the winnings, because they're now "worth" more on the market. Their reputations have been enhanced among all network executives who make such buys.

Howard, Glazer, and Krantz would have to apportion some of their winnings to several talented writers and producers who have been devising the clever, oddball situations that the trio are selling. Among them is Aaron Sorkin, who came up with the idea for the show and wrote several of its early episodes. Even before he did so, Sorkin's reputation in Hollywood was on the rise. He wrote the scripts for the movies *A Few Good Men* and *The American President.* If *SportsNight* was a big hit, Sorkin, too, would be "worth" more.

So when Eisner told Disney shareholders that *SportsNight* was one of the "building blocks" he was putting together to make ABC "Number One," the statement was not precisely true. Moreover, even if *SportsNight* had become a hit (which it didn't), Disney stockholders would not have been nearly as enriched by it as they might have expected. That's because, rather than sitting atop a bureaucracy whose "building blocks" are owned outright, Eisner is at only one point—albeit a big one—in a web of connections whose every point has choices about where it wishes to be connected in the future. This significantly dilutes the "winner-take-all" phenomenon, because it gives talented people like Aaron Sorkin—at another of those points—leverage to get whatever he's worth on the market. Unless Sorkin was compensated adequately, Disney's rivals could pull him away from ABC—which was exactly what happened in the fall of 1999, when he created a hit series for NBC, *The West Wing*.

The new economy has precious few lone players like Mo Vaughn who win it all, or nearly all of it. The rest of the people at or near the top are doing remarkably well, to be sure. They possess just the right combination of talents and connections, and have sold themselves adeptly. But they are not winning it all; they are sharing some of their winnings with talented people arrayed around them on whom they depend, and those people in turn are sharing some of their winnings with others on whom *they* depend, and so on, extending outward and downward in a vast network of interconnections. As talented people make names in their fields, they're worth more. The Aaron Sorkins of Hollywood are doing better all the time.

Rather than there being just a handful of people at the top and everyone else far below them, many talented people are on the rise. The top 1 percent is doing magnificently; the top 5 percent is faring better than ever before; the top 20 percent is living quite comfortably. But each rung on the ladder is spaced more widely apart than before. As noted, the middle has not progressed much, and those on the rungs below them are relatively worse off.

MARKET-DIRECTED MAN AND WOMAN

In the old economy, you got ahead by being well liked. Self-help books solemnly advised on *How to Win Friends and Influence People*.[24] The successful "organization man" was accepted by all. Arthur Miller's Willy

Loman advises his sons how to succeed: "Be liked and you will never want," he says. "[T]he wonder of this country [is] that a man can end with diamonds here on the basis of being liked!"[25]

David Riesman, the eminent sociologist of midcentury America, identified what he termed the era's "other-directed" personality, who sought above all else to be approved of by his peers. "One makes good only when one is approved of," Riesman observed about the quintessential midcentury American character. "Thus all power . . . is in the hands of the actual or imaginary approving group."[26]

In the new economy, you get ahead not by being well liked but by being well marketed. The goal is no longer to fit in or to gain the approval of one's peers. It's to stand out among one's peers, to dazzle and inspire potential customers, or people who will connect you to them. The old organization is vanishing, and in its place are men and women who not only believe deeply in themselves but can persuade others to believe in them. To this end, a generous dose of self-esteem is more important than gregariousness; beaming self-confidence, more useful than humble charm. In order to be powerful, it's necessary to *feel* powerful, to have *The Courage to Be Rich*,[27] says financial guru Suze Orman: "I do know that your net worth will rise to meet your self worth only if your self worth rises to accept what can be yours." Management consultant Tom Peters instructs that "starting today you are a brand. You're every bit as much a brand as Nike, Coke, Pepsi, or the Body Shop." If you are to succeed, your "most important job is to be head marketer for the brand called You."[28]

Financial and management consultants are America's new spiritual leaders—televangelists, psychologists, personal trainers, and coaches who preach spiritual self-actualization as economic advancement. Under the new ethic of self-motivated financial spiritualism, personal worthiness is measured by one's net worth. It's the Protestant ethic turned on its ear: You're worthy because the market rewards you; you succeed financially because you believe passionately not in God but in *yourself.* By making your personality into a marketable commodity and selling it successfully, you can increase your worth and thus gain worthiness in the divine eyes of the market.

Behind the financial spiritualists are legions of personal promoters, publicists, personal marketers, and image consultants able to turn pastry chefs into marketers of cookbooks, cable-television shows, appetizing Web sites, new lines of soups and spices, and kitchenware. "When you get a job as a chef," says Jacques Torres, pastry chef at Le Cirque 2000 in Manhattan, "you start at a certain salary. That salary will go up gradually, but if you really want to make a better living, you have to get into consulting, books, television."[29] Don Hobbs, who specializes in "personal marketing" of real-estate agents, advises that agents use advertising dollars to "market *me*—to create a distinction between me and 5,000 other agents." Not "'I'm Joe Blow, real estate agent,'" but "more like two little girls running up to Dad. Dad getting out of the car. Soft music. 'When it matters . . . it matters to Ron Kubek.' Those two darling blond babies in his arms—highly emotive music. You've got to get them emotional."[30]

Not many years ago, state laws barred doctors from advertising. It was assumed that doctors were not, and should not, be part of a commercial culture. After all, they adhered to a code of conduct first set down by Hippocrates. Now, with the help of "doctor publicists," some doctors market diet books, health advice, and a host of products extending from sugar-free maple syrup to the steroid hormone pregnenolone.[31] An increasing portion of this booty is marketed over the Web, where even Dr. Koop now resides. Dentists hire publicity agents to promote their high-tech gum lasers and state-of-the-art laminating techniques. One Dr. Larry Rosenthal is rolling out a consumer product line bearing his name, including an electronic toothbrush and dental floss that can remove stains between teeth.[32]

Talented people are even selling shares in themselves. Rock star David Bowie floated a personal bond issue, entitling investors to a fixed percentage of his future royalties and concert receipts, which was fully subscribed within an hour for more than $50 million.[33] Martha Stewart has incorporated, and is selling shares in herself. Stewart isn't simply lending her name to a specific product, like Minnie Pearl's Fried Chicken. She's selling her cheerful personality—her homespun but elegant taste, her adorable decorating ideas and homey recipes, and her pleasantly agreeable approach to life, in which everyone has time to make citronella candles from scratch. Her investors hope the Martha Stewart brand has significant value apart from her, but should she take her money and retire to the Netherlands Antilles, they may discover that the two are inseparable.

Aspiring politicians now market their personalities rather than their beliefs or platforms, relying on a growing number of political consultants for promotional assistance. The well-marketed politician has less need of a political party, just as the well-marketed professor has less need of a particular university, the up-and-coming journalist of a particular newspaper, the rising scriptwriter of a TV network or production house, the talented baseball player of a particular team, the star investment analyst of a particular financial house. Political parties, like all other organizations, are becoming collections of entrepreneurs. It should come as no surprise that today's politicians, divorced from party and platforms, find themselves in continuous mud fights. When a personality is being marketed rather than a party or a set of principles, competition almost inevitably turns personal. Electoral success depends on advancing one's own persona while destroying that of an opponent. "Opposition research," a euphemism for digging up personal dirt about one's opponent, is now a routine feature of American political campaigns.

THE SALE OF the self makes relentless demands on one's life. It also encroaches on one's personal relationships. When the personality is for sale, all relationships turn into potential business deals. Unlike David Riesman's "other-directed" man who wished only to be liked, the new market-directed man or woman wants only to make a deal. Yet when friends, relatives, and casual acquaintances become vehicles for selling oneself, all relationships can become tainted with ulterior motive. In Washington, New York, Hollywood, Silicon Valley, or any other center of dealmaking, it is often difficult to get together for lunch with a "friend" without its being assumed that one party or the other is selling something, or looking to buy. The assumption is often correct.

The market-directed person's value derives not from acceptance by his or her peers but from what others are willing to pay for his or her services. Hence the central importance of being in demand. In certain quarters, one of the first questions asked of someone long unseen is no longer "Are you well?" but "Are you *busy*?" It's assumed that if they're busy, they're in demand, and if they're in demand, they *must* be well. The apparent complaint "I'm so busy!" is not really heard as a lament, however sincere. The complainant may have almost no time or energy left for anything in life other than paid work—may even have sacrificed friends and family to the incessant demands of getting ahead—but is nonetheless presumed to be successful in the market, which is the ultimate test of market-directed success.

Riesman's other-directed person of midcentury America was in danger of losing his identity to the group. The market-directed person at the start of the new century is in danger of selling it. Which is the greater danger? Once, the worst thing that could be said of someone was that he had sold out. Now the worst thing that can be said is that he's not selling.

CHAPTER EIGHT

The Incredible Shrinking Family

THAT THE NEW WORK is taking a toll on family life is not in great contention. The more interesting question is how this is occurring, and what form it's taking.

The midcentury nuclear family—husband with steady job, wife at home caring for an average of 2.7 kids and cleaning compulsively, everyone home for meatloaf dinner—was a historical oddity. Go back to the mid-nineteenth century, before large-scale production, and you see complex and shifting living arrangements under the same roof: relatives who came and went, children who died in infancy, stepmothers taking the place of biological mothers who died while giving birth, stepfathers who stepped in when fathers died from one of an array of accidents, infections, and diseases. And it was often the case that all family members had to work—men, women, and children, in hard physical toil for long hours—in order to keep enough food on the table and a roof overhead. The economy was far more precarious than now, as was life itself.

The precariousness of today's living arrangements, here on the other side of the industrial era, comes not from death but from work, which takes family members away for longer periods of time or which, even when the family member is physically present, is intrusive, preoccupying, and unpredictable.[1] The new family, such as it is, exists within a complex set of logistical arrangements for getting various members to where they need to be in order to respond to the economy's new demands. Sociologists have even coined an acronym, DINS—double income, no sex—to describe modern stressed-out couples too tired to do anything in bed but sleep. As they try to coordinate their small slices of time together for maximum effect, such couples have caused a small boom in sales of ovulation-predictor kits. Once a child arrives, a third of working parents now divide up work and child care into shifts, with one partner working during the day while the other undertakes parental duty, and then switching roles for the evening.[2] They communicate with each other by notes, listing who called while the other was out, what happened in the baby's day, what's for dinner.

More homes are effectively vacant for longer periods of time. Both partners are on the road, or if working in the vicinity, they are away for more of the day. Small children are trundled off to day care. Elderly parents live alone or in nursing homes. Few families synchronize their schedules sufficiently to dine together. Working parents arrive home long after the stomachs of children demand to be filled. The portion of married Americans who say "definitely" that "our whole family usually eats dinner together" has dropped by a third in the last twenty years, from 50 percent to 34 percent.[3]

Some families have even got to the point where they schedule a weekly meeting. Craig Forman is the chief executive officer of myprimetime.com, a Web site intended to help busy working people make better use of their time. Every Sunday at 6:30 p.m., Forman meets with his wife, Cecile, and their seven-year-old son, Elliot. "My week doesn't have a beginning or an end," Forman told the editors of *Fast Company*.[4] "I live the startup life: I travel a lot, and I carry a bunch of cell-phones plus an Internet pager. This family meeting allows us to come together and update one another about what's on tap for the week ahead." At one weekly meeting, they discussed whether Elliot, who had always attended French-speaking schools before the family moved to their present home in San Francisco, should have a French tutor. "Our family meetings are like my company's project update sessions," Forman said. "We take turns telling one another what's on our schedule for the coming week and what's been nagging at us."

TAKE A SNAPSHOT of a typical group of people living together in the early 1970s, and compare it to a snapshot taken a quarter-century later. The biggest difference you will see is a sharp drop in the percentage of married people with children at home, from 45 percent in 1972 to 26 percent in 1998, combined with an *increase* in the percent of unmarried people without children, from 16 percent to 32 percent.[5] In short, the typical household has shifted from married with children, to unmarried without children. At midcentury, domestic sitcoms like *Father Knows Best* and *Leave It to Beaver* reflected the household norm; today, sitcoms revolve around the new style of unattached young singles like those in *Ally McBeal* and *Friends*.

Several developments, starting in the seventies, explain this change. First, women gained greater control over procreation. They got access to more effective contraceptives like the Pill.[6] And in 1973 the Supreme Court ruled that states couldn't prevent women from getting, and doctors from performing, abortions during the early stages of a pregnancy. Yet women's greater reproductive autonomy cannot explain all of the change. Surveys also show a significant drop in people's *desire* for large families. In 1972, a majority of adults (56 percent) thought the ideal number of children was three or more per family. By the late 1990s, less than 40 percent held this view.[7]

Something else began to happen in the 1970s, and it has been accelerating since. It's actually two things, closely related. Both pertain to the larger trends we've been looking at, but each of them warrants separate examination.

THE BIG FAMILY CHANGE (I)

The first thing driving some women into the workforce starting in the seventies was the relative decline in the earnings of their male spouses or partners. The shift from large-scale production toward innovative ideas and personal services has been particularly hard on men, who used to do most of the production work. As their earnings declined, their wives or partners began to work for pay in order to prop up family incomes.[8] (Of course, many poor women had never left the paid workforce.)

The drop in the earnings of blue-collar men has been well documented, although there is a debate over its steepness. In some ways, a blue-collar family in 2001 is still better off than it was in 1979 even if its dollar income has dropped according to standard measures of inflation. Given the new spirit of innovation, some products and services are cheaper than they used to be, many are better, and there are a lot of new ones. Long-distance telephone calls cost less, as do television sets, airline tickets, and a host of other things. You can now buy digital recorders, educational software, antidepressants, and Viagra. A doctor can have an MRI machine scan thin slices of your body, looking for tiny traces of cancer. Chances are, you'll live longer. And as I have stressed, you can shop more efficiently for terrific deals.

Yet even in an era of abundance, some people may feel *relatively* deprived compared to the status they used to have in society. As the overall living standard of Americans continues to rise, families who fail to gain ground understandably feel themselves to be losing ground. Both men and women in such families will want to work longer hours for pay because they perceive the need to gain some of that ground back. They are less motivated by envy of their better-off neighbors than by a sense of what constitutes a minimally acceptable standard of living for themselves and their families. Many blue-collar families feel that they have been running harder since the late 1970s just to stay in place. Women have been running especially hard.

THE BIG FAMILY CHANGE (II)

A second group of women has been moving into the workforce for a different reason. They're responding to the increasing rewards available to creative workers who develop new ideas, solve problems, and discover how to cut costs. These new opportunities for women began opening up in the early seventies when the economy began shifting in this direction, and they've been escalating since. In the future, expect even greater opportunities for talented women.

When I attended college in the late 1960s, most women who were attending at the time expected to become teachers or nurses. But by the early seventies only a small fraction still had their eye on these noble but relatively low-paying professions. Other options had opened up, some paying far more. This occurred in part because the crusading efforts of a group of highly able and forward-thinking women pried open many doors. Ensuing laws against employment discrimination also helped. But the doors would still be shut were it not for the stirrings of a new economy with an increasing need for brains and creativity. Since the 1970s, as the new economy has claimed more ground, the earnings and opportunities for well-educated women have soared.

This second group of women haven't entered paid work in order to maintain family incomes. When they have married, their husbands are usually well-educated men comfortably in the top fifth of male earners. Consider: In 1979, 55 percent of women with such wealthy husbands were working outside the home, earning an average of $15,800 (in 1996 dollars). By the late 1990s, 75 percent of them were working, earning an average of $27,175. That means their earnings have shot up 113 percent—far faster than the earnings of women whose husbands are not in the top fifth, and faster even than their own husbands' earnings.[9]

Quite apart from any inherent satisfaction they get out of working outside the home, these women have faced the steadily increasing costs of *not* working. As their job opportunities have become greater and their potential compensation has grown, the sacrifice entailed in rejecting careers in favor of home and family has grown in tandem.

This also suggests why more women than ever are enrolling in college—more women, in fact, than men. About 70 percent of young women are now heading to college from high school, compared to only 64 percent of male high-school grads. If the current trend continues to the year 2007, there will be 9.2 million young women in college and only 6.9 million young men.[10] This marks a stunning reversal from just a few years ago, when young men attended college in far greater numbers than young women. Midcentury parents who could not afford to put all their children through college routinely sent their sons and kept their daughters at home, assuming (correctly) that educated sons had better job opportunities than educated daughters.

Well-educated women still earn less than well-educated men, even when they're doing the same jobs. As noted, gender discrimination has yet to be wrung out of society. But if present trends continue, it seems a safe bet that sometime this century women will catch up. The new economy rewards traits that women are no less likely than men to possess: inventiveness and empathy, which I've previously described as belonging, respectively, to geeks and shrinks. Moreover, as I said earlier, education is highly correlated with future income (and with the valuable connections leading to good jobs), so as women match men in acquiring college diplomas, and the connections that come with them, the gap also will narrow. You already can see something of the trend: In families with two wage-earners, women have steadily gained ground on their spouses. In 1980, fewer than one in five working wives earned more than their husbands; by 2000, nearly one in three did. Among highly educated women, nearly half now earn more than their husbands.[11] Meanwhile, women are taking over a steadily larger portion of managerial and professional jobs. Excluding teachers and nurses, they held less than 20 percent of all managerial and professional jobs in 1970 but more than 36 percent in 1999. Among high-powered professionals, the increase went from 9.2 percent in 1970 to more than 25 percent in 1998.[12]

But here's the rub. As noted, high-powered jobs in the emerging economy tend to demand total commitment. It's all or nothing—fast track or slow track. If you want to remain on the fast track, you have to work late with customers and clients, be available at all hours, develop your contacts and connections, and stay abreast of new developments. Yet many women continue to be the major caretakers in their families. And, unfortunately for them, many men want them to be. It's almost impossible to be both the major breadwinner *and* the major caretaker in a family.

If men want to have children as much as potentially high-earning women do, those women will be in a position to strike a deal: Men will have to take on at least half of the caretaking responsibilities. On the other hand, if it turns out that men are more willing than women to forgo parenthood, women will continue to be faced with a shortage of prospective husbands and partners willing to do at least half the work of raising a family. So women will continue to have to choose between fast track or slow track with children, as many are doing now.

Women can't have it all. Nor can men. Not long ago, Alice Hector, then a partner in a high-powered Miami law firm (the same one where Attorney General Janet Reno once worked), lost custody of her daughters to her ex-husband, Robert Young. While she had toiled long hours at the firm, Young, an unemployed builder, had stayed at home with their girls. After the divorce and during the custody fight, Hector argued that she spent as much time with her daughters as most professional working parents spend with their children. Perhaps she did. But this line of argument didn't persuade the presiding judge. The judge was more interested in which parent spent the most time caring for the kids. "It is clear from the record," he said in awarding custody to the father, "that it is Mr. Young who is available to the children after school, takes the children to the doctor and dentist appointments and actively participates in the children's school and after-school activities." Added Young, after the judge's decision was announced: "The reason she was able to devote so much time to her vocation is that I made my vocation my kids. Dads can be moms, too."[13]

What happened in this case may offer a glimpse into the future. Even if both parents work full-time, presumably one of them will have to choose between the fast track and the slow track. Women who care more about keeping their children than about earning more money and holding on to the power and prestige that come with it won't make Alice Hector's mistake; they'll let their husbands get on the fast track, and they'll stay on the slower one in order to ensure that, if a split should occur, they will win custody.

Attitudes about marriage and work have changed as the economy has changed, but with a slight lag time. In the late 1970s, for example, most Americans felt that wives shouldn't even contribute to a household's income. By the late eighties, as the emerging economy bore down harder on families, a slim majority (51.7 percent) continued to hold this charmingly anachronistic view. But by the early nineties, a majority agreed that wives *should* contribute to household income, and by the late nineties, a generation of men and women fully adapted to the new economy pushed it up to two-thirds. Similarly, in the mid-1970s, almost two-thirds felt it was "much better for everyone involved if the man is the achiever outside the home and the woman takes care of the home and family." But by the end of the nineties, two-thirds disagreed with this view.[14]

THE BIG SQUEEZE

Regardless of whether women are heading into paid work in order to prop up family incomes or to pursue great opportunities, families have been shrinking in response. Women are having fewer children, or no children. This is either because women can't afford them or because they can't give children the time and energy they require, or both.

In an economy becoming ever riskier—where every enterprise is busily turning its fixed costs into variable costs and thus subjecting all jobs and incomes to greater uncertainty—many women (and men) simply don't want to take on the biggest fixed cost of them all, which is a child. To speak of children as a "fixed cost" is a cold-blooded way of making the point that children's needs are continuous. And a child's world requires some stability and reliability if the child is to grow and thrive. Yet the emerging economy is discontinuous, and is anything but stable and reliable.

So it's not surprising that, as the economy has shifted, the birthrate among married women has steadily dropped: from ninety-eight births per 1,000 married women twenty years ago to eighty in the late 1990s. In all likelihood, as the new economy claims more terrain, that rate will continue to drop. In fact, it's no longer unusual for a woman to decide to forgo children altogether. In the mid-1970s, only about 10 percent of middle-aged women had never had a child. Among them were teachers, nuns, or nurses who had dedicated their lives to their work. Their decision to be childless was respected but also set them apart, in their own childless subcultures. Now a decision to forgo children isn't so odd. Nineteen percent of women between the ages of forty and forty-five have never had a child. Some of them are happily married. They're just pursuing interests other than raising children.[15]

Even women who plan to have children are delaying. Births to teenagers have dropped dramatically, reaching by the year 2000 the lowest rate in the United States since the government began tracking births in 1906. The same pattern holds true for all racial and ethnic groups. Birthrates for women in their twenties, meanwhile, have been flat. The only increase in birthrates has been among women in their thirties.[16] In my home state of Massachusetts, more babies are now born to women over thirty than under thirty.

Women are waiting because that's a perfectly rational response to the emerging economy. Some poorer women hold off until they and their partners can afford a child. Professional women want to wait until they make partner, or otherwise establish themselves. All women sense that once they give birth they won't be on the same earnings trajectory as they were before, and they're probably right. Whether rich or poor, younger working women without children come closest to matching men's pay levels. But once a woman has her first baby and faces the choice of fast track or slow, she most often chooses the slower one, and thereafter starts losing ground relative to men. Unless, of course, she's willing to go the route of high-powered women like Alice Hector.

SMALLER OR DELAYED families can be understood in terms of the emerging economy, but why is marriage disappearing as well? Americans are now less likely to marry than at any time since statistics on marriages began to be tallied almost a century ago. Here's a clue: The sharp decline in marriage rates began in the 1970s. A snapshot in 1970 would show 68 percent of adults married and 15 percent never married (the rest divorced, separated, or widowed). A snapshot at the end of the 1990s would show only 56 percent of adults married and 23 percent never married.[17]

Recall that when the large-scale production economy began to shrink in the seventies, the wages of most blue-collar men began to stagnate or drop, relatively speaking, and they've dropped further since then. Even earnings that aren't dropping are becoming less predictable. As a result, men are nowhere near as good a deal for women as they used to be. Far be it from me to take the romance out of marriage, but most women are not completely irrational when it comes to making marriage decisions. They'll consider who's going to contribute what to the union. Twenty-five years ago, a man with a stable job in the old mass-production economy could contribute quite a lot. Moreover, most women lacked a separate source of income. Under these circumstances, a man's commitment to a stable marriage had significant value to a woman. Since then, such a commitment has steadily declined in value, like a share of stock in a company that's going downhill.

Consider also *her* own separate stream of income. Although starting from a much lower level than men and still lagging behind, her stock is generally going up. And consider, finally, that even if a man is doing okay now, there's no telling what will happen to him in this unpredictable economy. And if he loses his job and can't get another, or if the next job pays very little, who's to guarantee he won't take it out on her?[18]

So it would be rational for her to hedge her bets. Perhaps she keeps her options open by adopting a sort of "pay and stay" rule that goes something like this: Fella, you can stay as long as you contribute to household expenses, but when your contributions stop, or take a dive, you're outta here. I'm not suggesting that most unmarried women think about marriage in such a mercenary way. The point is that, in the new economy, such a calculation is entirely rational. And consciously or unconsciously, a growing number of women seem to be making it.[19]

Moralists are demanding stricter grounds for divorce. Several states now require that a couple first enter counseling if their marriage begins to falter. Some are calling for better preparation for marriage.

Florida offers a discount on a marriage license if the prospective couple has taken a "marital education" course. There's nothing wrong with efforts to make people think harder before they commit themselves to forming a more perfect union, and harder still before they abandon each other. But such efforts miss the basic point. The decline of marriage isn't due mainly to a slump in morality or a wave of carelessness. It's due, in large part, to a change in the economy, resulting in big differences in what men and women bring to the union. Many men no longer represent particularly good deals. Women no longer have to marry in order to have some economic security. In fact, marriage might even jeopardize their economic and personal well-being. The rising rate of divorce already has slowed, largely because fewer women are getting married in the first place.

LESS OF A MORAL CRISIS THAN YOU THINK

What really galls moralists is the sharp rise in the percentage of births that occur outside marriage. Consider that at midcentury a tiny 5.3 percent of births involved unmarried women. By the nineties, more than 32 percent of births took place outside wedlock. You can see the same trend in other nations. In Britain, for example, the proportion of children born outside marriage is now about the same as in the United States, quadrupling in the span of one generation.[20]

There is a serious crisis of illegitimacy, all right, but not quite the crisis it's often made out to be. Remember that fewer women are getting married, and that even when they do, they're having far fewer children. So it's increasingly likely that when children are born, they'll be born to women who are unmarried. This may be bad for the children (more on this in a moment), but it doesn't signal a marked trend toward illegitimacy. Imagine that a married woman gives birth to three children and an unmarried woman to one, so that one out of four of these children is born out of wedlock. Compare this to a situation where the married woman has two children and the unmarried woman has one, with the result that now one out of three children is born out of wedlock. Has the rate of illegitimacy risen? Only relative to the total number of children born. But in the second situation, the unmarried woman behaved exactly as she did in the first. In other words, some of the so-called "crisis of illegitimacy" is a by-product of the larger trends toward fewer marriages and fewer children born to married couples. As more women have begun to have fewer children, or no children, even the rate of births to unmarried women has begun to level off.[21]

Here's another misleading half-truth: Nearly 70 percent of black babies are born to black single mothers. What you don't hear is that black women are having fewer babies to begin with. The steepest drop has been among married black women, which, again, automatically increases the rate of black babies born out of wedlock, since when a black baby is born, its mother is now more likely to be single.[22] But even single black women are having fewer babies. Their rate of giving birth has been declining steadily since 1989, reaching a forty-year low in the late 1990s.[23] In short, there's no rising tide of "immoral" out-of-wedlock births among black women.

The interesting question is why black women are having far fewer babies overall. The answer is a slightly more extreme version of the answer for white women. Starting in the 1970s, the earnings of black men dropped sharply, with the result that black women have had to work longer and harder to make up the gap. At the same time, black women have gained more and better job opportunities. In consequence, the cost to them of having children and *not* attending to a job has risen, just as it has for white women who are doing better in the job market. In fact, the decline in the black birthrate has been steeper than the decline in the white birthrate, which has a lot to do with the fact that black women have moved up the earnings ladder faster than white women—while starting from a point far behind them. Black women with high-school diplomas now earn almost as much as white women with high-school diplomas ($926 for every $1,000 earned by a white). By contrast, black men with high-school diplomas are still far behind white men with diplomas, earning only $732 for every $1,000 earned by white men. Black women with four years of college behind them earn the same as white women with four years of college. And a growing percentage of black women are finishing high school and college.[24] In other words, the "opportunity costs" for black women of getting bogged down with the responsibilities of teen pregnancy are far greater today than they were three decades ago.

None of what I've written should be taken to minimize the tragically high incidence of poverty among children of single mothers. As I write this, almost 40 percent of all unmarried mothers are earning less than what's needed to buy themselves and their children adequate nutrition, clothing, and shelter. But these mothers' problem isn't that they're single. Many of them, in fact, are living with men. Some would be better off if they were married, but not all of them would be. Many of the men available to them as potential husbands are earning very little; some are abusive. These men are among those who have fallen deepest into the postindustrial hole. Rather than marry or remain married to one of them, it's sometimes smarter for these women to shop for temporary mates who will contribute more to the household for a time.

The problem of single-parent poverty is not due to an increasing percentage of poor women giving birth to children they cannot afford. As I've emphasized, the trend among all women is toward having fewer children, and this includes poor women. The real problem is that, inevitably, *some* women will have children they cannot afford. Some of these women may have behaved carelessly or irresponsibly. Others may have tried to plan their families beforehand but have hit upon bad luck, or been let down by men they thought they could count on, or been slammed by an economy that's become less predictable.

The basic reality is that jobs at the bottom of the income ladder don't pay enough to support a working woman and her children, even if she's living and sharing expenses with a working man who's also at the bottom of the income ladder. Doing away with our national system of welfare in 1996 may have made poor, nonworking mothers less "dependent" on government handouts, but it hasn't lifted them out of poverty. Although the employment rate for single mothers with children has risen since then, and a majority are now in paid jobs, the blunt fact is that, despite the best economy in a generation, poverty rates have barely changed. Most of the welfare poor have now become working poor. If, by the time you read this, the economy has turned sour, this problem will loom much larger.

In short, the real issue isn't so much a "moral crisis" within the American family as it is the growing asymmetry between what the emerging economy offers by way of work, and what children need by way of financial support, care, and attention. Many men are earning less relative to what society considers a decent standard of living, as well as what they had come to expect. More jobs require greater time and energy, regardless of whether a man or a woman is doing them. And all earnings are less predictable. Yet children's needs have not changed. This basic asymmetry has caused many women to give birth to fewer children, or to delay having children, or to decide against having them at all—not because women (or men) love children less or get less satisfaction out of parenting, but because children don't fit in easily with the demands of the emerging economy. In a different economic world, in a different time, children would be more welcome.

Yet most women are still having children. And most of these mothers are now in the workforce—either because they have to be, or because the cost to them of not working is becoming so high. Some of their children are very young. At midcentury, only 15 percent of women with children under age six were in paid work. By the 1970s, when the economy began shifting, 39 percent of them were working; by the end of the century, 65 percent. Expect the percentage to continue to rise.

Incidentally, this trend offers a way to understand why the American public stopped feeling sympathetic toward poor mothers who accept welfare checks rather than work. At midcentury, the norm was for the mothers of young children to remain home with them. Mothers with working partners relied on their partners' paychecks; single mothers relied on welfare checks. But by the end of the century, the norm was for the mothers of young children to have jobs outside the home. Once the norm had shifted from women as stay-at-home parents to women as paid workers, people began to ask why poor mothers should be subsidized by government to stay at home with their children while mothers who were hard up but not so poor as to qualify for welfare had to go to work. No one had a very good answer. Rather than subsidize all such women who stayed at home with their small children (as some European nations have done), America simply removed the supports.

THE OUTSOURCED FAMILY

In 1776, Adam Smith noted the inefficiencies of isolated homes scattered about the Scottish Highlands in which farm families had to be hugely self-sufficient. He used these poor and overworked families to illustrate the superior advantages of a division of labor, such as one would find in a town. We are now in the process of extending Smith's basic economic precept, to an unprecedented degree, into domestic life. All sorts of things that used to be done by families are now being subcontracted to specialists, including food preparation, cleaning, child care, elder care, even dog-walking. As we move further into the new economy, it seems likely that more family functions will be outsourced.

The test a family uses to decide whether to subcontract a particular task is just like the test used by a company considering whether to "outsource" a particular function. Can the subcontractor do the task as well as the family member can do it, but do it more cheaply, considering the alternative uses of the family member's time? Since the major alternative use of the family member's time is earning money, the calculation is straightforward: Figure your after-tax income for a given hour of paid work, add in whatever additional psychic satisfaction the paid work provides you, and consider also the possibility that if you didn't take the work, it might not be there tomorrow (make hay while the sun shines), or that contacts, connections, and your reputation for being dedicated to your work might suffer. Then compare all of this with the cost and the quality of the subcontractor's work, plus whatever psychic satisfaction you might otherwise get from doing that home work yourself. If the former sum exceeds the latter, you subcontract.

Families are making these calculations all the time—perhaps not quite as systematically, but surely with some feel for relative costs and benefits. And as both men and women work harder for pay, they're subcontracting out more of what were once family responsibilities. By 1996, spending on take-out meals from restaurants exceeded spending on meals consumed at restaurants. By 1997, spending on take-out meals *and* restaurants exceeded spending on groceries.[25] And even the supermarkets are offering more prepared food: roasted chickens, soups, grilled salmon, cooked vegetables, casseroles. If you wish, you can order your meals or your groceries by phone, fax, or Internet.

Atlanta-based Maid Brigade has expanded more than 20 percent a year for a decade. Working women constitute 80 percent of its clients. For a small membership fee, Streamline (www.streamline.com) will install a large box in your garage replete with refrigerator and security system, for picking up or delivering dry-cleaning, videos, film processing, groceries, pharmaceuticals, or just about anything else you want taken from or brought to your home when you're not there. Streamline's director of marketing explains that, "[l]ike businesses, families are rationalizing the number of relationships with their suppliers."[26]

Streamline doesn't yet pick up and deliver kids to piano lessons or play dates (the box is a bit stuffy for children), but other services do. Some families rely on private van services to shuttle their children from place to place. One luxury Manhattan condo offers "para-parenting" services, featuring a concierge mother or father on call to "direct [your child] to the nearest milkshake, schedule your doctors' appointments, or book the Spice Girls for your darling's deb ball."[27]

When I had a birthday as a young boy, my mother baked me a cake using flour, sugar, and other basic ingredients. By the time my kid sister had her first birthday, my mother had relented to the extent of using cake mix. Then came the big squeeze. By the time my own children were young and had birthdays, my wife or I ordered ready-made cakes with customized messages on top. Now, it's not unusual for parents to subcontract the entire party to restaurants that specialize in children's birthdays. These restaurants supply not only the cake but also the balloons, party favors, and games—plus the all-important supervision and cleanup. Pay extra and they get a clown, and even someone to take the video. Meanwhile, Mom or Dad can duck out to check for messages.

Upper-income families of the Gilded Age had their maids, chauffeurs, cooks, gardeners, and nannies, because they had a lot of money to exchange for leisure time. Today's upper-income families also have household staff. ("I have more people working at my house for me now than I do at work," says Diane Swonk, chief economist at Bank One Corp in Chicago, who employs a maid, a nanny, a cook, and a gardener. "I'm a small corporation, essentially."[28]) But the difference is that today's upper-income families aren't purchasing leisure. They're buying more time to put into paid work. They figure that the return they get from working is higher than the cost to them of subcontracting.

By far the biggest family subcontract is child care. Today most children under the age of five—more than ten million of them—need to be looked after while their mothers and fathers go to work. Forty-four percent of these children are cared for by relatives, including older siblings; 30 percent, by staff members of day-care centers or nursery schools; 15 percent, by other adults in private homes; and the rest, by nannies, neighbors, or baby-sitters.[29] A significant portion of these children don't get much personal attention within this hodgepodge of child-care arrangements, but as we'll see in more detail in the next chapter, the market is operating efficiently. The amount and quality of personal attention varies directly with its price.

On this subject, too, public attitudes have shifted as the economy has shifted. In the 1970s, before women with children streamed into the workplace, a majority of adults didn't think a working mother could establish "as warm and secure a relationship with her children" as a mother who did not work. But by the late nineties, more than two-thirds felt that she *could*.[30]

Increasingly, families are also subcontracting the care of elderly parents—another job traditionally performed by women at home—to nursing homes, residential long-term-care facilities, hospices, and personal attendants at home. Some families are even subcontracting the sort of personal care and attention one spouse or partner might give to the other had they more time and emotional energy: Now they rely on massage therapists, coaches, counselors, spiritual guides, personal trainers, and shrinks.

When all this caring, fixing, delivering, cooking, cleaning, raking, clipping, and birthday-partying was done inside the home, it wasn't included in the official "national product" because money didn't change hands. Women's work at home never appeared in the national accounts. But now that families are subcontracting more of what they used to do themselves, these tasks have suddenly emerged as growth industries, and the national product is that much larger. In fact, there's a multiplier effect. Many of the people—mostly women—who get paid to do these subcontracted tasks devote a portion of what they're paid to paying someone *else* to take on some of the tasks they no longer have time or energy to do within their *own* families.

When my mother baked my birthday cake, her labors contributed only indirectly to the economic statistics, showing up as a tiny addition to the agricultural production and retail sales of the ingredients she purchased. When she moved to using cake mix for my younger sister's birthday, the "processed foods" category of the national product grew a tad. Our own boys' ready-made cakes added to America's service sector the labors of ready-made-cake bakers. The modern subcontracted birthday party adds still more to America's bulging service sector, including the personal services of party planners, waiters, clowns, and attendants with video cameras. Each stage records greater prosperity, although the cakes have not noticeably improved.

WHAT'S LEFT

Underlying the legal definitions of a "family" are four simple criteria we used to take for granted: Members of a family were expected to remain committed to one another for life. They spent a lot of time together under the same roof. Families reproduced themselves biologically, and helped their offspring grow into adulthood. And they supported one another—financially and with caring attention.

Most families still conform to these four basic criteria, but to a lesser extent. And every trend line is moving in the opposite direction—largely because of the changes we've seen in how work is organized and rewarded. Connections are becoming more temporary, people spend less time together, couples are having fewer children, financial support between spouses is eroding, and care and attention are being subcontracted. Extend these trends into the future, and "family" may mean something entirely different from what it used to.

This does not necessarily signify a problem. People *want* this new kind of "family" life—at least in the superficial (and admittedly tautological) sense that they've chosen it for themselves. And their attitudes about the ideal family have changed to become better aligned with the choices they've made, as I've also shown. Yes, there are surely strains and tensions along the way. Finding good and affordable child care or elder care, for example, is a major hassle. Many people say they'd like to find a better "balance" between work and family. But, overall, they're accommodating to the new economy by downsizing and outsourcing the family.

ECONOMIC and technological forces can't explain everything, and I want to caution you against assigning all credit or blame to them for what has been happening to the family. Undoubtedly there are cultural shifts at work here as well. But it is striking that the changes in family structure and attitudes about family directly parallel the changes in our economic system that began in the 1970s and are now accelerating. The old system of large-scale production offered most men steadier work and more solid wages, and offered women fewer opportunities for paid work. The new system of continuous innovation features less predictable earnings from year to year or even month to month, and wider disparities in earnings. And it induces harder work in terms of time and emotional energy.

Undeniably, the emerging economy bestows great benefits on us as consumers and investors. We have more choice, and we can more easily switch to better deals. Our dollars go further, and productivity is rising. The emerging economy also generates more opportunities for talented women, as well as talented men, to earn more money. And it gives almost all women the option of having a job rather than being entirely dependent on a male breadwinner.

Given the new economy, the choices people are making about family are entirely rational. But the more fundamental choice has never been posed, and the more basic question never asked: Would we choose every aspect of this new reality if we fully appreciated its consequences for the family life we might otherwise have? In other words, as with other aspects of our personal lives, is the new economy worth what it costs us?

CHAPTER NINE

Paying for Attention

It's about the heart of the matter: your life. In the unique experience known as private banking at J. P. Morgan, we don't just nurture and manage your assets. We guide you through every facet of wealth management, which is really life management.

—Advertisement, March 2000

THE WAY work is coming to be organized and rewarded places a premium on personal attention. Personal attention is an ever-larger portion of the gross national product, an ever-bigger percentage of every dollar spent and earned. Among the fastest-growing job categories are attention-*givers*—people who care for, tend to, or oversee children, the elderly, the disabled, the depressed and anxious, as well as more or less healthy adults who want more attention for themselves and are able and willing to pay for it.

There are two specific reasons for the growth of the attention industry. First is the increasing number of people who are working harder and subcontracting more of what had been family responsibilities, many of which are all about giving attention. Second is the growing productivity of machines, including computerized machine tools and robots inside factories, and, in the service economy, automated bank tellers, automated gas pumps, voice-activated telephone answering systems, and digital devices that soon will do just about everything. Notably, one thing machines cannot do is provide personal attention. (Perhaps one day a robot will be capable of giving people a sense of being cared for, but I'm not betting on it.) So many people whose jobs have been supplanted by highly productive machines are selling their personal attention instead, and many more will do so in the future.

WHY THE HUMAN TOUCH MATTERS

People don't always prefer personal attention to technology. For making routine bank deposits and withdrawals, I'd rather deal with an automatic bank teller than a human one. Not only is the ATM down the street available all the time, but it also doesn't require that I be polite to it, or even speak to it. I'd prefer to save my scarce social energies for more important encounters. And give me self-service gas pumps over full-service any day. They're cheaper and faster.

Yet it's also true that personal attention can be pleasurable, and its lack distressing. I enjoy going to restaurants where waiters make a fuss over me, and detest large department stores where it's almost impossible to find a salesperson. The human desire for attention goes deeper than this. In fact, scientists hypothesize that human beings *require* some degree of personal attention in order to be healthy. In the 1940s, René Spitz, a French psychoanalyst, compared two groups of infants—one housed for the first few months of their lives in an orphanage, whose nurses kept them well fed and clothed but had no time to give them personal attention; the other, in a home for delinquent mothers, who gave their babies one-on-one attention—and found that only the second group developed normally.[1] Recently, Harvard's Mary Carlson elaborated on the Spitz study by examining infants in Romanian orphanages who had received adequate medical care and nourishment but very little personal attention. As a neuroscientist, Carlson was most interested in how these infants' brains were affected. She found the children to be mentally and physically retarded, many displaying repetitive body movements similar to those observed among baby monkeys that had been physically isolated from other monkeys.[2]

Human touch seems to be an important aspect of attention. One study compared two groups of premature infants. The first were placed in incubators, where they received all the nourishment and warmth necessary for them to mature into full-term infants. The second got something extra: For ten days, three times each day, their bodies were massaged by a nurse, who reached in through portholes in the incubator walls. The second group gained 47 percent more weight, and were released six days earlier, than premature infants who didn't get such massages. Years later, the children in the second group still weighed more than children in the first group, and performed better on standard tests of mental and motor skills.[3]

Personal attention appears to improve the health of adults as well. In one of the most ambitious research projects ever undertaken, epidemiologists tracked more than 4,000 elderly residents of Alameda, California, from 1965 to 1974. At the start, the researchers matched people with roughly the same health conditions and incomes. During the subsequent nine years, in every group, the death rate among those whose ties to friends, spouses, or extended families were weak was three times higher than the death rate among people whose ties to others were strong.[4] Another study of more than 1,000 elderly people found that the two most important predictors of physical and mental well-being were the frequency of visits with friends and attendance at meetings; the more contact and attention, the better the health.[5] A third study, sponsored by the MacArthur Foundation, measured changes in lower-body strength, coordination, and manual dexterity among a group of elderly men at intervals of two and a half years. The researchers discovered that the best single predictor of physical well-being was emotional support and attention from other people.[6]

Recently, researchers at Carnegie Mellon University investigated the psychological effects of Internet use.[7] They randomly chose 169 people in the Pittsburgh area and tracked their behavior over one to two years.[8] It turned out that the more time people spent on the Internet, the more depressed and lonely they became. This result surprised not only the researchers but also several of the computer and software companies that had funded the research, expecting just the opposite. Since the Internet allows people to connect easily with others through e-mail and "chat rooms," the researchers initially assumed that the Internet would provide a richer mix of relationships than were usually available face-to-face, and hence contribute to better psychological well-being. During the course of the study, participants reported that they did in fact use e-mail and Internet chat rooms. But they also noted that the more time they spent online, the fewer direct interactions they had with family and friends, simply because they had less time for them. So while the *quantity* of their interconnections with other people remained the same or even increased, the *quality* of their relationships declined. "Our hypothesis is there are more cases where you're building shallow relationships, leading to an overall decline in feelings of connection to other people," said researcher Robert Kraut, professor of social psychology at Carnegie Mellon's Human–Computer Interaction Institute. Relationships "over long distances without face-to-face contact ultimately do not provide the kind of support and reciprocity that typically contribute to a sense of psychological security and happiness."[9]

No one knows exactly why direct human contact seems to be so important to physical and mental health, but neuroscientists who study the brain have some guesses. Positive attention from another person reduces certain hormones normally associated with stress—in particular, epinephrine, norepinephrine, and cortisol. The urine of infants who are rocked or massaged contains lower levels of these stress hormones than does that of infants who aren't.[10] In the MacArthur study on aging I mentioned a moment ago, the elderly men with more human contact and attention also had lower levels of epinephrine, norepinephrine, and cortisol in their urine than the men receiving less contact and attention.[11]

From an evolutionary perspective, it shouldn't be surprising that human contact reduces stress. The human animal evolved in families and clans that offered protection as well as shared sustenance. The primitive parts of our brains probably remember that to be alone or out of contact with other people is literally dangerous, while to be showered with attention is the very essence of safety.

At the start of the twenty-first century, this need for personal contact poses something of a problem for human beings, who often can't freely give or get as much personal attention as they might like. The new work requires too much of their time, emotional energy, and psychological involvement. So what do they do? Increasingly, they pay for attention.

BUYING MORE ATTENTION, OR LESS

More than three million people in the United States, and a million in Europe, now spend their working days sitting in cubicles, wearing headsets, staring at computer monitors, and responding as best they can to a steady torrent of questions or complaints about electronic gadgets, pensions, credit cards, bank accounts, insurance, Internet purchases, or family problems. And the number of such call-center, help-desk, or customer-service "hot line" phone jobs keeps growing rapidly in places like Cincinnati, the British city of Leeds, and Dresden—places where factory jobs have disappeared but legions of reliable workers remain.

Why do companies keep hiring people to do this sort of work at a cost of about $5 per customer call when they could pay just 50 cents per call for an automated "voice-response unit" that would give customers just about the same answers (after the caller went through a sequence of "option menus" and pushed several telephone keys), or just a few *pennies* per inquiry for an Internet service requiring only that customers tap their questions or comments onto a computer keyboard? Because a friendly human voice builds customer loyalty. Says Howard McNally, AT&T's vice president for consumer product management, in discussing AT&T's new special "0-0" help line, "Our new directory assistance service has less to do with traditional notions of productivity than it does with using a personalized service to create a competitive advantage."[12]

But even as companies are staffing up call centers, they are simultaneously investing in cheaper ways to respond. It's a sure bet that in years to come they'll figure out how to separate their better customers, who want and are willing to pay for more personal attention, from lower-paying customers served by automated and Internet devices. To put it another way: Increasingly, customers will be getting the degree of attention they pay for.

Think of this as a kind of scale of attentiveness, depending on its price. The cheapest form of attention won't involve a human being at all, just some preassembled information off the Internet. Pay more, and you'll get a voice-activated robot, maybe even a three-dimensional hologram of a person. Pay still more, and you'll summon a real human being on the other end of a telephone, but only for a few moments. Pay even more, and you'll elicit the attention of someone at a call center who takes time to download some personal information about you and match it to a database—giving you some useful information as well as the comforting feeling that you're being specially cared for. Pay more than that, and you may even get a personal visit to your home or business. Pay still more, and you'll be pampered to your heart's content.

The brokerage firm of Merrill Lynch is busily creating a hierarchy of attentiveness. Its clients with accounts of less than $100,000 in assets are being herded toward its customer-service call centers, where they receive crisp, standard responses to their inquiries. This frees up Merrill's highly trained "financial consultants" to devote more time to affluent clients who generate larger commissions.[13] Not long ago, the director of Merrill's Long Island district, one of its most profitable, issued an e-mail to brokers setting out the new policy with admirable candor: "If we are to be Financial Consultants to wealthy and successful individuals and businesses, then we don't have time to provide personal services to the poor. . . . Remember . . . the game is still more assets in bigger accounts," he wrote. "If there are still F[inancial] C[onsultant]s that really enjoy servicing small accounts, please let me know, and I will get you a nice salaried job in the Investor Services Group where you can deal with poor people to your heart's content."[14]

What do the "wealthy and successful" get, exactly? Some of it is custom-tailored advice. But much of it is simply personal attention—a reassuring voice, a familiar personality, someone who may become a trusted friend. In the Gilded Age of the late nineteenth century, luxury meant Waterford crystal, Wedgwood china, and a staff of household servants. People with great wealth displayed their status through, in Thorstein Veblen's memorable phrase, "conspicuous consumption"— an ongoing demonstration of their exemption from industrial life, unfitness for manual labor, and almost infinite capacity for leisure.[15] Today's affluent, by contrast, are money-rich but time-poor. So for them luxury takes a different form: exquisite personal attention designed to make their frenzied lives as efficient and pleasurable as possible. People of more modest means, meanwhile, have access to increasingly efficient technologies that provide them much of what they need but, notably, with fewer human touches.

Michelle Siron, a thirty-eight-year-old management consultant, is picked up from her London hotel by a chauffeur driving a Range Rover for a smooth ride to Heathrow Airport. There she's met curbside by an attendant, who checks her in for her flight even before she emerges from the car, then escorts her to a private lounge, where she sips tea and nibbles on smoked salmon sandwiches while her hair is cut and blow-dried. Once on board, she gets a manicure and a neck massage. Flight attendants respond to her every wish. "It really takes the stress out of travel," Michelle (a real person, who in fact experienced this) reports.[16]

Contrast Michelle's experience with that of a discount air traveler—

call her Jennifer—who, weighed down with luggage, shuffles through a noisy and crowded Heathrow, waits an hour in a long check-in line, just barely manages to find a plastic chair to sit on in an overcrowded waiting room until her row number is called, is then squished into a small seat in the back of the plane, thrown a tiny snack by a harried flight attendant who disappears for the remainder of the trip, and finally, six hours later, commences a one-hour wait for her luggage to show up. By the end of the journey, Jennifer's stress hormones are at a fairly high level.

But Jennifer has no grounds to complain about her plight or her flight. The cost of her trip was far less than the cost of Michelle's. It was probably less, in fact, than Jennifer has paid ever before. Airlines are under increasing competitive pressure to reduce prices for budget travelers, and technological improvements like highly fuel-efficient engines, advanced aerodynamics, and computerized reservations and tracking systems have allowed them to do so. But Jennifer also received less personal service than before, because she and other budget-conscious customers like her are more interested in paying a low price than in being pampered. Jennifer chose to pay less, and so she got less attention.

"The principle 'you get what you pay for' is recognized in America and around the world," says Donald Casey, executive vice president of Trans World Airlines, in explaining the airline's new strategy.[17] TWA, like most airlines, is beefing up its business-class service—adding more flight attendants, more lounge attendants, more pampering services, more personal conveniences, more attention overall. But instead of hiring additional people to provide all this attention, most airlines are reallocating their existing personnel to focus more of their attention on customers who want to pay for it, and less on customers who don't.

There's a simple economic reason why airlines are lavishing more attention on elite business travelers like Michelle and less on budget travelers like Jennifer. It's the same reason why Merrill Lynch wants its brokers to shift their attention to the high rollers: because that's where the revenues are. In 1999, the top tier of business travelers represented just 9 percent of all airline passengers, but they contributed 44 percent of airline industry revenues. So even as airlines are battling to offer better bargains to budget travelers like Jennifer, they're also busily courting people like Michelle who will pay a lot for personal attention.

As long as the Michelles of the world continue to want more personal attention and seem willing to pay for it, they'll get it, along with higher fares. As long as the Jennifers want better bargains and are eager to shop for them, the cost of discount travel to them will continue to fall. Michelle will receive ever more lavish personal service; Jennifer will get the benefits of advancing technology with fewer and fewer personal frills. Michelle and Jennifer are, in effect, paying for two different products. Jennifer is paying just to get there. Michelle is paying both to get there *and* to be pampered along the way.

Incidentally, it's doubtful that Michelle paid for her luxurious trip out of her own pocket. It was a business trip, which means that it was paid for in part by Michelle's client (or, more accurately, its shareholders, if a publicly held company) and in part by other taxpayers, who always fill the gap that's left when companies deduct business costs from their taxable earnings. Michelle made the trip for business rather than for pleasure, even though she may have got some pleasure out of it. But the cost of the pleasure is a business cost, too. This is the coming pattern. Exquisite personal attention is lavished on people who are busy earning a lot of money, *as* they earn it. The pleasures of being pampered at a five-star hotel, joining clients to watch the World Series from a catered skybox, or dining with suppliers in a swank restaurant come as tax-free perks enjoyed in pursuit of money. Companies are willing to foot the bill for all this attention in order to attract and retain talented people, appreciative clients, and reliable suppliers, especially since the rest of the tax-paying public is picking up part of the tab.

PAYING TO BE PAMPERED

In a world of more technology and less time, the essence of luxury is to have time lavished on you by another human being—the charming concierge who personally arranges your stay; the hotel housekeeper who provides fresh flowers, folds the towels just so, fluffs the pillow, lays out the soft cotton kimono and plush terry slippers, and asks if you need anything else before bedtime; the wake-up call at 6 a.m. from a real human being instead of a voice-synthesized clock. It's the restaurant maître d' who knows your name and ushers you to your favorite table, where waiters hover and the wine steward offers his personal recommendation as the chef prepares your favorite dish. It's the doorman of your co-op apartment who obligingly hands you the package that has been delivered, and inquires after the family.

The most exquisite pampering, and the most expensive, comes in the form of a person who acts as a trusted friend and confidant. Jeffrey Kalinsky, owner of the exclusive Atlanta Mall fashion boutique, hand-picks items with a particular customer's tastes in mind, then ships them to the customer to try on. He mails follow-up notes advising the customer how to wear the new purchases, answers late-night emergency phone calls about what to wear, lavishes gifts on his best customers and accompanies them to Europe to view fashion shows. Several of Kalinsky's customers fly from New York to Atlanta expressly to visit him. "Jeffrey . . . encourages you to try things you'd never try. He has a total vision," gushes one. And he trains his twenty-eight employees to do the same, perfecting the art of providing exquisite personal attention, the art of making people feel cared for.[18]

If you're one of the growing number of people who pay several hundred dollars a month to a "personal coach," chances are you're after more than advice. You also want someone who's solely interested in your well-being—a *friend* you can count on to be there solely for you, perhaps because most of your real friends are too busy. "Best friends are wonderful to have. But is your best friend a professional who you will trust to work with you on the most important aspect[s] of your life and/or business?" asks an advertisement for the Personal and Professional Coaches Association. If you hire a personal coach, you can "[h]ave both—a best friend and a coach."[19]

That these "friends" have an ulterior motive besides friendship has not, apparently, dampened the enthusiasm of the people who seek them. The number of personal coaches has doubled each year since the early 1990s, according to Thomas Leonard, founder of Houston-based Coach University, which has already trained thousands of them. Valerie Olson, of Minnesota, earns close to six figures a year coaching thirty clients, each of whom pays her $250 a month for four half-hour sessions. "Coaches are trained to be completely focused on a client's agenda—in human relationships," she says. They don't try to psychoanalyze their clients. It's a matter of listening, providing empathy, giving total attention.[20]

In addition to personal coaches, there has been an upsurge in personal counselors, spiritual guides, spiritual advisers, and therapists. Bill

Clinton made use of several spiritual advisers during his White House years but, to the best of my knowledge, no therapists. That may be because it's perfectly acceptable to utilize a coach, counselor, spiritual guide or adviser. Most of us occasionally feel the need for an attentive confidant and cannot always find a friend or family member to do the job adequately. But someone who visits a therapist is still assumed to have a "problem."

Until recent years, health spas were places where people of leisure vacationed, sometimes for months. They "took the waters" at sulfur springs, inhaled pine-scented air in remote scenic locations, ambled off on long walks in the woods. But most of the people who can afford such things no longer have the time for them, and yet still yearn to be taken care of. This explains the growing popularity of urban spas with staffs who lavish attention on the stressed-out affluent. The number of personal trainers doubled in the 1990s to more than 100,000. Add in massage therapists, Rolfers, trainers, personal estheticians, stylists, pedicurists, aromatherapists, and aerobics instructors and you have a small army of personal caregivers to the affluent.

The new saying is "Be good to yourself," meaning that if you have the means to do so, you should not skimp on paying for such services. What's really being bought and sold is not a series of exercises (you could exercise alone in your home or apartment), nor is it advice (you could get it off the Internet or from a book), but the pleasant feeling of being cared for by another human being.

Recall how well premature infants responded to being massaged. When the body is stroked, rubbed, or held, stress hormones seem to be reduced in the same way they are when someone gets the full attention of someone else. Staff of the Pacific Athletic Club, headquartered in Redwood City, California, travel to executive meetings in Silicon Valley to provide in-chair massages. Chic environs like New York's Reebok Sports Club or the Elizabeth Arden Red Door Salon Spa send your clothing off for a quick dry cleaning while treating your body to such wonders as Sea Spa Pedicures (described as "facials for the feet"), Aromatherapy Salt Glow Escapes (coarse-salt body rubdowns, followed by a moisturizing lotion), Double Oxygen Treatments (cleansing the face with alpha-hydroxy fruit acid, exfoliation, and massage, followed by a fifteen-minute blast of oxygen that "boosts cell metabolism"), Hot Milk and Almond Pedicures (in which one's feet are placed in a large bowl of warm whole milk, then rubbed with a mixture of sea salt and almond oil to rid them of dead skin), and Ginger Rubs (arms, legs, and back covered with grated ginger mixed with oil, designed to "detoxify" the skin and heat the body). At New York's Felissimo, on West 56th Street, you can even treat your pup to aromatherapy designed to "revive your beloved dog with a euphoric feeling of happiness and joyful responsiveness."

What's also being bought and sold is a relationship—the easy familiarity with which your personal trainer greets you, the friendship of a massage therapist, the little confidences shared with your Rolfer or even the person who parks your car. "Members develop relationships with the [parking] attendants the way they do with their trainers. It really adds to that service aspect," says Phil Swain, director of operations at Los Angeles's Sports Club.[21]

ATTENTIVE CARE OR CUSTODIAL CARE

Busy people often lack the time and energy for giving family members the quality of caring attention they need—listening to them, talking to them, massaging their tired muscles, making them feel cared for, respected, loved, acknowledged. Some of this caring attention can be bought, even though the paid givers aren't motivated by familial duty. Familial bonds don't necessarily generate more caring attention than financial ones. Both can be nurturing; both can be abusive.

But personal attention is the first thing to go when a family can't pay any more than what's absolutely necessary, and when government insurance programs or employer-provided benefits are squeezed. No-frills medical care is coming to mean lots of technology but fewer humans offering caring attention. In fact, medical care is evolving into a two-tiered system—one comprising doctors paid directly by patients to provide them with lots of time and attention; the other, of doctors paid at a lower rate by health insurers to fix up patients as rapidly as possible. The income of doctors (as well as nurses and nurse's aides) in this second tier depends on how many people they deal with in a given period of time rather than on people's subjective feelings of how well they're being cared for. (Apparently female doctors in this second tier are generally more willing to sacrifice additional income for extra minutes with a client or patient than are male doctors. One recent study found that male doctors dispense with most of their patients in less than eleven minutes each, while female doctors match this remarkable pace with only a third of their cases.[22])

Yet, in fact, personal attention *isn't* a frill. The research cited at the start of this chapter suggests that people who are sick or disabled, as well as the elderly and young children (and perhaps all of us), are likely to benefit physically and emotionally from a caring relationship. Without it, they and their health may deteriorate. Sociologist Timothy Diamond tells of a night-shift nursing-home aide who popped in to check the vital signs of one eighty-seven-year-old resident, asking, "Is there anything I can do for you, Rose?" "Yes," responded Rose. "Stay with me." The aide couldn't comply with Rose's request because he had twenty-nine other residents to check on and record the vital signs of.[23] Yet all Rose really wanted and needed was human attention. Rose's vital signs will probably decline faster without someone keeping her company.

Nursing homes provide custodial care, but not much attentive care. Custodial care aims merely to keep people safe who might be endangered if left on their own. Attentive care builds a relationship with them, relieving them from the stress of isolation, interacting with them, sometimes touching and holding them. Working families are often hard-pressed to provide either form of care, but the attentive kind is a luxury.

The elderly population in the United States is growing by 2.7 percent a year and will soar when the baby boomers turn sixty-five, starting around 2011. This elderly boom will impose even more of a burden on working families already hard-pressed by a new economy to give adequate attention to their children. The nation as a whole will have fewer young people to take care of every older person. In other advanced nations whose populations of young people are flat or declining, as in Japan, the percentage of elderly is already rising precipitously. Keeping all these aging people safe will be difficult—bathing and feeding them, cleaning bedsores, lifting them out of bed, changing their diapers. (I recently heard about the invention of a robot for nursing homes, capable of doing some of these operations.) But giving the elderly adequate personal attention will be a larger challenge. Currently, the U.S. government pays two-thirds of the cost of caring for America's 1.6 million nursing-home residents (mostly through Medicaid), yet very little of the cost of long-term home care or community-based elderly day care—both of which would keep most elderly as safe, but also allow for more attentive care by friends and family members. And even when government insurance does pay for home health care (usually through Medicare), it's strictly for medical procedures, not for attention.[24]

Many children suffer the same attention deficit as the elderly. Custodial child care is inferior to the kind that builds a relationship with the child. But again, you get the attention you pay for. The cost of organized child care ranges from $4,000 a year per child to $20,000. All of it is called "child care," but the low end is fundamentally different from the high end. Low-end care may provide a safe environment but has fewer caretakers per child than at the higher end, the caretakers usually have less training, and they are more likely to leave for another job in a short time (because they're paid less and are more overworked). For these reasons, children in low-end care have less opportunity to form relationships with their caregivers than do children in high-end care. These differences in the amount, quality, and consistency of care can have significant consequences for children later in their lives.[25]

The effects appear to continue until adulthood. One study looked at children from 111 poor black families in Chapel Hill, North Carolina, all of whom, because of their poverty, were at risk of doing poorly in school, dropping out of high school, and creating another generation of poor children. The study began in 1972, when the children were infants. Fifty-seven of them, selected at random, were assigned to full-time child-care programs until they were five years old. The child care included a lot of personal attention in which the caregivers built personal relationships with the children. Ratios of child-care workers to children were very low (ranging from one for every three infants, to one for every seven four-year-olds); child-care workers had as much training as public-school teachers; almost none left or were replaced during the period; and they provided each child with a lot of intellectual stimulation and emotional support. The other fifty-four children in the study got nutritional supplements and some visits from social workers, to assure that they were healthy and safe, but no attention-rich child care. Once they reached the age of five, both groups of children attended comparable kindergartens, elementary schools, and high schools.

The study traced the children until they were twenty-one years old. Although they were treated no differently after the age of five, it turned out that, by their twenty-first birthdays, almost two-thirds of those who had received attention-rich child care were either still in college or in a good-paying job, while just 40 percent of the others were. The attention-rich child care had been costly—the equivalent of $11,000 a year for each child in today's dollars.[26] Given its long-term effects, you might conclude it is worth the cost. But the sad reality is that most families can't afford it.

Affording good-quality child care is one problem; another is making sure children receive the attention that's paid for. Toddlers don't know enough to complain to their parents if they're not, or if they're being mistreated. The same is true, of course, for the elderly and infirm, mentally ill, or retarded. Lack of proper custodial care in nursing homes is exposed with sad regularity. Many nursing homes are parts of big for-profit businesses, and child care is also becoming a big business. For-profit businesses have to give shareholders a good return on their investments, possibly at the expense of investments in the quality of attention. Some parents who fret about this sort of thing when they're at work now utilize innovations provided by trendy child-care centers: little Web-cameras mounted on the ceilings and walls of the centers that allow the parents to click open a little viewing box on one corner of their computer screens and watch their toddlers all day long.

THE NEW DIVIDE

If you (or your children) don't have the right innate talents, education, and connections to make it into the creative sector of the economy—devising and selling designs, concepts, plans, strategies, deals, and insights—chances are that you (or they) will end up selling personal attention, because that's the other arena where job growth is occurring. Yet you should know, if you don't already, that most people who sell personal attention do not earn a great deal of money doing it. There are several reasons. First, by its very nature, personal attentiveness is a relatively unproductive service. It's given one-on-one—and it entails giving *time*. In the hours it takes a software engineer, management consultant, or investment banker to create a product or change a service that may affect the lives of hundreds if not hundreds of thousands of people, the child-care worker, nurse's aide, or personal trainer may have worked directly with a few dozen human beings.[27]

Second, even in a tight labor market, the supply of people giving personal attention is growing as fast as if not faster than the demand for it, thus keeping a damper on wages. Although there are shortages, from time to time, in specific attention-giving fields, such as nurses or aides for home health care, the overall supply of attention givers is relatively abundant. Some of these personal-attention workers are women who continue to enter the workforce to prop up their family's finances. Many are new immigrants, both documented and undocumented, who are streaming to these shores. Some are people who are taking on more than one job or working longer hours because they need the money. Some have been displaced from their old service jobs as telephone operators, bank tellers, or retail workers by new technologies. Although most personal servers continue to be women, an increasing number are men whose former factory jobs have been downsized or outsourced out of existence.

Finally, personal-attention work is not especially valued by society. Traditionally, it was considered "women's work"—most of it unpaid, much of it taken for granted by the men, children, and aged parents who received it free of charge. It was expected of women, assumed to be their responsibility if not their special calling. Women first ventured into the workforce as nurses, nuns, teachers, and flight attendants, giving personal attention in exchange for low wages. Black women eked out a bare living as maids and nannies within middle-class homes.[28] Immigrant women have been heavily represented here as well, especially poor women from developing countries. Black and immigrant women are still the ones who give the kind of personal attention that's hardest: lifting the infirm elderly into their wheelchairs, cleaning their sores, and emptying the bedpans.

More than two million people work in nursing homes in the United States—as nurse's aides, dietary workers, and housekeepers. Most are women earning little more than the minimum wage, between $7 and $8 an hour in 2000. Another 700,000 people work as home health-care aides, or home aides, attending to the elderly, sick, or disabled at home. They're also mostly women, with pay averaging between $8 and $10 an hour. Another 1.3 million people work in hospitals as aides, orderlies, and attendants, at about the same rate. There are 2.1 million registered nurses in the United States, who are paid $10 to $25 an hour. The Bureau of Labor Statistics forecasts substantial increases in all these occupations.[29] One out five new jobs in the coming decade will be in health services, and most will entail giving personal attention.

An estimated 2.3 million people in the United States are now paid to care for children. About half of them work in child-care centers, others in organized play groups, as nannies, or as helpers. In 1999, their median wage was $6.17 an hour, usually without benefits, which was less than that earned by funeral attendants ($7.16 an hour) or pest controllers ($10.25 an hour). Most child-care workers are women.

Half a million people are social workers, and 200,000 more are classified as "human-service" workers. All attend to individuals and families with severe problems. Their pay averages between $8 and $15 an hour. Most of the people who attend to the mentally ill, however, are police officers who pick them off the streets on cold nights and put them into shelters or arrest them for petty crimes, and the guards who then watch over them in jail. In New York City, as elsewhere, it is a crime to be homeless and sleeping in the street; the homeless can either spend the night legally in a city shelter (many of which are dangerous), or they can be arrested and spend the night in a city jail (many of which are dangerous).

People who bestow personal attention on diners and hotel guests are also paid relatively little, although the pay and the tips get better at the higher end. Housekeepers at New York's Pierre Hotel begin at $11 an hour, and can earn up to $16 an hour, with two weeks of vacation and benefits.[30] Limousine drivers are in greater demand as well, earning $10 to $25 an hour. And there has been a surge in valet-parking attendants, earning the minimum wage plus tips. The Los Angeles Yellow Pages now have forty-five listings under "Parking Attendant Services."[31]

Also included among the fastest-growing occupations are personal trainers, exercise-class leaders, fitness instructors, massage therapists, manicurists, and others who firm up, poke, prod, pummel, knead, moisturize, and prune human bodies. Such jobs pay between $15 and $70 an hour. Top-of-the-line trainers or masseurs, who give exquisite attention to celebrity bodies, can earn more. In almost no case are benefits included. As noted, the number of personal coaches has been growing rapidly as well, with pay seemingly dependent on how much individual clients value the help.

IN THE OLD economy of large-scale production, the people who labored to produce the cars or television sets earned enough to buy them. Henry Ford famously argued that it made good business sense to pay his assembly-line workers $5 a day, a relatively large sum at the time, because they'd have enough money to buy the Model Ts they were turning out in large quantities. Similarly, service workers like bank tellers, telephone operators, and retail salespeople used the same services they supplied to the public when they themselves went to the bank, used the telephone, or visited the mall.

But increasingly, the tens of millions of people selling personal attention don't earn enough to buy the kind of services they're selling. So they're opting instead for "no frills"—budget travel without much personal attention, take-out food, visits to a doctor only when absolutely necessary (many can't afford health insurance), and care of children and the elderly that depends largely on relatives or friends. They don't belong to a health club, travel in limos, or dine in fancy restaurants. They park their own cars.

Many of them can't find a place to live within an easy commute of where they sell personal attention, because homes there are too expensive. People who staff the resorts, restaurants, and spas of Vail, Colorado, or Park City, Utah, for example, have to live so far away that even resort owners are becoming concerned. One survey calculated that an average worker in Vail, at $10 an hour, would have to hold down five full-time jobs in order to have enough money to live there. "In the service business, you want people who are warm, fuzzy, hands-on. If you ask people to commute 100 miles, it is not going to work out very well," says Myles Rademan, a resort consultant based in Park City, which imports half its workforce every day.[32] I suspect that few personal attendants actually commute a hundred miles each day, but the problem of transportation is real. The gardeners, health-care aides, massage therapists, and trainers who work in Greenwich, Connecticut, where the average price of a home is $1.1 million, necessarily commute in from the Bronx and similar low-rent districts.

The old monied class of the Gilded Age had servants from the other side of town, of course, and the servants cleaned rooms and drove carriages they never could have afforded themselves. But gradually large-scale industrialization changed all this, creating a mass market for mass-produced goods and standardized services while building a huge middle class along the way. That was one of the great achievements of modern capitalism, and it strengthened American society as well as the economy.

The emerging economy is not taking us backward, but it does seem to be moving us toward a new kind of social divide. The material well-being of most people is improving, to be sure. Jennifer, for example, could never have got her cut-rate airfare twenty years ago, because there wasn't enough competition among airlines, or the technology, to slash the costs of air travel. And the Internet will be available to more people, allowing even home health-care aides to get excellent deals on all sorts of things they need, so their dollars will go further. But these advantages notwithstanding, the allocation of personal attention is likely to become even more sharply skewed in years to come—toward those who can afford to pay for it, away from those who can't.

The way paid work is coming to be organized and rewarded in the new economy is inducing people to work longer and harder, and to sell themselves with ever-greater urgency. As a result, there is less room for families, which are being downsized and outsourced. Personal attention—once the province of spouses, parents, and the children of the elderly—is rapidly moving into the market economy, in which people receive the attention they can afford to buy. Ironically, the people who can't afford to buy it, or buy very much of it, are coming to include most of those who are selling it.

CHAPTER TEN

The Community
as Commodity

UNCLE BILLY [*emotionally, at breaking point*]: Mary did it, George! Mary did it! She told a few people you were in trouble and they scattered all over town collecting money. They didn't ask any questions—just said: "If George is in trouble—count on me." You never saw anything like it.
—*It's a Wonderful Life*, screenplay, 1946

THE FINAL CONSEQUENCE of the emerging economy for our personal lives concerns the communities we inhabit. Communities used to pick up where families left off. Home schooling gave way to the local public school; the very sick moved from home to the local hospital; libraries and playgrounds provided access to expensive facilities few families could afford on their own. Think of a "community," and you're likely to picture a place where people look after one another—a traditional neighborhood, church, voluntary association, New England town meeting, frontier barn-raising, quilting bee, volunteer fire department, charity supper. The last scene in Frank Capra's 1946 movie *It's a Wonderful Life* typifies the American ideal: Just as George (Jimmy Stewart) is about to give up in despair, he finds he can count on his neighbors' generosity and goodness, as they have always counted on his. They're bound together in common cause and friendship.

Contrast this imagery to a more recently heard lament: Americans lack community. We're no longer joiners. We don't know the people

194

next door. We "bowl alone."[1] Since most of us are working harder and selling ourselves with ever-greater gusto, no one should be surprised if we have less energy to spend with our neighbors.

But the view that we're no longer joining with others is not quite correct, and it fails to account for the most important aspect of what's happening. We're still joining together—for child care, elder care, schools, health care, insurance, health clubs, investment clubs, buying clubs, recreational facilities, private security guards, and everything else that's too expensive to purchase alone. But we're not joining as participants; we're joining as consumers. We're pooling our financial resources to get the best deal.

The same advances in communication, transportation, and information technologies that are giving us wider choices of products and investments are giving us wider choices of whom to join and for what purpose. And as with other facets of our new lives, we can abandon the community we choose almost instantly and switch to another in pursuit of an even better deal. Like personal attention, communities are becoming marketable goods. We get what we pay for, and we pay not a penny more than necessary for what we get.

NEW GROUPS

Through most of human history, community members didn't have much choice about whom they joined. They were born into their communities and usually died in the same ones. Some notably broke with theirs or were banished, but these partings were rare or traumatic. Even well into the industrial age, most people still congregated within extended families and clans that gave definition to city neighborhoods. Members of these communities stayed put for at least a generation or two.

These communities provided their members some security and care. Yet they often did so at the price of boredom and stifled opportunity. One of history's crowning achievements has been to give people a *choice* of community. An unprecedented share of Americans (and citizens of other modern nations) now enjoy the freedom to escape the communities they were born into. They can choose whom they join with, and then switch to another group if they wish—another residential community, spa, health plan, child-care center. They can abandon their cyber-communities with a click. As choice replaces random fate, surely community life will be richer, more harmonious, and happier. How could it be otherwise?

For one thing, membership in the older communities extended to many facets of a member's life. There were many different arrangements, of course, but mutual obligations and benefits tended to come in a big bundle: production, defense, care, nourishment, parenting, entertainment, and spirituality. As a participant, you contributed no less to the bundle than was expected of you, and extracted no more than you were expected to take. Clan members produced for the clan and took care of one another's children, sick, or elderly.

By contrast, the new communities offer highly specific benefits. You pick a community for exactly what you want from it. As with other aspects of your new life, you shop for the best community you can afford. Because exit is so easy and the benefits are so targeted, these new communities don't require nearly as much commitment as the old did, nor do they offer the same security to members who might need to depend on one another in a pinch. Sure, you develop friends in a child-care group, but you don't have to reveal as much about yourself along the way, and you can end the friendship instantly, as can they.

Here's the real catch. Given the range of choice and ease of switching, we're sorting ourselves into communities of people with roughly the same incomes, the same abilities, the same risks, and the same needs. Where we live has more to do with how much we earn than ever before. It's Vail and Greenwich versus the communities who attend to them—but on a much larger scale. People who are most buffeted by the new economy—whose incomes have eroded the most, whose earnings are the most precarious—are ending up together in the same poor communities.[2] Their schools are among the worst. They have less medical attention. Their insurance is more costly. Even when they pool what they can afford, the parents of toddlers still can't raise enough for good-quality day care. This sorting process started years ago, but it's become far more efficient, just when the people who are being sorted away into neglected communities need help the most.

THE SORTING MECHANISM

To understand what is taking place, you have to understand the sorting mechanism. All other things being equal, someone who buys into a community wants the highest return on his or her investment—the best value, best service, most enjoyable and stimulating peers, largest amount of prestige their money will buy. Those already *in* likewise want the highest return on every new member—people who will contribute as much as if not more than they, and who make minimum demands on the common pool of resources. Unless your motive is charitable, there's no sense joining a community composed of a lot of people who are more costly and needy than you, because you'll end up subsidizing them. And it's irrational for a group to go out of its way to attract members who will be a drain on it, or to provide benefits that will likely attract such people.

When a friend recently landed a job at the University of California at Los Angeles and his wife got a job in a financial firm in downtown Los Angeles, the two of them toured many different communities within a fifty-minute commute for both in order to find a good place to live. After they narrowed their pick of community, they examined a variety of condominiums and cooperatives. They finally settled on the best deal they could afford—within a condominium complex possessing its own security guards, maintenance crew, modest recreation facility, and even broadband Internet connection, in a neighborhood that was safe and attractive and contained a good elementary school for their daughter. In making their decision, they naturally considered the price of the condominium and the monthly fee that went along with it, as well as local taxes. They didn't consciously seek to live in a community containing few poor people whose children would need extra instruction in school and whose overall family needs would require more social services and hence higher local taxes to pay for them. And they didn't intentionally choose a condominium complex whose price would screen out poorer people with larger families that might use up more of the common amenities. They simply tried to find the best deal for their money. They had a lot of information and a wide array of choices (townships with different tax bases, private residential communities with different monthly fees).

The wider the choice and the greater the ease of switching to something better, the more efficient the sorting mechanism becomes. Individuals try to get into groups offering them the best deals—not only the best cities or townships and the best private residential communities they can afford, but also the best universities, primary and secondary schools, child-care centers, nursing homes and elder-care centers, insurance pools, professional partnerships, and companies. And such groups compete to attract the most desirable members—those who can contribute the most and demand the least. As a result, the most desirable end up clustering together, sometimes nationwide, even worldwide. And with ever-greater efficiency, they exclude those who are less valuable or more needy. The *next* most desirable cluster together as well, and exclude those who are more costly than they. And so on, down the line.

I've made it sound like a cold calculation—colder and more calculating than it usually is—in order to reveal a logic that's just under the surface of society, and likely to become ever more apparent as choices widen and information improves, and it becomes easier to switch to better deals. Few people employ the sorting mechanism consciously. It is, rather, the consequence of a large number of rational personal decisions.

RESIDENTIAL SORTING

Begin with the decision my friend and his wife made about where to live. In a world of wider choices and easier switches, more people like them are making such decisions according to how much they can get for their money, and implicitly choosing not to subsidize people who are likely to contribute less to, or use up a lot more of, common resources. As residential communities have become commodities—marketed, evaluated, and purchased like any other—it's easier for buyers to get just what they want. And sellers have stronger incentives to offer just such deals.

Local services in *private* residential communities—the fastest-growing part of the U.S. housing market—are supported by membership dues. Such services in exclusive *public* townships, like Vail or Greenwich, are financed by local property taxes. But private or public, the sorting mechanism is essentially the same. Private residential communities exclude large families that need a lot of schools and social services, and whose children may be noisy or engage in petty crime, by charging hefty prices for homes and high membership fees and by strictly limiting the number of bedrooms in each unit. Upscale townships do it by requiring two- to four-acre plots for each home and prohibiting multi-family housing. Despite Vail's labor shortage, its residents don't want low-income housing that might threaten their property values. The only affordable housing that hasn't drawn complaints is situated in an old gravel quarry on a flood plain, forty-five miles away.[3]

"Citizens' movements" against state and local taxes have been spear-headed by private homeowner associations whose members see no reason why they should pay to support families outside the gates when members are getting everything they need inside, through their dues. In 1990, the New Jersey legislature defused one such revolt by agreeing to reimburse residents of private communities the taxes paid for public trash collection, snow removal, street lighting, and other public ameni-ties because those residents were already paying for them privately. In other words, homeowners would pay only for what they got and no longer subsidize other communities needing more.

Depending on which is the more efficient means of sorting, private residential communities can morph into public townships, and vice versa. On March 24, 1999, the Leisure World retirement village in Orange County transformed itself from a gated community into one of Cali-fornia's newest municipalities: Laguna Woods, whose average citizen is seventy-seven years old. The change allows residents to keep more of their tax dollars for themselves, paying only for the swimming pools, tennis courts, riding stables, and lawn care within the new city's bound-aries rather than spending money on schools and social services for children in the rest of the county.

I once described this as the "secession of the successful," but in recent years the sorting mechanism has extended further down the economic ladder. As the proportion of married-with-children house-holds continues to shrink and that of elders rises, more school districts contain larger concentrations of older people who vote for lower taxes and lousy schools rather than the opposite combination. Meanwhile, American cities are creating all manner of "special service" districts for middle-class residents and business owners willing to pay assessments for more trash collection, cleaning, and police—so long as the extra services are performed solely inside the district. Exclusive communities are even becoming exclusively wired. In the not-too-distant future, they'll link all their households, schools, retail stores, and offices to sin-gle giant high-speed networks—allowing teachers to communicate more easily with parents, businesses with their employees, and everyone with their town officials.[4] Gated communities used to be just for the very rich, but now middle-income home buyers want in. In 1970, the nation had more public police officers than private security guards; now it hires three times as many private guards as public ones—in California, four times as many.[5]

The secession of middle- and lower-middle-income families is also leading America back toward racially segregated neighborhoods. The probability that a black student will have white classmates dropped during the 1990s. You can spot the trend in most of the nation's large metropolitan areas. At the start of the nineties, about 10 percent of Chicago's neighborhoods could still be described as integrated (with black families constituting 10 to 50 percent); by the middle of the decade, less than 3 percent.[6]

SCHOOL SORTING

As the stakes in getting a good education continue to rise, parents more aggressively seek the best education they can afford for their children. And the best deals are where *other* students are at least as intelligent, ambitious, and intellectually stimulating—and less likely to use up the scarce attention of teachers by being troublesome or needing a lot of extra help.

Peer effects among school-age children are significant—a fact that parents of teenagers will hardly find surprising. High-school students are more likely to go to college when more of their classmates are college-bound.[7] And whatever their level of ability, students do better in groups more able than they, on average, and worse in groups less able, although the process isn't symmetrical. Students of less ability are helped more by being together in classrooms with students of greater ability than the more able are hurt by being combined with the less.[8] New evidence strongly suggests that such childhood peer effects extend beyond schools to the communities surrounding them. After a random sample of poor inner-city families received housing vouchers that enabled them to move to higher-income suburbs, their children's behavior improved relative to children in families who wanted the vouchers but lost out in the lottery.[9]

Here too, the sorting mechanism is becoming far more efficient. Wealthier and more ambitious parents are choosing highly regarded private schools or good public schools in tony suburban communities where other students are likely to exert a positive influence, trouble-makers can be easily extruded, and slower learners are quietly isolated. ("Tuition" for a good public school in a wealthy neighborhood is, in effect, included in the purchase price of an upscale home there, and the corresponding property taxes.) Or they choose publicly funded "char-ter" schools with more leeway than public schools about whom to admit or expel. In most states, charters have little room explicitly to exclude or expel, but they can craft their offerings in such a way as to deter less desired students, for example by failing to offer services for children with learning disabilities or admitting children only from the surround-ing upscale neighborhood. (A recent study of charter schools in Michi-gan found that most of them excluded students who were especially costly to educate, such as those requiring special-education services; charter schools in many of the most affluent school districts refused to accept applicants from outside the district boundaries.)[10]

The same mechanism explains the upsurge of private "parents' foundations" in the wake of court decisions requiring richer school dis-tricts to subsidize poorer ones. Rather than pay extra taxes, parents are quietly shifting their support to these charitable enterprises, thereby keeping more of their money in the home district. Already about 12 percent of the more than 14,000 school districts across America are funded in part by such foundations,[11] paying for everything from a new school auditorium (Bowie, Maryland) to a high-tech weather station and language-arts program (Newton, Massachusetts).[12] "Parents' foun-dations," observed the *Wall Street Journal*, "are visible evidence of par-ents' efforts to reconnect their money to their kids."[13] And not, it should have been noted, to kids who are needier and more costly.

As a result of all this sorting, poorer children who require a lot of attention from good teachers are increasingly bunched together with other poorer children who also need a lot, within schools that have rel-atively few resources to begin with.[14] It shouldn't be surprising that parents in poor communities tend to favor school vouchers, because vouchers at least give them a means of separating their children from troublemakers who use up even *more* of the scarce time and attention of teachers, and who exert the worst influence on their own kids. Schools in a voucher system are freer to expel children who are particu-larly unruly. Parochial schools have always had that option, which partly explains why poor kids who attend them do better on standardized tests than poor kids in the public schools. The aggressive use of "zero tolerance" codes of school behavior makes the extrusion of troublesome children all the more common. Where do all these children go? They're bunched together at the bottom of the entire educational system in schools that are essentially custodial institutions. If the children are too unruly even for these precincts, they may end up in juvenile detention centers. The sorting mechanism is complete.

No one designed the educational system this way. Well-meaning parents think of their reliance on private schools, good public schools in upscale communities, charter schools, local foundations, or school vouchers as means of obtaining as good an education as they can afford for their kids—not as means of excluding children more costly to educate than their own. But in fact, these individual decisions add up to a large-scale sorting mechanism. And once under way, the mechanism has its own momentum—as is strikingly clear in California, which in the 1960s had been among the heaviest spenders on public education per pupil and had one of the best school systems, yet now spends among the least and has one of the worst. As residents segregated into richer and poorer communities, the poorer schools began to deteriorate. After Proposition 13 placed a cap on local property tax rates in 1978, and a court decision required rough parity in spending across districts, California moved to pool educational funds statewide—transferring tax dollars from rich towns to poor. This lessened the educational payoff to better-off parents of choosing a wealthier town in which to live, so they began sending their children to private schools and withdrawing their support from the public school system. As a result, overall public spending on education dropped, and almost all public schools began to deteriorate.

In the emerging economy, success will depend most on talent, ingenuity, the ability to sell oneself, and connections. The quality of a child's early education and the character of the child's community are centrally important in these respects. Yet with ever-increasing efficiency, the sorting mechanism is separating children according to the communities and the schools their parents can best afford. Individual parents are acting rationally, but what's rational for individuals is not necessarily rational for society as a whole. Nor is it the outcome we might choose as citizens concerned for the future of the nation.

UNIVERSITY SORTING

Say you're a bright high-school senior, considering college. Twenty years ago your sights would have been on the best university in your state, perhaps your region. Now you've got far better comparative data about national colleges, starting with *U.S. News*'s ratings and a flood of information over the Internet. Besides, your state university may no longer offer the cheapest deal. State support for higher education is no longer as generous as it used to be (we'll come to the reason later).

This shift toward a national (and in many respects a global) market in higher education has put all colleges and universities into more direct competition with one another. In order to maintain or enhance their reputations, they've got to attract the smartest young people from around the nation, even the world. They, too, have more and better information about high-school stars. And as competition for these stars intensifies, colleges are offering them more lucrative scholarships.

Parents of the stars are wising up and conducting bidding wars similar to those conducted by prized employees. Carnegie-Mellon University explicitly encourages star applicants to bring back offers from other colleges so that it can match or surpass them. *We'll beat any price!* Harvard makes the same offer more delicately, as is Harvard's wont: "We expect that some of our students will have particularly attractive offers from the institutions with new aid programs," it writes its new admits, "and those students should not assume that we will not respond."

But as a result, there's less scholarship aid left over for needier students. "Need-blind admissions"—by which universities admitted applicants according to merit, and made sure that anyone who got through the door received enough financial help to stay—is fast disappearing. More of the scholarship aid is now going to the best and brightest. "It used to be, providing aid was a charitable operation," says Michael S. McPherson, president of Macalester College in St. Paul. "Now, it's an investment, like brand management."[15]

This means that students who are especially talented, well organized, and motivated are clustering more than ever together in the same prestigious universities. Their chances of doing well in life are already high before entering college. The clustering further bolsters their prospects of success. Not only are their talents and ambitions mutually reinforcing, but their wealth of contacts and connections provide the whole group with access to even better job opportunities. And as they cluster together, the prestige of their university brand grows steadily higher. Young people who are somewhat less disciplined, motivated, or capable of doing well on standardized exams attend "second-tier" universities, and their experience reinforces those almost-but-not-quite-good-enough inclinations and connections. And so on down the line. (As noted in a previous chapter, however, university rankings don't perfectly correlate with the talent found in any given institution of higher education. And some of the best small universities are establishing reputations for excellence in particular niches, to which world-class faculty and students are attracted.)

The trend has been gathering momentum for several years. What's new is the efficiency of the sorting mechanism. Fiercer competition on both sides—prospective students seeking admission to the best universities, and the universities seeking out the best students—is resulting in an ever-greater concentration of talents and abilities. This helps explain why inequality of earnings is rising even among college graduates.[16]

RISK SORTING

One traditional function of a community was to spread the risk of misfortune among its members. All contributed against the possibility that any single one might be in particular need. By the early decades of the twentieth century, it was assumed that nations as a whole should provide all their people with social insurance. Every American citizen would "receive old-age benefits direct from the insurance system to which he will belong all his life," said Franklin D. Roosevelt of the system he was signing into law. "If he is out of work, he gets a benefit. If he is sick or crippled, he gets a benefit."[17]

But the sorting mechanism is eroding social insurance. To understand why, you need to understand two basic things about your incentive to insure yourself and your family: First, the reason you buy insurance—either privately, from an insurance company, or publicly, through tax payments to the government—is that you don't know whether or how much you'll be needing it. If you knew, it wouldn't be insurance; it would simply be the specific cost of whatever you anticipated needing, like a new car every five years. Second, the amount you actually pay to be insured—your premium or your tax payment to cover the cost of the insurance—corresponds to the average riskiness of everyone within the group to be insured. As long as every group reflects roughly the same mix of more or less risky individuals, or the group is a national risk pool like Medicare or Social Security, the cost to you is about the same. You can't get a better deal, so you have no incentive to shop for one. Inevitably, then, people on whom fortune smiles end up subsidizing the people on whom fortune scowls. To the extent that fate is random, this seems only fair.

Absent strong social bonds, your incentive to contribute to an insurance pool will erode if you believe the likelihood that you'll need to draw from it is significantly less than the likelihood someone else will. "Welfare," as originally conceived in FDR's plan of social insurance, was for mothers whose income-producing husbands had died. As such it was popular, because the misfortune could happen to almost any family. But when welfare began to be seen as income support for unmarried mothers, a large portion of whom were black, the program no longer seemed like insurance. It looked more like a handout to the "undeserving" poor—who appeared even less deserving as more married mothers of young children had to get jobs. Political support for welfare dried up, and welfare shriveled.

 Broad-based social insurance programs remain popular with the elderly (witness the quadrennial political grandstanding about Medicare and Social Security), but the wealthier and healthier are having second thoughts. Many are beginning to see that they can get a better deal by joining together and leaving the poorer and sicker behind.

Selfishness isn't the new force at work here. It's technology, which is revealing more about one's riskiness. For example, the genetic codes carried within your cells can reveal the odds that you'll develop any number of life-threatening diseases. Your family history—how long your parents and grandparents lived, and what they died of—reveals more information. And the way you live your life—the kind and amounts of food you ingest, how active you are, where you live, your income, your education, your personal habits and addictions—can be analyzed to provide still more specific information on the odds that you'll get sick, have an accident, or otherwise invite misfortune. In short, it's no longer the case that you and the community that insures you are in the dark about your chances of needing to be bailed out. The odds can be known with increasing precision.

The sorting mechanism for insurance operates exactly as it does with social services and education: The best deal is one where your dollars don't subsidize anyone riskier than you. Americans spend tens of billions of dollars a year insuring their health and their lives in the private insurance market. Insurers who compete for this business have every incentive to "cherry pick," pursuing people with lower risks and charging them lower premiums. As more and better information becomes available, such people—who tend to eat better, get better medical treatment, have higher incomes and better educations—will be charged progressively less; people with higher risks—the converse in every respect—will pay more, and the gap in price will widen.

The sorting mechanism is already slicing up private health insurance. Health maintenance organizations (HMOs) actively market themselves in wealthier suburbs and to high-paying companies whose employees are also less likely to need a lot of costly medical care. Employers, meanwhile, are narrowing or dropping coverage of their lower-paid and more risky employees even as they enhance coverage for their most valuable. Rather than continue purchasing group health insurance to cover all its employees, Xerox announced at the end of 1999 that it would give its employees vouchers to buy their own—a move that will cut Xerox's costs and also end the implicit subsidy of higher-risk employees by the lower-risk. And as many large companies that used to offer all their employees group health insurance continue to downsize and subcontract their operations to smaller companies, the only employees remaining within the parent-company group insurance plans are core managers, who are generally wealthier and healthier than the rest.

Meanwhile, the "managed care" revolution is reducing medical care for the uninsured poor. City hospitals used to provide a kind of last-ditch health insurance for the neediest and riskiest—free care for those who couldn't pay; emergency trauma centers and burn units; treatments for drug-resistant tuberculosis; units devoted to AIDS, drug addiction, family violence; and health care for recently arrived immigrants. The hospitals could afford these services because health insurers indirectly subsidized them, paying the hospitals a bit more than insured patients actually cost. But increasingly, HMOs are competing furiously against one another to rein in costs, thus leaving city hospitals without the extra funds. In fact, the new competition is also encouraging hospitals to compete for low-risk patients with ample coverage— middle-class women delivering babies, for example—while shunning the uninsured drug addicts and the traumatized. And it's causing doctors to spend less time on charity care. One recent study showed that in communities with the most competition among managed-care plans, doctors provided about 25 percent less charity care than did their counterparts in communities where managed care had not yet taken hold.[18]

As originally conceived, Medicare offered every retiree a certain minimum guaranteed health insurance, financed by the contributions of all workers. Because no individual worker knew for sure how much medical attention he or she would require when reaching retirement age, the system seemed reasonably fair. But now that the wealthier and healthier have a much better idea, many would prefer individual "medical savings accounts," enabling them to get a better deal on their own rather than subsidize the chronically ill. Their preference is perfectly rational. Yet this sorting mechanism, adopted by all, would leave the sickest and poorest elderly behind in their own expensive publicly supported insurance pool, highly vulnerable to budget cuts.

Similarly, the original idea behind Social Security was that some of the payroll taxes paid by higher-wage workers would be tapped to raise the benefits of lower-income retirees. Since workers couldn't be certain at the start of their careers how much they'd earn over the course of them, this seemed a fair arrangement. But now, well-educated and well-connected young people rightly figure they'll amass considerably more wealth during their careers than will workers with poor educations and connections, most of whom will accumulate no wealth at all. It's understandable that they'd prefer to merge their savings with those of other similarly promising young people within a mutual fund, and collect the full returns on that pool of private investment, rather than subsidize poorer retirees. Yet "privatizing" Social Security by this sorting mechanism will leave lower-income retirees with less.

LEADERSHIP AS COURTSHIP

The old job of leadership was to make decisions. The new job of leadership is to attract (and keep) money and talent. This is because money and talent are more mobile than ever. Leaders of companies, universities, museums, hospitals, and other institutions want to create virtuous circles in which money and talent join together with a lot of other money and talent and, as they link up, capture the mutual benefits of the group's prestige, its capacity to innovate, the teaching and learning that occurs within it, the quality of services available to its members, or the low costs and risks of being a member of such a group. The problem is that at some point a virtuous circle may reverse itself and turn vicious. The most talented may leave for an even better deal elsewhere, prompting others to leave as well. There may even be a rush for the exits, resulting in stampedes like "brain drains" and "capital flight." Wider access to information and easier exit are likely to set off more stampedes in the future. The job of the leader is also to stop vicious circles before they gather momentum.

Private-sector executives no longer make big strategic decisions. Their time is spent reassuring stock analysts, venture capitalists, and institutional investors about the enterprise's rosy future, and persuading valued individuals to come or to stay by enticing them with stock options and interesting projects. Many of these solicitations must be done in person for maximum effect. After IBM made its $3 billion hostile takeover bid for Lotus in 1994, Louis Gerstner, Jr., IBM's chairman and chief executive officer, made a personal pilgrimage by helicopter from the company's world headquarters in Armonk, New York, to Cambridge, Massachusetts, to convince Ray Ozzie, one of Lotus's most creative minds, to remain with the company. Ozzie had devised the original idea for Lotus's premier software product, called Notes, which enabled employees anywhere in a company's far-flung operations to share documents. Gerstner's personal intervention bought a three-year commitment from Ozzie, who quit in late 1997 to form a new company.[19]

Nonprofit leaders, likewise, are immersed in continuous efforts to lure talent and money. "To direct an institution nowadays you have to be an opportunist," says Marcia Tucker, former director of the New Museum of Contemporary Art in New York. "You have to use every social situation to think about fund-raising and social contacts."[20] While university deans busily court faculty stars (increasingly, as has been observed, in Barro-type bidding wars), most college presidents are consumed by the task of raising funds. "One has to be a beggar, a flatterer, a sycophant, a court jester," notes Leon Botstein, president of Bard College.[21] The great visionary university presidents who once changed America's thinking on weighty matters—such as James Conant, who, as Harvard's president from 1933 to 1953, instructed the nation on the importance of civilian control of atomic energy; and

Robert Maynard Hutchins, who led the University of Chicago from 1929 to 1951 and bombarded the nation with provocative ideas about education and justice—have been replaced, for the most part, by a generation of leaders whose vision is focused on raising large donations. Harvard's president at the turn of the millennium, an unassuming man named Neil Rudenstein, was almost unknown to the world outside, but proved himself adept at extracting big sums from people eager to have their names chiseled into a Harvard pediment. In order to do his job well, Rudenstein pointedly eschewed controversial stands on large issues of the day. "I have to think very, very hard not about where I should be positioned, but about where Harvard should be positioned," he explained.[22]

GOVERNANCE AS SALESMANSHIP

Government officials must court on a grander scale. Governors and mayors hustle to attract or to keep within their borders residents with high skills and high incomes, on whom virtuous circles of growth depend—who will attract others like themselves, and with them, global capital. The mobility of such individuals corresponds with their educations. While only 1.6 percent of high-school dropouts move to another state each year, almost 4 percent of college graduates do so.[23] Not only do the better educated have a greater choice of jobs in different locations than the less educated, and many more connections, but, as noted, they can sell their services in cyberspace from almost any locale.

How to attract and keep better-educated, creative workers? By lowering their taxes, furnishing them safe and attractive surroundings in which to live and work, and granting them easy access to airports and vacation spots, museums, and sports arenas with fancy skyboxes. Otherwise, they'll leave for better deals elsewhere, as evidenced by the legions of Massachusetts high-tech workers who in recent years have decamped to New Hampshire in pursuit of lower taxes.

This courtship partly explains why the burden of state and local taxes is quietly shifting from higher earners who are more mobile to lower earners who have fewer choices about where to live. Income taxes—which take a larger proportion of the incomes of higher earners—are being replaced by sales taxes, taxes on gas, cigarettes, and alcohol, and lotteries, all of which take a larger proportion of the incomes of lower earners. Since 1993, as state treasuries have grown flush, governors have cut taxes, but notably, more than two-thirds of the tax cuts have been income taxes rather than sales taxes.[24]

It also partly explains the decline in state support for higher education. After all, given the relationship between education and geographic mobility, if a state helps one of its young people obtain a college degree rather than drop out of high school, it doubles the probability of losing that worker to another state. "We've been experiencing a brain drain," complains Nebraska governor Ben Nelson, noting that the higher Nebraskan students score on standardized tests, the more likely they are to abandon the state.[25] Nebraska now pays state tuition costs only for those students who agree to work in Nebraska for at least three years after graduating.

Governors and mayors must also persuade businesses to come and to stay. With products becoming lighter, and transportation and communications steadily cheaper, one place on the map increasingly substitutes for any other. Thus, bidding wars for businesses are escalating, with states and cities competing more fiercely to lure or keep them by means of generous subsidies and tax breaks. All over the world, corporate taxes are plummeting.

A few years ago, I helped officiate at the solemn signing of a "treaty" among officials of New York City, New Jersey, and Connecticut in which they agreed to refrain from poaching companies from one another. The deal lasted ten days before one of the three succumbed to the blandishments of a company that quietly suggested it would move if properly motivated. Now the three jurisdictions are spending more than $2.5 billion annually bidding against one another for essentially the same jobs. New York's governor and mayor have proudly announced a record $720 million package of tax breaks and subsidies for the New York Stock Exchange to build a sixty-story office tower right across from its current home, at Broad and Wall Streets, where it has been since 1902. New Jersey had tried to lure the Big Board with a generous package of its own, although the lure seemed less than compelling. No insult to the Garden State intended, but it's hard to imagine much luster from a listing on a "New Jersey Stock Exchange." Besides, within a few years, electronic trading systems are likely to replace bricks and mortar, wherever the bricks are piled up. Nonetheless, "[t]he reality," explained a *New York Times* editorial, "is that if New York City refuses to play this game, other, hungrier cities and states will take advantage of that passivity. Then Manhattan, in particular, will see its prestige and residents lured away like so many free agents."[26]

Worse, the tax breaks and subsidies offered to business come at the expense of public services needed by many of these areas' less fortunate people, like good schools. State and local governments gave businesses more than $17 billion in tax rebates and subsidies in 1999; this is an amount that, were it spent on schools, would have been enough to educate one and a half million elementary school students at *double* 1999's average rate per pupil.[27]

Public officials are even trading schools for sports stadiums. The stadium bidding wars are heating up, to the detriment of schools in poorer areas. In 1999, Pennsylvania approved $160 million for new stadiums for the Eagles and Phillies in Philadelphia and the Pirates and Steelers in Pittsburgh, replete with parking garages and skyboxes. Meanwhile, Philadelphia's public schools were overcrowded, their roofs leaked, and they were out of supplies; Pittsburgh's schools faced a $30 million budget shortfall.[28] In 1995, Cleveland made a $175 million bid to keep the Browns from moving to Baltimore, even as the city closed eleven public schools for lack of funding.[29] As I write this, the vociferous owner of the Yankees is demanding that New York City build the team a new multimillion-dollar stadium, and the mayor seems eager to oblige. Yet New York's schools, starved for funds, are overcrowded and dangerous. Why are political leaders making this tradeoff? Because the sports teams will leave town if they don't get new stadiums, but inner-city kids have nowhere else to go.

It's happening on a global scale. More than a century ago, the United States asked the world to send it their "tired . . . poor . . . huddled masses yearning to breathe free,"[30] but now we're more intent on attracting the smart, well-educated software engineers yearning to be rich. Although there's growing unease about the influx of poor immigrants to these shores, American high-tech firms have lobbied furiously, and successfully, to lift quotas on U.S. visas for foreign high-tech workers. Other nations are also trying to lure talent their way. Ireland attracts best-selling authors with generous tax cuts. In 1998, the leaders of Iran were offering former Soviet scientists who once worked in labs linked to germ warfare up to $5,000 a month—more than these scientists earn in a year in Russia. Iran explained that other nations in that volatile region would attract the talent if it didn't do so first.[31]

On the other hand, Canada is losing managers, doctors, nurses, scientists, and other professionals, partly because taxes claim half their incomes.[32] Sweden's scientists and engineers, facing a maximum tax rate of 59 percent, plus a 1.5 percent wealth tax on property valued at more than $120,000, are leaving home, too; global companies head-quartered elsewhere are happy to have them. It's only a matter of time before Canada and Sweden feel compelled to reduce taxes on their most prized citizens.

Heads of state are also courting global investors. Diplomacy used to be about treaties, alliances, and delicate balances of power, and the most important meetings took place among heads of state. Now it's about attracting investment and avoiding capital flight, and the most important meetings take place between heads of state and world bankers and fund managers. Like carnival barkers trying to herd the throng into their assorted tents, presidents and prime ministers are try-ing to lure (and keep) global investors by promising whatever they can in return for global capital. They are fawning over and ingratiating themselves with those who direct the money flows. Almost all are busily cutting taxes on companies. Where necessary, they're slashing budget deficits—including public spending on social insurance, health care, and schools—in order to gain investors' confidence.

REPRISE: THE SORTED COMMUNITY

As a result of all these maneuvers, the burden of paying for the things that the less fortunate members of every society most need is being shifted more squarely onto them. This is the ultimate consequence of the sorting mechanism.

People with the greatest bargaining power—able to strike the best deals for schools, universities, child care, health care, insurance, taxes, returns on investments—are already the best off. They're likely to be well educated (or have well-educated parents), healthy, wealthy, and economically secure. Those with the least bargaining power—on whom the burdens of economic change are falling the heaviest—must settle for the poorest schools, little or no access to universities, minimal or no child care, poor or no health care, and no insurance against the vagaries of the market. And as they become more socially isolated, they also lose connection to a wider economy that depends ever more on connections. The bargaining power of everyone between these extremes is also inversely related to their need.

No one designed the system this way, nor intended this result. It's the product of a large number of separate decisions by individuals seeking to do the best for themselves and their loved ones. It doesn't suggest that people who are wealthier and more fortunate have become less charitable toward people who have less. The better off may sincerely want to help those who are falling behind. Many contribute to a host of worthy causes. They may in fact disapprove of the sorting that's occurring, to the extent they are aware of it. But the sorting itself may reduce their awareness of how others live who are less fortunate than they. And even if they are fully aware, the sorting mechanism has raised the stakes. For them to act on their own to join a poorer community would require them to sacrifice comfortable neighborhoods, good schools, access to excellent universities, high-quality health care and child care, valuable connections, and all the rest of the benefits that come from belonging to the more exclusive community. A decent society should not have to rely on saintliness.

The sorting mechanism further increases the pressure to earn as high an income as is possible. High incomes buy you and your family memberships in excellent communities. Low incomes force you to reside in poor communities with inadequate schools, few parks or playgrounds, unsafe streets, and a host of social problems. As the sorting mechanism becomes more efficient, the benefits of membership in a desirable community and the costs of having to settle in an undesirable one diverge more sharply, further raising the stakes.

This is not the end of our story. We are not slaves to present trends, nor captives of the sorting mechanism. We can, if we want, assert that our mutual obligations as citizens extend beyond our economic usefulness to one another, and reorganize ourselves accordingly. In this, as in other aspects of the new economy, we have choices.

PART THREE

CHOICES

CHAPTER ELEVEN

Personal Choice

To love and to work.
 —Sigmund Freud, on what a person should be able to do well[1]

M OST OF US are more prosperous than ever before. We own more. We're able to get terrific deals. Yet the deepest anxieties of this prosperous age concern aspects of our lives that can't be bought. Many of us worry about the erosion of family, about our own inadequacies as spouses or parents, about the difficulty of sustaining genuine friendships, about the brittleness of our communities, and about the challenge of keeping intact our own integrity.

Paid work is demanding more of our time, often more emotional energy and psychological preoccupation. As noted, the typical American is working 350 more hours a year than the typical European, more hours than the Japanese. And this feverish pace doesn't even include the time taken up with the ever more ubiquitous intrusions on personal life—phones, faxes, beepers, e-mails, business trips. Nor does it account for the preoccupations, exhilarations, and anxieties that overflow paid work and flood the rest of waking life and sometimes even sleep. Many of us don't run out of time as much as we run out of juice. Constantly being *on*—creating, teaching, convincing, and selling—can be emotionally draining. Burnout can occur well within the bounds of a forty-hour week. Even if there's physical time for friends, family, community, and personal reflection, there's no psychic space left. Alternatively, we're so juiced up by work that we don't want to spare juice for anything else. The rest of life is becoming downsized, outsourced, and sorted.

Is this the choice we've made? Is this the future of success?

WHAT DO WE REALLY WANT, ANYWAY?

Economists and most social scientists assume that the best way to measure what people want is to watch what they do. Psychologists and psychoanalysts assume that, regardless of what people say they desire, the real test is what they choose. If people wanted to live according to different priorities and were willing to accept the sacrifices that those different priorities entailed, presumably they'd do so.

Some people are compelled by economic necessity to work harder and more obsessively, but necessity can't explain much of the trend. American managers and professionals who were already living well grew far wealthier between the mid-1980s and the end of the century. And yet over the same period of time, the proportion of them working more than fifty hours a week rose by one-third. In fact, as noted earlier, the higher your earnings, the more likely it is that you'll work hard. It's not that you earn more *because* you work harder; you work harder because of what you can earn by doing so. Nearly 40 percent of male college graduates and 20 percent of female college grads work more than fifty hours a week for pay. College graduates earn considerably more than people who don't graduate from college, yet they're four times more likely than nongraduates to be putting in more than fifty hours a week at their jobs.

There's even evidence that the higher your earnings, the more likely it is that your teenage children will feel that their lives are more frenzied than yours. In one poll of young people aged thirteen to seventeen, affluent teenagers, regardless of race or gender, were substantially more likely than nonaffluent teenagers to report that their lives were harder and more stressful than their parents' lives.[2] Perhaps this is because the poorer teenagers hear stories of their parents' toil and struggle and feel that their own lives are easier by comparison, while the more affluent teenagers hear stories of "making" it, with an implicit warning about the danger of sliding backward. I'm reminded of a Roz Chast cartoon in *The New Yorker* (a magazine whose readers are rarely impecunious) picturing two boys with baseball caps and

backpacks, under the caption "Most Likely to Succeed." One boy is saying to the other, "I'd love to come over and hang out, but now that
we're competing in a global economy I can't."

Attitudes of college students seem to be shifting toward wanting to
work even harder for more money. As has been noted, only 41 percent
of college freshmen in 1968 listed being "very well off financially" as a
very important personal objective. Then, most were more interested in
"developing a meaningful philosophy of life." But financial well-being
steadily gained ground and philosophy of life steadily lost it until, by
1998, 74 percent of college freshmen listed being "very well off financially" as essential. As I've emphasized, this shouldn't be taken to mean
that today's students are greedier than previous generations. Record
numbers of college students are volunteering to work in their communities. They just have a more pecuniary focus for their lives.

Adult Americans also seem more intent on children's working hard.
A large sampling of Americans has been asked annually to choose the
one attribute that is "the most important for a child to learn to prepare
him or her for life" out of a list of five: to think for oneself, to obey,
to work hard, to help others, or to be well liked and popular. Since
1986, when this question was first asked, about half the sample has continued to choose "to think for oneself." But over the years, the only
attribute to have steadily *gained* in importance has been "to work
hard"—from 11 percent in 1986 to 18 percent in 1998.[3]

From the viewpoint of social scientists, who assume that the best
way to understand what people want is to watch what they do, the easiest conclusion to be drawn from all this is that Americans are choosing
hard work for themselves and their children because they *want* to. Forget a "better balance." All the talk about making room for the rest of
life—about the importance of family, friends, community, personal
callings, and spiritual fulfillment—is just superficial posturing in front
of the cameras.

Yet personal choices don't occur in a social vacuum. We choose one
way or the other because certain consequences attach to those choices,
consequences that depend partly on how society has chosen to organize itself. That a prisoner chooses to scale a high wall topped by barbed
wire doesn't mean she *wants* to scale high walls and traverse barbed
wire, but only that her circumstances have led her to do this dangerous
thing. Were the conditions of her imprisonment to grow steadily
harsher, or the world outside the prison to become far more comfort-

able, she might choose to scale even higher and more dangerous walls. But to conclude from this that she is developing a preference for higher walls is to fail to understand the essence of what's happening. Her increasing effort is due to the widening contrast between her life inside the walls and the life she could lead outside them.

REPRISE: THE BIG CHANGE

Why do most Americans work harder than they did three decades ago? Not because they are more dedicated to work now than before, or have progressed to a different point on the evolutionary scale. Something else must have happened, and must still be going on. Why does the average American work 350 more hours a year than the average European, and still want to work harder for more money? Not because Americans' brains are differently wired than European brains. There must be another reason, having more to do with the situations Americans and Europeans find themselves in than with their genes.

Why do college students today place greater value on financial well-being than did college students three decades ago? They aren't greedier. What's changed? Why do today's adults place greater store on children's learning to work hard than did adults only a few years ago? Here again, something must have happened to make adults more concerned about the consequences of not working hard.

Why are people having fewer kids? Not because they love children less than they used to. Again, there must be another explanation. Why is your choice of community much more important now than it was years ago? Not because citizens have become more intent on living in pleasant neighborhoods with good schools than they used to be. Here, too, something has happened to change the calculation and raise the stakes. In these and other examples I've offered in these pages, personal choices about work and life are taking place within a larger set of societal changes.

We must be careful to avoid placing too much responsibility for these trends on technological and economic changes alone. Human animals are complicated creatures, influenced by many different things. Yet the preceding pages do suggest how changes in technology and the economy are altering how work is organized and rewarded, which in turn influence how you lead your life. Let me summarize.

• Your earnings are less predictable than they were before. You can't be nearly as confident today about what you'll earn in the future as you could be in the old system of large-scale production. Even if you work diligently and are good at what you do, the demand for your services may drop unexpectedly because customers find better deals elsewhere. This puts you in a dilemma, because many of your costs of living are fixed—mortgages, rents, car payments, insurance, and the like. So what do you do? How does your behavior change from what it used to be when your earnings were steadier? Now, you must make hay while the sun shines. You work harder when the work is available against the risk that your income may drop in the future.

• If your skills are in great demand now, you're likely to be paid more than were people near the top of the income ladder in the old system. Pay used to depend largely on rank or seniority. Now you're paid for your ideas and your ability to sell. If you're a truly superb geek or shrink, you can earn vast sums. You're also likely to have generous employment benefits and a great work environment, maybe even a gym and a Jacuzzi downstairs. And your work is likely to be interesting, even fun. On the other hand, if you've been in a job that's rote or routine, which a large number of people here or around the world can do just as well—or your job can be done by computerized machines or by software over the Internet—you're likely to be paid less than you used to be paid for doing it, and you may be losing your benefits. And forget the gym and Jacuzzi. In fact, you may lose the job entirely. Unless you have the education and skills to become a geek or a shrink, there's a good chance that your new job will involve providing personal services at relatively low wages. Some of this work is satisfying, perhaps even ennobling; much of it is difficult or frustrating.

• If you're in the latter category and losing ground relative to the standard of living that most people deem acceptable, you have to work harder to prop up your family's income, and your spouse or partner may be working longer hours as well. If you're on the winning side and earning a lot, you may want to work longer and harder, too, but for a different reason. The sacrifices you'd make by *not* working so hard—the income and perks you'd give up, as well as the challenge and the fun—are much bigger than they were under the old system. For the same reason, you're more likely to go after one of those high-paying jobs rather than, say, teach school; were you to settle for the more modest income, you'd be giving up far more than you'd have given up making the same choice years ago.

• Even if you're doing well, you've got to continue to hustle. The market is changing quickly, customers are being offered a lot of new alternatives to which they can switch easily, and competition is intense. There's no relaxing, no cruise control, no resting on your laurels or seniority. Today's great idea might not last more than a few days or weeks, because rivals will be quick to copy it or try to come up with something even better.

• Furthermore, you're either on the fast track or you're not. Either you remain in close contact with your clients and customers, develop your connections, and stay up-to-date with new developments in your field, or you'll earn a lot less money and perhaps have a lot less interesting work. Yes, the new organization of work gives you more flexibility in how and when you do your job. Sure, it's easier than ever to work part-time, go on a long vacation, or take a year or several to be at home with a new child. But beware. If you do any of these things, you'll pay a big price. Don't expect to get back on the fast track easily, because while you were gone too much will have happened, and other people will have moved in to take over your clients and connections and develop new expertise.

• You're no longer in a big organization that will steadily promote you up the ranks because you do your job competently and well. Increasingly, you're on your own, which means you've got to promote *yourself.* It's not enough to be smart or creative or have a cool idea; a lot of people are smart and creative, with cool ideas, and they're competing with you for business. You've got to attract and keep customers. You may have to use all of your connections—including friendships and even distant acquaintances—to expand or keep up with the demand for your services. You've got to make a name for yourself rather than invest a lot of time and effort in a particular company or organization. You need to put yourself into "play" by orchestrating bidding contests for your services.

- The sorting mechanism is becoming ever more efficient. If you work hard, sell yourself effectively, and do well, you'll be able to pool your winnings with others who have done well. This means you can live in a charming, safe community; send your kids to a nurturing child-care center, an excellent school (a public school in an exclusive upscale community or a top-tiered private school), and then on to a superb university; belong to a comfortable health club (a "public" facility in your tony township, or a private spa); have comprehensive insurance at a reasonable cost, and good health care with an attentive doctor and access to a highly reputed medical center. But the sorting mechanism will treat you far less well if you have less to bring to the table. If you're at or near the bottom of the earnings scale, your community is apt to be blighted and dangerous, the schools lousy, the health care minimal or nonexistent.

In short, you work harder than a typical European or Japanese works, in large part because work is organized and rewarded in America in a manner that induces harder work: There's more uncertainty, wider inequality, more sorting, and more intense competition. You also work harder than you used to work, because in all these respects the stakes have become higher. Young people in college are more interested in being well off financially than they used to be because the potential financial rewards are greater than they were years ago, and the consequences of failing to pursue financial well-being are more onerous. Adults are more intent on children's learning to work hard for the same reason. People are choosing to have fewer children because paid work is crowding children out. Where you reside and with whom you join have larger consequences than before because the sorting mechanism is more efficient.

Of course, the choice is still up to you. No one is *requiring* you to work so hard for pay or to dedicate so much concentration and emotional energy to it. You could choose, if you wished, to work less, and have more left over for yourself, friends, family, and community. You could decide to have more kids and not to subcontract their care. You could choose against buying personal attention for yourself, including "friends" in the form of coaches and counselors. You could choose to live in a poorer community than the best you can afford to buy into.

On one level, these are all your personal choices. But at another level, they are not really personal choices at all, because the advantages of working harder for pay and the disadvantages of not doing so, as well as the benefits and the costs of living in one community or another, are larger today than they used to be, and larger in America than in many other countries. You don't have to scale the wall, but the consequence of not doing so is harsher, and the reward for doing so is sweeter, than you have ever encountered before. And both the harshness and the sweetness are intensifying.

This is not to suggest that you abandon all personal effort to achieve a better "balance" between work and the rest of your life. It's only to warn you that any such wholly personal pursuit will require greater fortitude now than it did years ago, and if the trends discussed in this book continue, even greater determination in the future. Repeatedly we're told, or we tell ourselves, that "balance" is within our grasp if only we become better aware of what's truly important to us, or if we better manage our time, or if we simplify our lives. These are noble aspirations, but we deceive ourselves if we believe that such approaches will resolve the anxieties of this prosperous age. To view what is happening to us and what we can do about it as private matters divorced from the larger trends in our economy and society is to miss much of the truth, and to limit our range of options unnecessarily.

SELF-AWARENESS

By all means, become more aware of what's truly important to you. Many of us know more about how we're doing on the job than about how we're doing in the rest of our lives. Job performance is constantly rated, evaluated, and appraised. We know our economic worth with ever-greater exactitude, because our paychecks now rise or fall to reflect it. If our star is rising, we get performance bonuses, stock options, and better job offers; if falling, our pay package shrinks. Yet the quality of the rest of our lives often eludes appraisal. Off the job, we're not nearly as sure of what's expected of us or what we should expect of ourselves. We may have a vague and uneasy sense that something's lacking, but how do we recognize what doesn't exist?

Society as a whole suspects that something is awry when it's shocked by events like children in an upscale suburb opening fire on other children at school. Such events are sadly expected in poor inner-city schools, but not in tony, carefully sorted suburbs. For a time, pundits, preachers, and politicians wonder publicly if our values are wrong, if we lack "balance" in our lives, if we're failing to spend enough time and energy on the "important things," such as our children. Then the crisis subsides, the headlines disappear, and we all go back to paid work, often more frenzied than before.

Many women are fully aware that their lives are becoming tightly compressed, but they're confused about what they (and others) should expect from themselves. Most of them continue to bear the major responsibility for taking care of children, a husband or male partner, and elderly relatives, as well as maintaining the home, even when they have full-time jobs.[4] Some feel they have to work even harder on the job to preserve what they consider to be an adequate standard of living; others feel they have to work harder if they want to stay on the fast track—cultivating connections, keeping up to speed in their fields. Today's woman is fortunate if she can squeeze into her day everything she feels she has an obligation to do. Her painful discovery is how often she cannot.

For many men, the painful discovery comes when something in their lives explodes. It may be their marriage, or their health, or their child who suddenly gets in trouble. Or it happens when their job begins to demand so much that they wake up in the middle of the night in a cold sweat. Or when their job becomes so rewarding that they suddenly discover the other parts of their life have all but disappeared. (That's what happened to me.)

Is there a more reliable way to become aware of the implicit choices we're making? Do we have to await a painful discovery? Recently I spent the better part of two weeks poring over some of the burgeoning self-help books, audiocassettes, home-study courses, newsletters, and guides for finding a "better balance" between paid work and the rest of life.

One recommended technique is to make lists or draw graphs representing what you most like or dislike about your life right now, or list what's most and least important, and then reflect on what you're actually spending your time on or devoting energies to. What have you allowed to become your priorities despite your resolve that they aren't or shouldn't be? A macabre version of the exercise is to imagine yourself nearing death, pondering what your life's priorities should have been. What will you look back upon that was most and least important? What would you want your legacy to be? How would you wish people to remember you? Then compare this to how you're actually living. I'm repeatedly assured by these guides, although I cannot find reliable statistics to support the assurances, that no one on his deathbed regrets spending too little time at the office.

These exercises in self-reflection are not harmful, and they may do some good. The basic point of all of them is simple: We're always making a choice, although we may prefer to deny we have choices; we might not want to accept the trade-offs they imply. When I worked in Washington, I didn't want to acknowledge that my life outside work was disappearing, because I loved the job so much that I didn't dare think about what it was taking away from me. Yet I was choosing just the same. The people who buy the books or the audiotapes, who enroll in support groups and consult with personal coaches, have already reflected enough to decide that something in their lives must change. The far harder part comes in deciding exactly what to change, and then actually following through.

TIME MANAGEMENT

Some people try to manage their time better. They buy into another small industry of time-management books, audiotapes, guides, coaches, and groups. Ever since the management-efficiency expert Frederick Winslow Taylor's time-and-motion studies in the first decades of the twentieth century, it's been assumed that human activity can be made more efficient by eliminating unnecessary steps. For starters, calculate precisely what you do in a typical day, breaking every task into measurable units. Make a "time diary."

Up, wash, quick exercise, dress . . . 40 minutes
Gulp down breakfast . . . 10 minutes
Check news headlines . . . 8 minutes
Pick up after dog . . . 4 minutes
Take son to school . . . 11 minutes
Drive to work . . . 28 minutes
On phone during workday . . . 2 hours, 25 minutes
Respond to e-mail . . . 2 hours, 15 minutes
Meetings . . . 3 hours, 40 minutes
Random chats . . . 1 hour, 15 minutes

Drive home . . . 24 minutes

Walk dog . . . 14 minutes

Straighten up house, empty wastebaskets, take out garbage . . . 18 minutes

Help prepare dinner . . . 19 minutes

Family dinner . . . 22 minutes

Clean up . . . 18 minutes

Time with son . . . 4 minutes

Do bills and family finances . . . 13 minutes

On phone at home . . . 32 minutes

Write, read, watch TV, listen to music . . . 2 hours, 18 minutes

Work on e-mail at home (including note to son at college) . . . 45 minutes

Read newspapers, magazines, portion of a book . . . 1 hour, 14 minutes

Say good night to son . . . 7 minutes

Quick exercise . . . 12 minutes

Wash, shower . . . 12 minutes

Into bed, talk with spouse . . . 14 minutes

Next, analyze the typical day. Note where you're spending too much time and where too little, according to your ideal priorities. What can be efficiently compressed in order to make room for expansion elsewhere? Three hours for e-mail, yet only twenty-two minutes with your son and thirty with your wife (not counting dinner prep)? That's out of whack. Cut e-mail down to two hours, and give your son and your wife thirty more minutes each. You're out of contact with your friends, so cut thirty minutes out of random chats at work and add thirty at the end of the day for phone calls to friends outside work. And what happened to your resolve to get more involved in the community? Make time for that. By the way, you're not getting nearly enough sleep. So cut an hour off meetings (you're sleeping through some of them anyway), and add an hour to bed. Add some exercise.

It didn't work. It's easy to decide what to devote less time to, but nearly impossible to stick to the new schedule. I know someone who has a small digital timer attached to his belt that vibrates whenever he's supposed to move on to his next event. I don't believe he has become more efficient, but he has definitely become more jittery.

One problem is that work doesn't present new opportunities and crises only when you block out time for them. This is especially true in the emerging economy, which is nothing if not a series of fresh surprises. Fierce competition and constant innovation inevitably give rise to things that can't be planned for in advance—a client with a crisis, a "killer app" from a competitor, a key employee on the verge of defecting. The more responsibility you have—the closer you are to the tumult—the less control you have over demands that will be made on your work time.

Another problem is that the actual time devoted to paid work is only one of its compressing forces. There's also the emotional energy and psychological concentration it requires.

Finally, the other people to whom you may want to relate outside of paid work—the very people who may have been shortchanged because of it—don't respond on a precise timetable. A spouse doesn't share intimate thoughts or feelings on a prearranged schedule. One of the best things about an intimate relationship is its spontaneity. Dedicating a specific unit of time to it is like trying to store a puppy in a box. Keep it in there too long, even with adequate food and water, and you take the life out of it.

Children don't operate on a fixed schedule either. While I know nothing about raising girls, I can tell you with authority that boys don't function by itinerary. As I've noted elsewhere, teenage boys are like clamshells. They open up just for a moment, in order to take in a little nourishment or expel some dirt. But then they clam up tight again. If you're around when they open up, you have a chance to see something wondrous inside. And you have a quick chance to connect.

But you have to be there for the moment. The clam shuts in an instant, and then you can't see or do a thing. Forget what you've heard about "quality time." Teenage boys don't want it, can't use it, have better things to do. When I came home from Bill Clinton's cabinet and suddenly had weekend time to spare, I waited for one of my boys to take me up on my offer of hours of quality time with them. "Sorry, Dad. I'd really like to go to the game with you, but . . . well, you see, David and Jim and I are going to hang out in the Square." "That's a cool movie, Dad, but . . . well, to tell you the truth, I'd rather see it with Diane." I suggested we make a plan, mark our calendars. But when the time came, there was always someone or something else. Teenage boys can't be scheduled.

SIMPLICITY

Some people decide to simplify their lives. There's even a "voluntary simplicity" movement that comes with yet another set of how-to books, conferences, newsletters, and support groups. The basic idea is as simple as the espoused goal. The jacket on one recent book in the series says it all: "Less—less work, less rushing, less debt—is more—more time with families and friends, more time with community, more time with nature."[5] First, decide how much money (or power or status) you really need. Can you do with a smaller house? Fewer restaurant meals? Less *stuff*? Assuming you can, cut back on the work you do for no reason other than to generate more of those things. Live more simply, and have more life left over.

These books remind me of diet plans. They view acquisitiveness like a compulsive eating disorder. The stuff you buy but don't need is like the food your body can't absorb, which turns into fat cells. Unless you want to become as big as a house, you have to cut back and stick to the diet. Discipline those yearnings. There's even the equivalent of a twelve-step diet plan for simplifying your life, and support groups to help you keep your resolve.

In reality, how much you buy isn't like how much you eat. Your body can absorb only so much, but there's no necessary limit to how well you can live by purchasing goods and services. The voluntary-simplicity approach assumes that "needs" can be fairly easily distinguished from "wants," necessities from luxuries. But beyond the bare minimum required to live, needs are entirely subjective.

Human beings don't really need very much in order to survive—about 1,000 calories a day, including a certain mix of vitamins and minerals; a quart or two of water; enough wrapping to keep the body at 98.6 degrees Fahrenheit; some exercise. As noted earlier, personal attention is helpful. So are antibiotics. Beyond this there are degrees of comfort. "That man is the richest whose pleasures are the cheapest," Henry David Thoreau wrote in 1856.[6] Thoreau, the unofficial head of the nineteenth century's "voluntary simplicity" movement, tromped off into the woods near Concord, Massachusetts, and lived in a bare cabin on Walden Pond, eating whatever he could grow or trap. "Our life is frittered away by detail. . . . Simplify! Simplify! Simplify!" he wrote. "I say let your affairs be as two or three and not a hundred or a thousand, and keep your account on your thumb nail."[7]

Beyond the bare minimum, what people "need" is relative to what most people in their society count on having. Necessity is an elastic concept, as is deprivation. "Most of the luxuries, and many of the so-called comforts, of life are not only not indispensable, but positive hindrances to the elevation of mankind," wrote Thoreau.[8] Someone can feel (and appear) deprived in modern America who would be considered well-off in sub-Saharan Africa. Here, a television is not exactly a life support system, but many people would put one on their list of necessities. A car is a necessity for many families, particularly where there are no buses or trams. Indoor plumbing qualifies, although upscale vacationers have been known to pay large sums of money to mountain outfitters to lead them to places where it doesn't exist. Computers aren't yet necessities, but they're coming close—children who grow up in families without one are digitally deprived, and may end up economically disadvantaged.

Ironically, how much you think you need becomes greater the more you already have. Turn the question of how much you "need" on its head, and ask yourself how much extra income would free you from concern about money. Your answer probably depends on how much you earn. In one recent poll, a sample of AOL subscribers whose annual incomes exceeded $100,000 said they needed far more extra money in order to stop worrying about money than did people who earned less than $40,000. Higher-earners were five times more likely to say they had to have more than $90,000 extra each year than were the lower-earners.[9]

A new magazine called *Real Simple* (another product emerging from the great maw of Time Inc.) is dedicated, according to its founding editor, "to helping you simplify every aspect of your life: your home, food, money, clothes, health, looks, work, family, and holidays. . . . About getting rid of what you can and keeping what you have."[10] The first issue—brimming with glossy ads for such bare necessities as Nieman Marcus pearls, De Beers diamond jewelry, Atencio sterling silver, Todd & Holland tea (a quarter pound for $56), Ralph Lauren sheets, and the Cadillac Catera—contains all sorts of handy suggestions for simplifying your life, like reducing the number of your credit cards and wearing plain woolen T-shirts costing $365. *Real Simple*, it turns out, isn't about getting rid of anything. It's about helping women with lots of money but little time unclutter their lives by buying a few exquisitely tasteful things.

IF YOU THINK cutting your costs of living will simplify your life, think again. Deciding on your "needs" doesn't avoid the difficulty of making a hard choice, because the choice isn't really between paid work and the rest of your life. It's between one kind of busy-ness and another. The readers of *Real Simple* have the money to live as "simply" as they like, but most people don't have that luxury. If you want to free up more time and energy for the rest of your life by working and earning less, then some of the things that now make the rest of your life easier or more pleasurable will have to be jettisoned, because you won't be able to afford them. Thoreau's luxury is my necessity. I don't want to live in a cabin in the woods and trap my food, thank you.

If you read Thoreau's journal, you'll see he was busy all the time. In order to keep himself warm and adequately nourished without relying on anyone else or paying for things, he had to work extremely hard to do it himself. Thoreau didn't have a family out there in his cabin, and as far as I can tell, he didn't have many friends. It's a wonder he had time and energy to write in his journal.

Simplicity isn't simple. A college friend who settled in Vermont years ago with her family in pursuit of a simple life rises at 4:30 a.m. to start the chores, which end late in the evening. She and her husband don't rely much on paid work to make ends meet, which means that they have to do almost everything for themselves.

Without specialization, all our lives would be far more squeezed than they are now. I specialize in teaching and writing. A few days ago, I used some of my earnings from teaching and writing to pay someone to repair the computer I'm now using to write on. Not only do I not trap my own food, but I also don't repair computers. A system of specialized food processing and computer repairing is far more efficient than one in which everyone traps his own dinner and repairs his own computer.

It's one thing to want to bake bread and trap small animals because you find these activities enjoyable, but quite another to do it because you have to if you want to eat. The same can be said for repairing computers. "Simplicity" offers no guide for how to find more time for what you want to do, unless you wish to spend more of your time doing the kinds of things you now pay other people to do for you more efficiently than you can yourself. The simple life based on homemade things is just too complicated for me, and probably for you.

BY ALL MEANS, become more reflective about what you're actually doing with your life as compared to how you'd like to live it. Reset your priorities. Manage your time better, if you can. Live on less money, if that's what you want to do. Make new resolutions. Ask your spouse or partner to take on more chores around the house. Walk in the rain. Take a hot bath. Stop watching television. Use a personal coach. Buy inspirational books. Do any and all of this, and maybe you can get a life. But don't bet on it.

We are personally responsible for the choices we make in life. But we operate within a system of incentives that make certain choices easier or harder. Seeking a "better balance" on our own, without reference to such incentives, overlooks the larger forces that are responsible for our being out of balance in the first place. Social choices frame personal choices. A full accounting of the choices before us, therefore, must also inquire into the choices we face together.

CHAPTER TWELVE

Public Choice

For to what purpose is the toil and bustle of this world? What is the end of avarice and ambition?
　　　　　—Adam Smith, *The Theory of Moral Sentiments* (1759)

Though we cannot know for certain the shape of the future, many of the trends that will carry us there are already clear. Today we can see the emergence of a vibrant new economy brimming with innovations. In the near future, consumers will be able to get exactly what they want, from wherever, at the best price and value. And when a better deal comes along, they'll be able to switch in the blink of an eye—or the click of a mouse. Investors will be able to shift their money instantly to better deals around the world. People whose services are in great demand will be able to move to better opportunities with exuberant ease. Jobs will be abundant, many of them exciting and well paid.

There is much in this picture to celebrate, yet there is also much that should at least give us pause. The economic dynamism we're beginning to see also brings financial insecurity, work that's more frenzied and intrusive, widening inequality of income and wealth, and greater social stratification—all of which is eroding personal, family, and community life. It seems an opportune moment to ask whether we are headed in the direction we wish to go—that is, to examine the social choices that lie before us.

BIG CHOICES

It may seem odd to use such language, to speak of the new economy in terms of social choices. The emergence of the global, high-tech economy seems largely out of anyone's hands. One development seems to have sparked the next, without any clear decision having been made about consequences. No one explicitly decided that technologies of communication, transportation, and information would advance as quickly as they have. Or that these technologies would push the economy from large-scale production toward a wide array of innovative products and services, with easy switching to better ones. Or that this would in turn sharpen competition and spur more innovation, resulting in faster economic growth and terrific deals on all sorts of purchases. Nor, especially, did anyone decide to accept the downsides of all this progress.

Imagine that several decades ago a giant genie appeared in the American sky, offering the nation a big choice: "Either you keep the economic arrangements you have now, stay working as you are, or—do I have a deal for you! By the start of the next century, some of you will be extraordinarily rich, most of you will be better off in terms of what you can buy, and the economy will balloon. But that's not all. [*The genie cackles.*] The other part of the deal I'm offering is this: Your jobs will be less secure, your incomes less predictable; there will be wider disparities of earnings and wealth; and your society will fragment. You will work much harder, and the rest of your lives will be tightly compressed. [*The genie cackles again.*] It's your choice! Thumbs up or down in fifteen seconds! I'll abide by the majority! [*The genie laughs again. His laughter grows louder and his face becomes larger until the laughter fills the air and his face fills the sky. And then everyone in America raises their hands in the air, thumbs up or down.*]

Knowing everything you now know, how would you vote? Is unprecedented prosperity worth the price? America never made the choice, of course. At least not directly—not in any way we understood ourselves to be making it.

In fact, societies *do* make all kinds of choices about their economic arrangements, whether we recognize them as such or not. The "free market" doesn't exist in a state of nature. It wasn't created by God on any of the first six days, nor is it maintained by divine will. It is a human artifact, the shifting sum of a set of judgments about individual rights and responsibilities. What's mine? What's yours? What's ours? How do we define and deal with actions that threaten these borders—theft, force, fraud, extortion, or carelessness? What should we trade, and what should we not? (Drugs? Sex? Babies? Genes? Votes?)

The answers are not found in logic or analysis alone. Different cultures, at different times, answer them differently. The answers depend on the values a society professes, the weight it places on solidarity, prosperity, tradition, piety. As a culture accumulates its answers to these questions, it creates its version of the market. To the extent that political rhetoric frames the issue as one grand choice—between government and market—it befogs our view of the series of choices about the wisest and fairest of an endless set of alternative ways to structure the rules of ownership and exchange. The absence of such rules is not a free market, it's no market at all. Just look at Russia.

The evolution of our economy has depended not only on innumerable clever and hard-working people—there are clever and hardworking people all over the world—but also on countless decisions about commercial contracts, the organization of banks and securities markets, what's taxed and what's not, patents and copyrights, antitrust, labor, zoning, and international trade (to name only a few pertinent areas). None of these decisions turns on whether the government should "intervene" in the market, but on how the market should be organized. It's impossible *not* to make these sorts of decisions. A failure to decide simply forces a reliance on prior decisions, or else creates uncertainty in areas where prior decisions offer no clear guidance.

What criteria should frame these and other market-making choices? Judges, legislators, editorial writers, and average citizens alike typically form their opinions on the basis of what alternative best promotes economic growth or best advances the well-being of consumers by lowering prices and generating better products. Or they decide on the basis of fairness. But in addition to growth and equity, they might also consider the likely consequences of such choices for the overall character of our lives. They might ask, for example, which arrangements best promote economic security, personal integrity, strong families, and good citizenship.

THE BIG CHOICES OF THE INDUSTRIAL ERA

At the start of the industrial era, in the latter decades of the nineteenth century and the beginning of the twentieth, Americans faced a dilemma roughly comparable to the one we face today. The emerging industrial economy posed enormous advantages in terms of cheaper and better products. Large-scale production, based on the new technologies of that era, put appliances, cars, shoes, clothing, kitchen utensils, processed foods, and a lot more within the reach of a growing middle class. But these advantages came at a price. Before then, we had been a nation mostly of small towns and self-contained communities whose economies were largely based on farming, and whose inhabitants knew one another well as friends and neighbors. Within a half-century, America was transformed into a society of large cities teeming with immigrants and the poor, of giant corporations and trusts, of widening disparities of income and wealth, and of big factories employing thousands of wage workers.

No genie asked Americans to decide if the benefits of industrialization were worth it. Instead, Americans of that era made innumerable personal choices about how they would lead their lives, based on the attractions as well as the repulsions of the new industrial order.[1] Would they leave the farm for the factory, the town for the city? Would they abandon what was comfortable and familiar in favor of what might yield a higher standard of living and would surely be more interesting? Would they encourage their children to do so?

It didn't end there. These personal choices also informed the *public* choices of the era. For example, technology expanded the scope of valuable production by nimble-fingered children, posing a starker choice than the farmwork children had always done before. Was childhood to be preserved for learning and play, or was it to be devoted to factory production? The choice could have been left to individual families, and for several decades it was. Some families chose the factory for their young children. But in time, the nation as a whole decided against child labor.

There was also a widespread belief that industrial workers needed better protection. The nation became appalled by sweatshops, in which young men and women worked long hours in unsafe conditions for little pay. Laws were passed that set minimum wages and maximum hours, with time and a half for overtime; that recognized unions and required collective bargaining; and that guarded worker health and safety through building codes, sanitation codes, and mining regulations.

As the new industrial order exposed working Americans to new kinds of economic uncertainties, there was a perceived need for social insurance—against injuries on the job, unemployment, the untimely death of an employed spouse, and inadequate retirement savings.

Economic inequality rose rapidly with industrialization. What was the newly industrialized nation to do? It seemed clear to reformers that success within the new industrial order required education beyond eighth grade. The "high-school movement" of the first decades of the twentieth century extended free public schooling through the twelfth grade, and required children's attendance until they were sixteen. Kindergartens were added as well.

In 1913, a federal income tax was initiated, and it became steadily more progressive in subsequent decades. By 1950, the highest job compensation listed in the public records of the Securities and Exchange Commission—$626,300 in 1950 dollars—was paid to Charles E. Wilson, the president of General Motors. The federal income tax on this sum (had GM paid it to Wilson in one lump) would then have been $462,000, leaving Wilson with just $164,300.[2]

Debate also raged about how to preserve and protect the habits of citizenship from the large industrial combinations that appeared to threaten it. Woodrow Wilson feared that the giant companies would erode the moral and civic foundations of American democracy unless the combinations were broken up. Theodore Roosevelt argued that a better means of keeping the advantages of large-scale enterprise while minimizing its dangers was to regulate it.[3] "Combinations in industry are the result of an imperative economic law," Roosevelt declared. "The effort at prohibiting all combination has substantially failed. The way out lies, not in attempting to prevent such combinations, but in completely controlling them in the interest of the public welfare."[4] In the end, the nation settled, as it often does, on a compromise: Antitrust laws were to be enforced in moderation, and regulatory agencies were to set rules in consultation with industry. Other nations enacted similar laws.

All these debates were, in effect, about how to achieve as much of the benefits of the new order as possible while eliminating its excesses and tempering its injustices—that is, how to attain a new social balance.

The laws, rules, and social conventions appropriate to the nineteenth-century preindustrial economy were mostly irrelevant to the new challenges of a national economy organized around wage work and dominated by giant companies. Yet it was impossible to know the path industrialization would take. The nation had to make choices based on the best information at hand, hunches about the future, and its own enduring values.

Now, we must do so again.

THE BIG CHOICES OF THE NEW ECONOMY

We are now moving rapidly into a new economy and a new society in which some of these older choices are less helpful, or obsolete. As I have noted in preceding pages, many of the regulations designed to control big corporations have been discarded because economies of scale are no longer necessary, and smaller entities can now compete effectively with large enterprises. Trust-busters are now less concerned about mere size or dominance in a given market—the economy is changing so quickly and so much of it is exposed to global competition that such static concepts are becoming irrelevant—than about "excessive stickiness," where firms gain dominance over a standard for interconnectedness, such as Microsoft's operating system. There are related debates over the future of intellectual property: Should patents be granted on genes? On business methods like one-click Internet sales? Should copyright protection be granted on mathematical formulas? on methods for cloning?

It's also dawning on many that, as I've also discussed, laws placing responsibilities on employers for wages, hours, working conditions, collective bargaining, and other aspects of employment do little to help the growing numbers of contract workers, contingent workers, free-lancers, e-lancers, commission-sales workers, managerial and professional workers, and everyone else selling their services directly in the new economy. In many parts of the economy, it is becoming difficult even to determine who's the "employer" and who's the "employee."

Similarly, the old systems of social insurance were designed for large and stable groups of people who didn't know what sorts of risks they faced individually. But the sorting mechanism is now giving wealthier and healthier citizens better private alternatives. As a result, many of the wealthier and healthier are seeking to opt out—and leave the poorer and sicker behind. There is an intensifying debate about whether Social Security should be privatized, and whether Medicare should be turned into a system of reimbursable "individual medical accounts." There's also a growing debate about group health insurance—how the groups are picked, and what happens to older or sicker people who can't get in.

Finally, as Americans self-segregate according to income, the sorting mechanism is undermining communities. Schools, parks, public recreation, libraries, and other amenities in poor and working-class areas that depend largely on local property taxes are being shortchanged. The old reliance on local funding was more appropriate when towns were composed of both rich and poor, but it is generating vast inequities today, when rich and poor are more likely to live in separate towns. The problem extends beyond financing. The schools children attend and the communities in which they are raised are critically important to their futures. Large concentrations of poor and near-poor are compounding the barriers they must overcome. Socially isolated at a time when connections count more than ever, economically segregated when career paths are blurring and manufacturing jobs disappearing, bereft of role models and social supports in a system that depends on both, young people in poor communities have limited means of gaining footholds in the new economy.

The anxieties of our time are not fundamentally different from those that surfaced at the start of the industrial era—about the stresses and insecurities of a new economy, the erosion of families and communities, widening inequalities of income and wealth, and the undermining of community. It's just that the answers the inhabitants of that era devised for dealing with these concerns—the balance they struck between what the new economic forces offered and what they cost—don't fit the economy and society that we are entering.

A debate is emerging all over the world about the merits of the new economy in terms of the quality of the lives people lead within it. The debate surfaces only sporadically and partially, like the tip of a giant floating iceberg into which all sorts of other, more particular, debates crash. French workers walk out on strike in pursuit of a thirty-five-hour maximum workweek, or against it. German industrialists, concerned about high wages and regulations making it hard to fire or demote employees, threaten to move jobs abroad. Americans march in Seattle against the World Trade Organization. In a national poll, a majority of Americans say they believe the global economy hurts average people; two-thirds worry that good jobs will move overseas, leaving Americans with jobs that don't pay enough.[5] Meanwhile, smaller nations complain about "hot money" rushing into and then suddenly out of their economies, wreaking social havoc. Right-wing movements in several countries fulminate against immigrants and foreigners, and occasionally against poor minorities in their midst; left-wing movements, against global elites who seem to float over and above nations, parking their money in tax havens, vacationing in idyllic spots, living and working in "urban glamour zones."[6] No one, it seems, is particularly fond of global corporations whose top executives appear to be greedy and rapacious, or Wall Street moguls busily "restructuring" businesses in seeming disregard of the communities they uproot or destroy in the process.

But much of the debate is misguided, and much of the blame misplaced. To the extent that there's an enemy, we've seen it, and it's us. Most of us *want* the new economy's terrific deals. All of us are consumers, and an expanding number are investors. Rapidly evolving technologies are creating a global network in which we can get exactly what we want from almost anywhere at the lowest price and highest value. We can choose widely and switch on a dime (or yuan, peso, or rupiah). In short, the culprit isn't out *there*—not in the global corporations, greedy executives, insensitive elites, immigrants, or poor minorities. It's in *here,* in our own appetites, in what we want to buy, in the great deals we want to get. People within cultures that aren't as materially prosperous as most Americans view on their satellite televisions all the gadgets and glitter of middle-class American life, and say: *We want that.* And quickly, please.

Yet the social price for all this is mounting, too. If we understood what we are really paying, we might be less enthusiastic about the deals we're getting. And so would others around the world.

Thumbs up? Thumbs down? Consider two extremes: At one extreme, this and any other society could embrace neo-Ludditism—pass laws to unplug the computers, burn the software, erect a huge tariff wall to keep out cheap foreign goods, place a chain-link fence around our borders to keep out inexpensive foreign labor, block flows of global capital, bar hostile takeovers, disempower shareholders, grant exceedingly long patent protections, preserve all our jobs just as they are, freeze-frame our neighborhoods, and stop innovation in its tracks. The society we would create by doing all these things might be serene and stable, inequalities might be diminished, and citizens might be free to devote themselves to quiet contemplation. But such a society would be very poor materially, relative to the wealth it could otherwise generate, and in various ways it would be profoundly oppressive. (By the way, do not assume that such a neo-Luddite strategy is impossible in an era of global technology. Fundamentalists, Puritans, zealots, and fanatics of many stripes have done it before; somewhere, someday, they will attempt to do it again.)

At the other extreme, we could put our foot on the accelerator and let 'er rip. We could choose the path of fastest growth, widest choice, quickest switch. Pursue this path to its logical end, and we all would be working in a giant global network. Each of our incomes would depend on continuous spot-auction bids for our services. All government supports—regulations, insurance, pooled benefits—would be dismantled as the sorting mechanism became perfectly efficient worldwide. The spectrum from exceedingly rich to exceedingly poor in every nation would exactly reflect the widest spectrum of wealth and poverty in the world. Your own position on that spectrum would depend on how hard you worked and sold yourself (and your children's eventual position, on how hard they worked to become little paragons of ambition and potential commercial value). We would overflow in material wealth, but no one would feel economically secure. And in the meantime, our society will have been pulled apart, sharply sorted, rendered indistinguishable from any other spot on the globe.

Thumbs up? Thumbs down? What do we choose? For most people, neither extreme is especially attractive. So, in the end, we're left with the question of balance.

A NEW SOCIAL BALANCE

What's the best position between these two extremes? What's the best social balance? There's no simple answer, because there's no single "best" trade-off between economic dynamism and social tranquillity. But in pursuit of an answer, you might ask yourself the same basic question Americans asked themselves a century ago when they were struggling to come to terms with what was then a new industrial order: How can we reap the advantages of the new economy while preventing its excesses and tempering its injustices?

Recall that the benefits as well as the burdens of the old industrial economy arose from stable, large-scale production. That's why reformers a century ago focused on improving the conditions of employment and constraining raw economic power. The benefits of the *new* economy, by contrast, arise from innovation and the increasing ease with which buyers can switch—to better, faster, or cheaper products from anywhere around the world, to higher-returning investments, and to the joint amenities constituting the modern "community." As we have seen, these same features of the new economy are also contributing to financial insecurity, more frenzied work, widening gaps in income and wealth, an ever more efficient sorting mechanism, and the consequent erosion of personal, family, and community life.

One way to a better social balance might be through a great moral and spiritual "reawakening" in which people rose en masse to renounce the excesses of acquisitive individualism. Such surges have occurred from time to time in history. But history reveals that their consequences have not been altogether positive. Moral fervor, once unleashed, is not easily contained. It seems safer, and more practical, to explore more modest avenues of reform. Some of these will have to be pursued by government; others are more properly left to the nonprofit sector, to faith-based institutions, universities, and social entrepreneurs.

In essence, rather than seek to preserve and protect the old jobs, old communities, and old relationships, or go to the opposite extreme and let 'er rip, a balanced society would seek to accomplish several goals:

Cushion people against sudden economic shocks. To protect individuals and families against the volatility of the new economy, there are many possibilities short of neo-Luddite measures to block choices and bar switches. One way to alleviate the sudden pressure of job loss would be to ensure that anyone who needed a job would have one. If no jobs were currently available, public-service jobs would make up the shortfall. In addition, unemployment insurance (a legacy of the industrial era, when "employment" was the norm) could be replaced with earnings insurance, designed to smooth out what might otherwise be abrupt drops in income.[7] Say your earnings dip 50 percent from one year to the next. The earnings insurance would make up half the difference. If your earnings doubled from one year to the next, you would pay some percentage of the gain into the earnings insurance fund. Such earnings insurance would help not only the poor, but also middle- and upper-income people anxious about the possibility of suddenly losing their economic footing. And such insurance would be extended to anyone, including part-time workers. We could also guarantee that all job holders receive a minimally decent income. Anyone who works at least forty hours a week would be eligible for an income supplement that brought their total earnings up to at least half the nation's median income.

To further cushion against shocks, employee benefits could be made fully portable. That is, rather than attach health and pension benefits to particular jobs through tax-favored treatment of health and retirement benefits (another vestige of the industrial era), we could uncouple such benefits from specific jobs and attach them to people instead. The tax savings could be used to supplement the health and retirement needs of workers directly, regardless of where they worked; low-income workers would get proportionately more help. All citizens would have access to affordable health insurance.

We could reduce sharp shocks to a community when business or financial capital suddenly departed by instituting *community* insurance. For example, if a community or region were to lose more than, say, 5 percent of its economic base in the course of a year, it would automatically get funds to help smooth the transition—to retrain people for different jobs, to help providers of local services slim down, to soften the decline in property values. Such insurance could be financed by a small tax on businesses or capital suddenly moving into a particular community or region. The same idea might be extended to entire nations, in the form of a small "transactions tax"—say, one tenth of 1 percent—on the value of all fast-moving global financial transactions. Not only would such a small tax throw a bit of sand in the speculative wheels of international finance, but it could also finance a stabilization fund to smooth the ups and downs of national currencies.[8]

Trade laws could be amended to provide greater relief from sudden surges of imports than is available through the so-called escape clause under current trade treaties. Now nations are eligible for such temporary trade protection only if a domestic industry is competitively injured by the surge. But *social* injury should count as well. Workers and their communities should be able to petition for temporary relief when a sudden surge of imports threatens substantial job dislocation and community abandonment.

Widen the circle of prosperity. Inequalities of income and wealth are wider than they have been since the early years of industrialization, in the late nineteenth and early twentieth centuries. What can be done? Most of the people who have been losing out are those lacking an adequate education—the first prerequisite to success in the new economy. So the best investment in their future prosperity is to improve their store of "human capital." More on this in a moment. But education takes considerable time. And even if children from poorer homes were learning like mad, they'd still start off their adult lives at a severe disadvantage. Education doesn't address their social disadvantages, their isolation and lack of connections. It also doesn't address their lack of capital assets.

Another means of extending prosperity, therefore, would be to make capital assets more accessible. For many years, the capital-asset elevator has been lifting America's wealthy ever-higher without their moving a muscle (except, perhaps, to speed-dial their brokers). The biggest single consequence of the 1990s bull market was to make those who were already rich before 1991 fabulously richer. Even if and when the stock market sags, the long-term outlook for capital assets is unremittingly bright. So in addition to better schools, we might consider providing every young person in America, upon reaching the age of eighteen, a financial "nest egg" of, say, $60,000, which he or she could then reinvest in additional education, a business venture, stocks and bonds, or some combination of these. Such endowments would be financed by a small wealth tax on the very richest among us.[9]

Give caring attention to those who need it most. How can we ensure that children, the elderly, and the disabled receive the caring attention they need? As I've noted, people who are paid to provide such caring attention—nurse's aides, home health-care aides, nursing-home aides, child-care workers, schoolteachers, social workers—do some of our society's most important and humane work. Society as a whole could pay them substantially more, provided they meet adequate standards of performance. Beyond higher pay, these workers also deserve higher status in society, and more respect. Higher pay and more respect would make these jobs attractive to skilled people, and give people more reason to get the skills these jobs really require.

Furthermore, we could take up where Progressive reformers left off a century ago when they created kindergartens. Given the demands of the new economy upon families, it would seem reasonable to extend schooling downward to include three- and four-year-olds and offer them safe and stimulating preschool programs. It also seems reasonable to extend the school day outward for all school-age children, with supervised play and study until most of their parents have finished work in the evening.

Businesses should be encouraged—perhaps required—to offer parents flexible time to do their work, and paid leave to care for a young child or an elderly relative in need. Many firms already offer these amenities to their high-paid creative workers, but few such benefits are available further down the hierarchy. And businesses, as I've pointed out, are quickly transforming themselves into contractual networks in which fewer workers are "employees" in the old sense. Thus, such requirements on employers may be less effective over the long term than direct public supports for people who work. One such support could be made available through the tax system. Because the costs of child care (and, often, of caring for an elderly relative) are literally "business expenses" that would not be incurred absent paid work, such expenses might be made fully deductible from income taxes.

A society intent on giving caring attention to its young children would, in addition, acknowledge that parenting isn't just a private role but also an important social responsibility. Any parent who decided to remain at home with a child under the age of three would be eligible for financial support equaling half the nation's median income. Such support could come in the form of a refundable tax credit.

Reverse the sorting mechanism. The sorting mechanism is at its most pernicious when it comes to schools, whose quality now largely depends on the incomes of the families residing in the school district. Because families are sorting by income into different townships, and because about half of school funding still comes from local property taxes, families whose children are most at risk of failing in the new economy cannot afford the schools they most need. A society intent on reaping the advantages of economic dynamism while minimizing its social injustices would shift school financing away from local property taxes. One option would be to replace local property taxes by a national education trust fund, financed by a small tax on the net worth of all citizens.

School vouchers might improve the quality of schools, but we would need to guard against the possibility that the poorest children with the biggest learning or behavioral problems would get sorted together into the least desirable schools. One way to avoid this would be to make the size of the voucher proportional to family needs. Children from the very poorest families would have the largest and most valuable vouchers, thereby making the children sufficiently attractive for good schools to want to compete for them.

A way to break up high concentrations of poverty would be to give all poor families housing-assistance vouchers, enabling them to afford homes in higher-income communities. Preliminary evidence suggests that poor children of families who have the opportunity to move to higher-income neighborhoods do better than the children who remain behind in the poor ones.[10] In addition, we could require that housing developers include in their plans for upscale communities a certain proportion of low-income residences. "Inclusionary zoning" like this has met with considerable success in specific places around the nation. And we could bar private insurers from imposing higher-risk premiums on people because of where they live, what they earn, or their genetic makeup.

We could seek many other opportunities for different communities of race, income, and age to interact with one another. In fact, such bridging could become an overarching goal of community-based non-profit organizations. Faith-based institutions would seem uniquely qualified to reach across such divides. Universities could link up with poor high schools and grammar schools in their region; their undergraduates could tutor in such schools, university faculty could teach occasional classes and keep the faculties of the schools apprised of new research, and promising high-school seniors could be given university scholarships.

PROPOSALS such as these are points of departure rather than a full agenda of reform. They are merely a sampling of what might be done, fodder for debate about what should be done. The basic idea common to all of them is this: Rather than preserve and protect the old, or go to the opposite extreme and let rip with the new, a balanced society would ease the economic transitions and bring most of its people along, so that citizens' lives could be materially better, more cohesive and equitable, and psychologically saner. Although this path won't be paved cheaply, a dynamic economy can well afford the cost; and I believe the cost is worth accepting for the sake of social and personal tranquillity.

Some will argue that the better-off members of society should not be required to foot most of the bill for initiatives like these, and that they will refuse to do so if they are asked. In a pinch, they'll move themselves and their personal fortunes to the Netherlands Antilles, or to any other comfortable retreat around the world. But I think this view is far too cynical. The sorting mechanism is a powerful force, to be sure, but the vast majority of better-off citizens feel allegiance to their society, and want to keep it from becoming further fractured and stratified. In fact, the sorting mechanism may itself have discouraged some people from taking a more active role, since any singular sacrifice on their part—say, moving into a poorer community than they could afford to live in, or sending their children to one of its schools—would impose a larger burden on them than would be the case if richer and poorer were better mingled to begin with.

Sorting may also have blinded the better-off to the conditions in which the less fortunate actually live, allowing the better off to pretend that almost everyone else is "like them." Reversing the sorting mechanism would help restore a sense of common ground. In addition, the better off will be more willing to contribute if they understand that the likely alternative is an eventual backlash against economic dynamism—including trade protections and neo-Luddite controls on technology—that will be far more costly to them in the long run. A yawning gap between rich and poor threatens the peace and stability of society, including its better-off members. Finally, it seems likely that some of the better off would prefer more economic security in their own lives, and a lower risk that they or their families might suddenly lose economic ground.

THE THREE CONVERSATIONS

We stand at the precipice of a new era. The economic and technological forces that have been building for more than two decades are about to crest, and thereby change our personal and social lives even more profoundly than they have been affected so far. There is no turning back to the old jobs and the old securities, to the old families and the old communities. So where do we turn? We delight in the terrific deals of the new economy. We stand in awe of its technological prowess. We are dazzled by the instant opportunities it presents for vast wealth. Yet where is the moral anchor? To what do we attach ourselves, our loyalties and our passions? Where do our friends, families, and communities come in? In what do we invest our integrity? How, in the end, shall we measure success—our own, as well as our society's?

The measure of a successful life surely goes beyond what we can acquire or the extent of our net worth; the test of a successful society extends beyond its gross national product. Success depends on our spiritual grounding, the richness of our relationships, the sturdiness of our families, and the character of our communities. Yet most of us are racing into this new era with remarkable insouciance—blindness, perhaps—toward what it means for our lives beyond our roles as consumers and investors.

Rather than debate the larger trade-offs, we're engaged in at least three separate conversations. The first is a breathlessly enthusiastic one, about the wonders of the new economy. That economy's terrific deals are very real, and will vastly improve those aspects of our lives that can be enhanced by what we buy. In a few years, through broadband and wireless Internet connections, as well as advances in molecular and genetic research, today's terrific deals will be overshadowed by even better ones. Many products and services will be cheaper, faster, more powerful. Some will enable us to live longer, or be more readily entertained, invigorated, stimulated, and interconnected. The dizzying exuberance of the new economy is justified. But the terrific deals alone don't prove that the price we pay for them with the rest of our lives is worth it.

The second conversation is a fearful one, about the dangers and depredations of unfettered capitalism, the power or greed of global corporations and international finance, and, sometimes, the encroachments of immigrants, foreigners, and ethnic minorities. These concerns can be heard with increasing vehemence on both the left and the right of the political spectrum, in America and elsewhere around the world. Given the scale of the dislocations wrought by the new economy—dislocations and upheavals that are only beginning—it's entirely understandable that many people will be afraid or disoriented and many others will feel unfairly burdened. For several decades, factory workers in advanced economies have experienced job loss and declining incomes. What happens when many salaried, professional, and service workers experience the same things? But this fearful conversation misplaces the blame. It assumes that the cause of the upheavals lies in corporations, globalization, international capital flows, or in the flows of immigrants and ethnic minorities. It thereby confuses causes with consequences. Corporations, capital flows, and immigrants are responding to the widening range of choice open to consumers and investors around the world, the increasing ease by which all can switch to better deals, and the intensifying competition that results. Some of those who complain loudest are simultaneously reaping great benefits from the new economy.

The third conversation is a private one, about the difficulties of achieving a balanced life in this new era. As we work harder and sell ourselves more intensely, and as we adopt the market-directed (have the "Courage to Be Rich"!) ethos of our age, many of us are anxious about what's becoming of our families, our friendships, our broader communities, and even our innermost selves. Yet we tend to view this unease in solely personal terms. To the extent that we feel we're failing in one domain or the other, we blame ourselves for being "inadequate" parents, spouses, workers, friends, or citizens. We thus overlook the larger forces that are making all such personal attempts to achieve "better balance" more difficult or complicated.

These three separate conversations are different responses to the same set of phenomena. Some of us might even be engaged in all three conversations simultaneously without seeing the connections between them. We may delight in the terrific deals we can obtain, while we also fret about what seem like encroachments by global corporations, trade, and immigrants, and at the same time worry about the personal demands our work is exacting from the rest of our lives. But if we are to deal effectively with the larger trade-off before us, we must understand the connections between these three conversations.

It is time for a larger discussion about what combination of economic dynamism and social tranquillity we want for ourselves, our families, and our society; and about the public choices we need to make in order to achieve this balance. What is the proper measure of success in the Age of the Terrific Deal? The new economy confers vast benefits, but it also generates social dislocations and personal stresses. All are intensifying. We will shortly be presented with vastly better deals and greater opportunities. Yet we, and every society, will have to cope with a much greater degree of social upheaval, and to struggle more arduously with the escalating demands of work on the rest of our lives.

This cannot be—it must not be—solely an economic conversation. It is more fundamentally a moral one. We are not mere instruments of the new economy. We are not slaves to its technological trends. And we should not misdirect the blame for its less desirable, more worrisome consequences. As citizens, we have the power to arrange the new economy to suit our needs, and in so doing to determine the shape of our emerging civilization. Every society has the capacity—indeed, the obligation—to make these choices. Markets are structured by them. Families and communities function according to them. Individuals balance their lives within them. It is through such decisions that a society defines itself. The choices will be made, somehow. They cannot be avoided. The question is whether we make the most important of these choices together, in the open, or grapple with them alone and in the dark.

INTRODUCTION

1. Data mentioned in this introduction are included in more detail within the book, as are the relevant citations.

ONE: THE AGE OF THE TERRIFIC DEAL

1. This discussion owes an intellectual debt to the eminent political economist Albert Hirschman, who once listed "exit" as one of three rational responses by individuals to firms, organizations, and governments that were in decline. By "exit" he meant abandonment of a failing firm, organization, or government, in pursuit of a better situation elsewhere. The two other responses he listed were "voice" and "loyalty." Rather than abandon a difficult situation, the individual either would voice his concern and seek improvement through negotiation, deliberation, and compromise; or would simply stay put out of loyalty to the firm, organization, or political entity. Arguably, of the three responses, exit has been America's preferred one. The nation was founded by individuals who had left other places where life was proving difficult in pursuit of something better. In the emerging economy, as I argue, exit is not a response reserved only for organizations that are failing or deteriorating. Now, and increasingly in the future, people will exit quickly from any commercial relationship, regardless of how satisfactory, when a better deal comes along. See Albert Hirschman, *Exit, Voice, and Loyalty: Responses to Decline in Firms, Organizations, and States* (Cambridge: Harvard University Press, 1970).
2. The data show that Americans continue to be on the move, although not necessarily at a higher rate than thirty years ago. See *Statistical Abstract of the*

United States, 1999, Section 1, Table 30. See also Sally Ann Schumaker and Daniel Stokols, "Residential Mobility as a Social and Research Topic," *Journal of Social Issues,* vol. 38, no. 3 (1982), pp. 1–19. See also data cited in *The Economist,* September 20, 1997, p. 27.

3. Frederick Jackson Turner's notable essay is called "The Significance of the Frontier in American History," 1893, reprinted in Turner, *The Frontier in American History* (New York: Henry Holt, 1920), p. 38.

4. Horace Greeley popularized the phrase "Go West, young man," but did not originate it. It came from John Babsone Lane Soule, in an article first published in the *Terre Haute* (Indiana) *Express* in 1851. Moreover, Greeley did not urge every young man to go West, but only those with nothing better to do. "The best business you can get into you will find on your father's farm or workshop," he advised. "If you have no farm or friends to aid you, and no prospect open to you there, turn your face to the great West, and there build a home and fortune." In "To Aspiring Young Men," quoted in James Parton, *Life of Horace Greeley* (1855).

5. The essential elements of the planning system for mass production are described in John Kenneth Galbraith's *The New Industrial State* (Boston: Houghton Mifflin, 1967).

6. Readers interested in a more detailed description of the shift from the stable high-volume production system of the industrial age to the "high-value" system of the information age can find it in my book *The Work of Nations* (New York: Alfred A. Knopf, 1991), especially chapter 7.

7. Adam Smith, *The Wealth of Nations* (1776), Book 1, Chapter III (New York: Modern Library, 1994), p. 19.

8. For an abundance of evidence of the declining costs of moving objects, services, people, and messages across distances, see Frances Caincross, *The Death of Distance* (Cambridge: Harvard University Press, 1997).

9. Even such business services as advertising, marketing, law, finance, and consulting, which used to be provided in close proximity to clients and customers, are moving greater distances away. Evidence can be found in Jed Kolko, "Can I Get Some Service Here? Information Technology, Service Industries, and the Future of Cities," unpublished ms., Harvard University, November 1999.

10. The calculation is credited to Federal Reserve chairman Alan Greenspan. See David Wessel, "From Greenspan, a (Truly) Weighty Idea," *Wall Street Journal,* May 20, 1999, p. B1. See also Alan Greenspan, "Goods Shrink and Trade Grows," *Wall Street Journal,* October 24, 1988, p. 21.

11. Even as search engines become quicker and more sophisticated, the number of Web sites continues to mushroom. There's no reason to suppose that search engines will ever be able to assess more than a small percentage of the sites. Lisa Guernsey, "Seek—But on the Web, You Might Not Find," *New York Times,* July 8, 1999, p. B8.

TWO: THE SPIRIT OF INNOVATION

1. One commendably candid example of neo-Luddite logic is Jeremy Rifkin's *The End of Work* (New York: Putnam, 1995). "Caught in the throes of increasing global competition and rising costs of labor, multinational corporations seem determined to hasten the transition from human workers to machine surrogates" (p. 6).

2. Further discussion of the relationship between unstable markets and changes in the organization of the firm can be found in my book *The Next American Frontier* (New York: Times Books, 1993), and also in M. Piore and C. Sabel, *The Second Industrial Divide* (New York: Basic Books, 1994). A formal treatment can be found in Masanao Aoki, "Horizontal and Vertical Information Structure of the Firm," *American Economic Review*, vol. 76, No. 6, pp. 971–83. See also D. Thesmar and M. Thoenig, "Creative Destruction and Firm Organization Choice: A New Look Into the Growth Inequality Relationship," unpublished ms., presented at the National Bureau of Economic Research Summer Institute, Cambridge, Mass., July 19, 1999.

3. For more on Joseph Schumpeter, see Robert Heilbroner's insightful treatise on the lives of notable economists, *The Worldly Philosophers* (New York: Simon & Schuster, 1953), p. 238.

4. Schumpeter's glum predictions can be found in his *Capitalism, Socialism, and Democracy* (New York: Harper & Brothers, 1942).

5. The number of new patent-related lawsuits exploded from 800 in 1980 to more than 2,100 in 1997, according to a review of federal court records by Eugene Quinn, Jr., of the Franklin Pierce Law Center. Reported in Richard Korman, "Lo! Here Come the Technology Patents. Lo! Here Come the Lawsuits!" *New York Times*, December 27, 1998, Section 3, p. 4.

6. Company value per employee is found simply by dividing the total capitalization of the company by the number of employees. By the time you read this, both the numerators and the denominators are likely to have changed, but the value per employee is likely to remain in the same broad range.

7. For more on the small, entrepreneurial companies of southern California, see Joel Kotkin, "The Rise and Fall of the Big Bureaucratic Organization," *American Enterprise*, January 1, 2000, pp. 30–33.

8. See Sam Allis, "Harvard Ponders Marketing on the Net," *Boston Globe*, September 19, 1999, p. A1.

9. Microsoft obviously disagrees with the proposition that its operating system should be available to all competitors and all product developers free of charge because it has become a basic standard akin to a generic name like "aspirin." In this respect, it's not without irony that Microsoft demanded that AOL establish a common standard for "instant messaging" so that Microsoft users could gain easy access.

The rise of industrial standards and the importance of standards for spurring innovation during the first decades of the twentieth century have not received the attention they deserve. The best discussions I've found are in Robert H. Wiebe, *The Search for Order 1877–1920* (New York: Hill and Wang, 1967); Louis Galambos and Joseph Pratt, *The Rise of the Corporate Commonwealth* (New York: Basic Books, 1988); and Ellis W. Hawley, *The New Deal and the Problem of Monopoly* (Princeton, N.J.: Princeton University Press, 1966).

THREE: OF GEEKS AND SHRINKS

1. For a formal argument that increases in the supply of skills more than proportionately increase the demand for skilled people by altering research and development activity, see Daron Acemoglu, "Why Do New Technologies Complement Skills? Directed Technical Change and Wage Inequality," *The Quarterly Journal of Economics,* vol. 113, No. 4 (1998), p. 1105.

2. For evidence on the effects of information technologies for magnifying good ideas and allowing them to spread more quickly through organizations, and to diffuse more rapidly to clients and customers, see T. Bresnahan, E. Brynjolfsson, and L. Hitt, "Information Technology, Workplace Organization, and the Demand for Skilled Labor," National Bureau of Economic Research Working Paper no. 7136, May 1999. See also L. Katz, "Technological Change, Computerization, and the Wage Structure," in E. Brynjolfsson and B. Kahin, eds., *Understanding the Digital Economy* (Cambridge: MIT Press, 2000).

3. Ellen Langer's provocative book is entitled *The Power of Mindful Learning* (Reading, Mass.: Perseus Books, 1997), and the quote is found on p. 114.

4. The passage by Annie Dillard is found in her small, lovely volume on the craft of writing, *The Writing Life* (New York: HarperPerennial, 1990), p. 56.

5. Quoted in Nina Munk, "The Eminence of Excess," *New York Times Magazine,* August 15, 1999, pp. 47–8.

6. Research analysts are spending more of their time advising and less of their time gathering information, which is what you'd expect as they shift from being information brokers to becoming knowledge brokers. In one study of major investment research firms in the late 1990s, conducted by Tempest Consultants for Reuters Group, analysts were asked how they allocated their time. The amount of time spent on fundamental research, including company visits, steadily dropped, while the amount of time spent advising institutional clients steadily rose. See Gretchen Morgenson, "So Many Analysts, So Little Analysis," *New York Times,* July 18, 1999, Section 3, p. 1.

7. "Ink," *The New Yorker,* April 6, 1998, p. 41.

FOUR: THE OBSOLESCENCE OF LOYALTY

1. For evidence on the declining importance of corporate headquarters in relation to their "hometowns," see Charles H. Heying, "Civic Elites and

Corporate Delocalization: An Alternative Explanation for Declining Civic Engagement," *American Behavioral Scientist,* vol. 40, no. 5 (1997), pp. 657–68.

2. Quoted in *Fortune,* October 1951, p. 98.

3. Quoted in Ian Somerville and D. Quinn Mills, "Leading in a Leaderless World," *Leader to Leader,* Summer 1999, p. 32.

4. Data on executive compensation are available in the proxy statements filed with the Securities and Exchange Commission. These data have been accumulated and analyzed by Graef Crystal, who for many years published his findings in a series of "Crystal Reports." At this writing, Crystal distributes his studies through Bloomberg Business News. See, for example, Graef Crystal and Brian Rooney, "CEO Pay Soars, Supercharged by Options: Bloomberg Pay Survey," Bloomberg Business News, at Bloomberg.com, April 19, 2000.

5. A study of 1,300 occasions between 1980 and 1996 when chief executives at Fortune 500 firms left their jobs revealed that one-third left involuntarily. Controlling for level of performance, a chief executive appointed after 1985 was three times more likely to be fired as one appointed before that date. See Rakesh Khurana, "Transitions at the Top: CEO Positions as Open and Closed to Competition," Sloan School of Management, Massachusetts Institute of Technology, working paper, 2000. See also Jay Lorsch and Rakesh Khurana, "Changing Leaders: The Board's Role in CEO Succession," *Harvard Business Review,* vol. 77, no. 3 (1999), p. 96.

6. Quoted in Steve Lohr, "Compaq Computer Ousts Chief Executive," *New York Times,* April 19, 1999, p. A17.

7. Quoted in Ellen Schultz and Susan Warren, "Pension System Ousts Company's Board in Big Victory for Institutional Investors," *Wall Street Journal,* May 29, 1998, p. A2.

8. Evidence that the growing threat of hostile takeovers has resulted in more cost-cutting, including lower wages for employees and a higher likelihood of plant closures—thus improving productivity but hurting incumbent workers and managers—has been documented by Marianne Bertrand of Princeton and Sendhil Mullainathan of MIT, who undertook a number of studies using state antitakeover laws in the 1980s as "exogenous" measures of changes in takeover threats facing firms chartered in different states. See M. Bertrand and S. Mullainathan, "Micro-evidence of the Effects of Corporate Governance," Massachusetts Institute of Technology, 1999; and M. Bertrand and S. Mullainathan, "Executive Compensation and Incentives: The Effect of Takeover Legislation," National Bureau of Economic Research, No. 6830, December 1998. See also Paul Osterman, "Work Reorganization in an Era of Restructuring: Trends in Diffusion and Effects on Employee Welfare," *Industrial and Labor Relations Review,* vol. 53, no. 2 (January 2000), p. 179.

9. Quoted in "Xerox to Cut 9,000 Jobs, Saving $1 Billion," *New York Times,* April 8, 1998, pp. D1–D2.

10. Quoted in Constance Hays, "Coca-Cola to Cut 20 Percent of Employees in a Big Pullback," *New York Times,* January 17, 2000, p. A1.

11. Described in Marcia Stepanek, "How an Intranet Opened the Door to Profits," *Business Week,* July 26, 1999, p. EB32.

12. Described in Aaron Bernstein, "Welch's March to the South," *Business Week,* December 6, 1999, p. 74.

13. Commission on the Future of Worker-Management Relations, "Fact Finding Report" (Washington, D.C.: U.S. Department of Labor, May 1994).

14. For evidence on the growth of non-unionized sectors of the economy, see Henry Farber and Bruce Westera, "Round Up the Usual Suspects: The Decline of Unions in the Private Sector, 1973–1998," Industrial Relations Section, Princeton University, Working Paper No. 437, April, 2000.

15. See analyses by the Securities Industry Association, Washington, D.C., which are drawn from the Federal Reserve System's "Ownership of Long-Term Securities Benchmark Survey." The most recent data are from 1999.

16. Pohle and Chirac are quoted in Greg Steinmetz and Michael Sesit, "Tighter Ship: U.S. Investors Bring More than Cash on European Tour," *Wall Street Journal Europe,* August 4, 1999, p. A1.

17. Ibid.

18. From Alan Friedman, "Executives in Europe Demand Reforms," *International Herald Tribune,* August 2, 1999, p. 1.

19. The extent of layoffs at Nissan, NEC, and Sony is from company reports and briefings.

20. Quoted in Annalee Saxenian, "Beyond Boundaries: Open Labor Markets and Learning in Silicon Valley," in Michael Arthur and Denise Rousseau, eds., *The Boundaryless Career* (New York: Oxford University Press, 1996), p. 28.

21. Heath Row, "This Virtual Company Is Real," *Fast Company,* December–January 1998, p. 48.

FIVE: THE END OF EMPLOYMENT AS WE KNEW IT

1. Laurence Zuckerman, "Agent to the Software Stars," *New York Times,* September 8, 1997, p. D1.

2. Orestes Brownson, "The Laboring Classes" (1840), reprinted in Joseph L. Blau, ed., *Social Theories of Jacksonian Democracy* (Indianapolis: Bobbs-Merrill, 1954), pp. 306–7, 309–10.

3. Abraham Lincoln, "Speech at Kalamazoo, Michigan" (August 27, 1856), in Roy P. Basler, ed., *The Collected Works of Abraham Lincoln,* vol. II (New Brunswick, N.J.: Rutgers University Press, 1953), p. 364.

4. The Knights' grand master, Terence Powderly, explicitly called for an abolition of the wage system in his "Address to the General Assembly of the Knights of Labor" (1880), reprinted in Powderly, *The Path I Trod* (New York: Columbia University Press, 1940), p. 268.

5. *Historical Statistics of the United States, Colonial Times to 1970*, vol. 1 (Washington, D.C.: U.S. Government Printing Office, U.S. Bureau of the Census, 1975).

6. "Testimony Before the Industrial Commission," Washington, D.C., April 18, 1899, reprinted in Gompers, *Labor and the Employer* (New York: E. P. Dutton, 1920), p. 291.

7. "Labor and Its Attitude Toward Trusts," *American Federationist,* vol. 14 (1907), p. 881.

8. Woodrow Wilson, *The New Freedom,* ed. William E. Leuchtenburg (Englewood Cliffs, N.J.: Prentice-Hall, 1961), pp. 26–7.

9. 198 US 45, 61 (1905).

10. 108 US 412, 418 (1908).

11. National Conference on Social Welfare, The Report of the Committee on Economic Security of 1935, 50th Anniversary Edition, Washington, D.C., 1985, p. 56.

12. U.S. Office of Management and Budget, Special Analysis of the Budget of the U.S. Government (Washington, D.C.), various issues.

13. William H. Whyte, Jr., was an editor of *Fortune* magazine when his book about the conformist culture of America's emerging white-collar class, *The Organization Man* (New York: Simon & Schuster, 1956), was published.

14. The 1952 survey was included in a book published by *Fortune* called *The Executive Life* (Garden City, N.Y.: Doubleday, 1956), p. 30.

15. Whyte, op. cit., pp. 143, 145.

16. Ibid., p. 146.

17. Sloan Wilson, *The Man in the Gray Flannel Suit* (Mattituck, N.Y.: Amereon House, 1955).

18. E. P. Thompson, "Time, Work Discipline, and Industrial Capitalism," *Past & Present, A Journal of Historical Studies,* no. 38 (December 1967), pp. 56–97.

19. Quoted in "Norman Vincent Peale Answers Your Questions," *Look,* March 6, 1955. Cited in Whyte, op. cit., p. 282.

20. *Sales Management,* January 15, 1952. Cited in ibid., pp. 288 n.3, 394.

21. J. Kahl, *The American Class Structure* (New York: Holt, Rinehart, 1956), pp. 109–10.

22. Evidence shows that earnings have become less stable, although not necessarily jobs. Researchers usually focus on several variables—"job stability," meaning the duration of jobs or the probability of retaining or leaving one; "job security," meaning the likelihood of experiencing involuntary job loss; and "earnings stability," meaning the variation in earnings from one time period to another. In the industrial economy of wage work the three typically went together, but that has become less the case. For a sampling of recent research, see Daniel Aaronson and Daniel G. Sullivan, "The Decline of Job Security in the 1990s: Displacement, Anxiety, and Their Effect on Wage Growth," *Economic Perspectives,* First Quarter 1998, pp. 17–43; Henry Farber,

"Trends in Long Term Employment in the United States, 1979–1996," *Industrial Relations Section Working Paper* no. 384 (Princeton, N.J.: Princeton University, July 17, 1997). See also U.S. Bureau of Labor Statistics, "Employee Tenure in the Mid-1990s," January 30, 1997; and Peter Gottschalk and Robert Moffitt, "The Growth of Earnings Instability in the US Labor Market," *Brookings Papers on Economic Activity*, no. 2 (1994). For an attempt to reconcile what seem to be several conflicting strands of evidence, see David Neumark, "Changes in Job Stability and Job Security: A Collective Effort to Untangle, Reconcile, and Interpret the Evidence," *National Bureau of Economic Research Working Paper* no. 7472 (January 2000).

23. Measures vary considerably, depending on how such work is defined. The Labor Department's Bureau of Labor Statistics has estimated that a relatively small portion of the workforce falls within these categories—no more than 8 to 10 percent—while other estimates range as high as 30 percent. See Barry Bluestone and Stephen Rose, "Overworked and Underemployed," *The American Prospect*, March–April 1997, p. 60.

24. Variable pay plans are rapidly becoming the norm. In a survey of almost 3,000 U.S. and Canadian employers conducted by the American Compensation Association of Scottsdale, Arizona, in August 1998, 86 percent said they already had variable pay plans, and 35 percent planned to place more emphasis on variable pay over merit pay. In a summer 1998 survey of 1,069 employers by Hewitt Associates of Lincolnshire, Illinois, 72 percent said they offered at least one variable pay plan (up from 61 percent in 1996), 63 percent offered stock and stock-option plans, and 55 percent planned to extend stock options down the organizational ladder in 1999. See generally "Pay Is Rising, Thanks to Sweeteners in a Tight Labor Market," *New York Times*, August 30, 1998, p. B11.

25. Dale Belman and Erica Goshen, "Small Consolation: The Dubious Benefits of Small Business for Job Growth and Wages," Washington, D.C.: Economic Policy Institute, June 30, 1998.

26. Barry Bearak, "Behind the Wheel: Long Hours and Hard Feelings," *New York Times*, May 15, 1998, p. A1.

27. Substantial political and journalistic attention has been paid to the increasing number of Americans lacking health insurance, less to the increasing number who must pay higher premiums, co-payments, and deductibles for the health care they do receive. The consequence of these higher payments is often to deter people from using medical services. For data on the decline in employer-provided health coverage, see Lawrence Mishel, Jared Bernstein, and John Schmitt, *The State of Working America, 1998–99* (Ithaca, N.Y.: Cornell University Press, 1999), pp. 146–7.

28. For evidence on universities' increasing dependence on contract workers, see Michael S. McPherson and Morton Owen Shapiro, "Tenure Issues in Higher Education," *Journal of Economic Perspectives*, Winter 1999.

29. David Marcotte, "Evidence of a Fall in the Wage Premium of Job Security," Center for Governmental Studies, Northern Illinois University, 1994; see also Barry Bluestone and Stephen Rose, "Overworked and Underemployed," *The American Prospect*, March–April 1997.

30. A survey conducted by the National Science Foundation and the U.S. Census Bureau shows very high levels of attrition among software engineers. It was cited by Normal Matloft, "Now Hiring! If You're Young," *New York Times*, January 26, 1998, p. A23.

31. One reason older and middle-aged people who lose their jobs are having more trouble finding new ones that pay as well as the old is that firms seem to be reluctant to invest in new training associated with new technology for older workers for whom there will be a shorter payoff period. For evidence, see William J. Baumol and Edward N. Wolff, "Speed of Technical Progress and Length of the Average Interjob Period," Jerome Levy Economics Institute, Working Paper no. 237, May 1998, Annandale-on-Hudson, N.Y. See also a survey by Exec-U-Net Outplacement Service, Norwalk, Connecticut, of 400 executives who had searched for a new job. The older the applicant, the fewer the interviews and the longer the search. Applicants aged forty-one to forty-five took 18 percent longer to find a job than applicants thirty-five to forty; those forty-six to fifty took 24 percent longer; those fifty-one to fifty-five, 44 percent longer; those fifty-six to sixty, 66 percent longer. Reported in Daniel M. Gold, "In Executive Job Hunts, Experience Doesn't Matter," *New York Times*, October 25, 1998, Business, p. 10.

32. Every March, Census Bureau researchers conduct a large-scale survey of American incomes. The Current Population Survey, as it's called, uses a very broad definition of income, including public assistance and other cash-transfer payments, as well as wages and salaries. But it does not measure capital gains or the benefits of home ownership, and incomes are measured in such a way as to understate very large ones. Thus the CPS can be assumed to be a very conservative measure of inequality. Data are collected on "families" (two or more related people living together) and on "households" (not just families, but also people living alone and unrelated people living together). Average income for families is higher across the spectrum than for households, since people living alone drag down the household figures, and inequality is likewise more pronounced among households.

33. A close reading of the data suggests that the increase in wage and income inequality may have been somewhat greater during the 1980s than in the 1990s. That makes sense, to the extent that the strong economic expansion that began in 1991 and continued through the nineties entailed a substantial increase in the demand for labor, and a corresponding decline in the rate of unemployment. As a result, workers at the bottom rungs of the economic ladder were paid more than they would be if demand were softer, and they also had more opportunity to work longer hours. The 1990s comparisons are

a bit distorted by the redesign of the Current Population Survey in 1994 (beginning with 1993 incomes), which led to a one-time large jump in income inequality in 1993.

34. U.S. Department of Commerce, Bureau of the Census, *Historical Data from the Current Population Survey,* revised September 1999 and supplement.

35. The analysis of who gained from the stock-market boom of the 1990s is from Professor Edward N. Wolff of New York University, who regularly analyzes data from the Federal Reserve Board's surveys of consumer finances. Edward Wolff, "Recent Trends in the Size Distribution of Household Wealth," *The Journal of Economic Perspectives,* vol. 12, no. 3 (1998), p. 131.

36. *Report of the 1994–96 Advisory Council on Social Security,* vol. 2 (Washington, D.C., 1997), p. 30.

37. People who deny that inequality is a problem also allege that inequality data from the Current Population Survey ignore the significant effects of taxes and transfer programs. But it turns out that inequality increased between 1980 and 1998 to an even greater degree when measured after taxes and transfers are figured in. See Census Web site, www.census.gov/hhes/www/income.html, Table RDI-5.

38. Studies that track consistent sets of people over time show only limited mobility. Relatively few families in the lower rungs move upward. Roughly six out of ten children who started life in families in the bottom fifth of income in the early 1970s were still there ten years later. See Peter Gottschalk, "Inequality, Income Growth, and Mobility: The Basic Facts," *Journal of Economic Perspectives,* vol. 11, no. 2 (Spring 1997).

39. Scott Thurm, "Silicon Valley Reveals Signs of Growing Disparity," *Wall Street Journal Europe,* January 11, 2000, p. 6, summarizing a report by Joint Venture: Silicon Valley Network, January 2000.

40. *The Economist,* February 26, 2000, p. 43.

SIX: THE LURE OF HARD WORK

1. The estimate of just under 2,000 hours a year for pay, for the average adult working American, comes from dividing total hours worked in the entire economy during the year by the average level of employment over the year. Because some people enter and leave the workforce during the year, however, the actual number of people with work experience is larger than the average level of employment—which means that *average annual hours for everyone with work experience* during the year is correspondingly lower. Either way you figure it, there's been a substantial increase in hours worked. Calculated the first way, average annual hours go from 1,905 in 1979 to 1,976 in 1999—an increase of almost two weeks. Calculated the second way, they go from 1,637 in 1979 to 1,776 in 1999—an increase of almost three and a half

weeks. See generally *Report on the American Workforce* (Washington, D.C.: U.S. Department of Labor, 1999).

2. Nations use different means to measure work time. In the United States, the measurements depend on people's subjective assessments of the time they put in on the job. Many European countries measure only "official hours" as reported by employers. Nonetheless, since every nation's measures are used consistently over time, there's no reason to doubt the trends. See "Key Indicators of the Labour Market, 1999" (Geneva, Switzerland: International Labor Organization, September 1999).

3. Data are as of 1997, the most recent date for which they're available at this writing. From 1969 to 1997, the proportion of married couples in which both partners work for pay grew from 36 percent to 68 percent. These and other related data are summarized in "Families and the Labor Market, 1969–1999: Analyzing the 'Time Crunch,'" a report of the President's Council of Economic Advisers, Washington, D.C., May 1999.

4. Among the first researchers to point out what appeared to be a trend toward increasing hours in paid work was Juliet Schor, in *The Overworked American* (New York: Basic Books, 1991). Her conclusions have been disputed by John Robinson and Geoffrey Godbey, *Time for Life* (State College: Pennsylvania State University Press, 1997). But debates among researchers about precisely how many hours Americans are putting in for pay, and whose hours are growing the most or the fastest, extend beyond Schor and Robinson-Godbey.

5. Robinson and Godbey, *ibid.*

6. Alice Walker, *In Search of Our Mothers' Gardens* (New York: Harcourt Brace Jovanovich, 1984), p. 238.

7. Lawrence L. Knutson, "Oldest U.S. Worker, at 102, Says His Job Still a 'Pleasure,'" *Boston Globe*, March 13, 1998, p. A3.

8. Ellen Langer, *The Power of Mindful Learning* (Reading, Mass.: Perseus, 1997), p. 58.

9. Arlie Russell Hochschild, *The Time Bind: When Work Becomes Home and Home Becomes Work* (New York: Henry Holt and Co., 1997).

10. Quoted in Fritz Stern, *Einstein's German World* (Princeton, N.J.: Princeton University Press, 1999).

11. Henry David Thoreau, *Walden,* conclusion (1854).

12. The data, from 1997, are cited in Julia Lawlor, "Minding the Children While on the Road," *New York Times,* July 12, 1998, Business, p. 10.

13. The data come from Ed Griffin, chief executive of Meeting Planners International, and are cited in Edwin McDowell, "The Many Amenities of Corporate Retreats," *New York Times,* September 12, 1999, Business, p. 16.

14. "DDB Needham Life Style Survey" (DDB Needham, Inc.), and National Opinion Research Center, "General Social Survey," various years.

15. See Norman Nie and Lutz Erbring, "Internet and Society: A Preliminary Report," February 17, 2000 (Stanford Calif.: Stanford Institute for the Quantitative Study of Society, Stanford University). The survey was conducted in December 1999 and was based on a nationwide random sample of 4,113 adults over the age of eighteen.

16. Christine Temin, "People Who Live in Glass Houses," *Boston Globe,* August 19, 1999, p. F1.

17. S. Bianchi, G. Weathers, L. Sayer, and J. Robinson, "Are Parents Investing Less in Children? Trends in Mothers' and Fathers' Time with Children," Center on Population, Gender, and Social Inequality, University of Maryland, working paper, unpublished, 2000.

18. The calculation requires that dollars be adjusted for inflation. But readers should be warned that earnings comparisons over time are tricky. In an era of great innovation such as we are now in, a dollar of income often buys better or better-quality goods and services than it did before. Standard measures of inflation may fail to capture these improvements.

19. U.S. Department of Commerce, Bureau of the Census, Current Population Survey, "Households by Type and Selected Characteristics," various issues.

20. Data show that the wives of husbands who are in jobs with less stable earnings and higher rates of unemployment are more likely to work, and to work longer hours, than wives of husbands with more stable earnings and lower rates of unemployment. See, e.g., J. Berry Cullen and J. Bruber, "Spousal Labor Supply as Insurance: Does Unemployment Insurance Crowd Out the Added Worker Effect?" National Bureau of Economic Research Working Paper, no. 5608 (June 1996).

21. Another factor that may partially explain why more workers volunteer for overtime is that fewer working men are now married. So perhaps they have less reason to go home than before.

22. See Phillip L. Jones, Jennifer M. Gardner, and Randy Ilg, "Trends in Hours of Work Since the Mid 1970s," *Monthly Labor Review,* vol. 120, no. 4 (April 1997).

23. Jerry Jacobs and Kathleen Gerson, "Who Are the Overworked Americans?" *Review of Social Economy,* vol. 56, no. 4 (1998), p. 442.

24. Interview in *Fast Company,* August 1998, p. 158.

25. Researchers compared the progress of 523 full-time managers within a large financial-services company who took leaves in the early 1990s with their peers who did not. Controlling for age, gender, and education, they found that leave-takers were 18 percent less likely to be promoted to positions with more responsibility and received lower performance ratings and smaller salary increases. The researchers also found that managers receiving early promotions tended to enter an especially fast track, rising more rapidly to higher levels of responsibility. See M. Judiesch and K. Lyness, "Left Behind?

The Impact of Leaves of Absence on Managers' Career Success," *Academy of Management Journal,* vol. 42, no. 6 (1999), p. 641.

26. In pondering the speed with which the wives of high-income men have been moving into the workforce, account must also be taken of changes in the tax code. It is not without irony that the same social conservatives who preferred that wives remain at home were among the most ardent backers of the 1980s drop in marginal tax rates facing wealthy stay-at-home wives—which encouraged them to run out the door and into the job market even faster than they were going before.

27. Report of the President's Council of Economic Advisers, op. cit.

28. "A Nation Prepared: Teachers for the 21st Century," Carnegie Forum on Education and the Economy (New York: The Carnegie Corporation, 1986), and subsequent surveys.

29. Report of the President's Council of Economic Advisers, op. cit.

30. This and the following are calculated from Current Population Survey data. I'm indebted to Professor John D. Donahue, of Harvard's John F. Kennedy School of Government, for this illustration.

31. Linda J. Sax et al., "The American Freshman: National Year Trends, 1966–1995," and "The American Freshman: National Norms" for each year thereafter (Los Angeles: Cooperative Institutional Research Program Survey of American Freshmen, Higher Education Research Institute, University of California at Los Angeles).

32. Linda Bell and Richard Freeman, "Working Hard," paper presented at the Conference on Changes in Work Time in Canada and the United States, Ottawa, Canada, June 1996.

33. International Social Science Programme survey, cited in ibid., p. 3.

34. John Maynard Keynes, "Economic Possibilities for Our Grandchildren," *Saturday Evening Post,* vol. 203 (October 11, 1930), p. 27.

35. Bell and Freeman, op. cit.

SEVEN: THE SALE OF THE SELF

1. William H. Whyte, Jr., *The Organization Man* (New York: Simon & Schuster, 1956), pp. 76, 147, 150.

2. David Riesman, *The Lonely Crowd: A Study of the Changing American Character* (New Haven: Yale University Press, 1950).

3. Whyte, p. 448.

4. Arthur Miller, *Death of a Salesman* (1949; London: Penguin, 1998), p. 65.

5. In 1997, the U.S. Department of Education released data from a survey of young people in full-time jobs who had received their college degrees in 1992 and 1993, asking how they found the jobs. Personal connections led to jobs three times more often than did college "placement" offices or job recruiters, and twice as often as want ads or official postings. See "Early Labor Force

Experiences and Debt Burden," Department of Education, National Center for Education Statistics Report No. 97–286, July 1997. See also Barber, Daly, Giannatonio, and Phillips, "Job Search Activities: An Examination of Changes over Time," *Personnel Psychology,* vol. 747, no. 4 (1994), p. 739.

6. The proposition that in the emerging economy financial success turns more on motivation and creativity than on elite credentials is consistent with the findings of Alan Krueger and Stacy Dale, comparing the earnings of students who were admitted but declined to attend certain elite colleges (whose average student scored relatively high on the Scholastic Aptitude Test) with students who did attend such colleges. A few years after they had graduated, the two groups' average earnings were about the same. See A. Krueger and S. Dale, "Estimating the Payoff to Attending a More Selective College: An Application of Selection on Observables and Unobservables," *Industrial Relations Section Working Paper,* no. 409, Princeton University (July 1999).

7. In the same study, Krueger and Dale found that students from low-income families, presumably less well connected than their peers from higher-income families, benefited more substantially than did higher-income students from being educated at the more prestigious and selective institution.

8. Stanley Milgram's famous experiment is summarized by him in "The Small-World Problem," *Psychology Today,* vol. 2 (1967), pp. 60–67.

9. On the importance of high-status "connectors," see P. Marsden and J. Hurlbert, "Social Resources and Mobility Outcomes," *Social Forces,* vol. 66 (1988), pp. 1038–59. See also Mark S. Granovetter, *Getting a Job* (Cambridge: Harvard University Press, 1974).

10. Charles Babcock, "Clinton Friend Referred Lewinsky for Internship," *Washington Post,* January 1, 1998, p. A12.

11. Eric Eckholm, "China's Colleges: A Rush to Party, as in Communist," *New York Times,* January 31, 1998, p. A1.

12. Jill Abramson, "The Business of Persuasion Thrives in Nation's Capital," *New York Times,* September 29, 1998, p. A22.

13. Ibid.

14. At this writing, Rundgren's music can be found at www.tr-i.com.

15. The rise of Mary Meeker is chronicled by John Cassidy in "The Woman in the Bubble," *The New Yorker,* April 26 and May 3, 1999, p. 48.

16. Meeker's reported compensation for 1999, and Morgan Stanley's reported earnings, are found in Charles Gasparino and Randall Smith, "Wall Street Scores in '99. Now for the Big Bonus Round," *Wall Street Journal,* December 9, 1999, p. C1.

17. Quoted in Bernard Weinraub, "Hollywood Raises Curtain on 2000," *New York Times,* February 20, 1999, p. A7.

18. See Alison Leigh Cowan, "Lessons: Questions in a Change of Heart," *New York Times,* February 23, 2000, p. A23.

19. Interview with John Isaacson, president of Isaacson, Miller, Boston, September 23, 1999.

20. Quoted in the *Boston Globe,* November 12, 1998, p. C1.

21. The Barro episode (including quotes cited in these pages) is described by Sylvia Nasar, "New Breed of College All-Star," *New York Times,* April 8, 1998, pp. C1, C3.

22. The thesis is nicely explicated in Robert Frank and Philip Cook, *The Winner-Take-All Society* (New York: Free Press, 1995).

23. Quoted in Kyle Pope, "For TV's Hottest Item, It's Let's Make a Deal," *Wall Street Journal,* April 5, 1999, p. B1.

24. Dale Carnegie, *How to Win Friends and Influence People* (New York: Simon & Schuster, 1936).

25. Miller, *Death of a Salesman,* op. cit., pp. 21, 65–6.

26. David Riesman, *The Lonely Crowd: A Study of the Changing American Character* (New Haven: Yale University Press, 1950), pp. 47–9, 83.

27. Suze Orman, *The Courage to Be Rich: Creating a Life of Material and Spiritual Abundance* (New York: Doubleday, 1999).

28. Tom Peters, "The Brand Called You," *Fast Company,* August–September 1997, pp. 83–94.

29. Quoted in Bryan Miller, "Serving Chef Under Glass," *New York Times,* October 10, 1998, p. B1.

30. Quoted in Tracie Rozhon, "The Agent as Hot Property," *New York Times,* April 19, 1998, p. C1.

31. See Ann Jarrell, "Doctors Who Love Publicity," *New York Times,* July 2, 2000, p. F1; Abigail Zuger, "Doctors' Offices Turn into Salesrooms," *New York Times,* March 30, 1999, p. F1.

32. The self-promoting dentists are described by Rick Marin, "Polishing Their Image," *New York Times,* January 31, 1999, Section 9, p. 1.

33. Bruce Orwall, "Wall Street Bets on Entertainment Idol's Earning Power," *Wall Street Journal,* September 26, 1997, p. B1. Martha Stewart's incorporation is a matter of public record.

EIGHT: THE INCREDIBLE SHRINKING FAMILY

1. Unless otherwise indicated, data on the changing structure of the American family are found in "The Changing American Family," in *Economic Report of the President,* Council of Economic Advisers, Washington, D.C., February 2000; see also "Families and the Labor Market, 1969–1999; Analyzing the 'Time Crunch,'" a report of the President's Council of Economic Advisers, Washington, D.C., May 1999.

2. On the increasing tendency for husbands and wives to exchange shifts of work and child care, see the National Study of the Changing Work Force,

1997 (a survey of more than 3,500 working men and women), cited in Julia Lawlor, "For Many Blue-Collar Fathers, Child Care Is Shift Work, Too," *New York Times,* April 26, 1998, p. 11. See also Jacqueline Salmon, "A Tag-Team Approach to Wrestling with Child Care," *Washington Post Weekly Edition,* April 10, 1998, p. 30.

3. For evidence on this point, see Robert Putnam, *Bowling Alone* (New York: Simon and Schuster, 2000), p. 100.

4. Amy Wilson, "All in the Family," *Fast Company,* March 2000, p. 72.

5. No other household grouping changed very much over the interval. The percent of households composed of unmarried people with children increased only slightly, from 10 to 11 percent. The proportion composed of married people without children went from just under 30 percent to just over 30. See U.S. Bureau of the Census, Current Population Reports, P20–509, and earlier reports; and unpublished data. See also General Social Survey, cited in Tom W. Smith, "The Emerging 21st Century American Family," National Opinion Research Center, University of Chicago, General Social Survey Report, no. 42, November 24, 1999.

6. For a view that assigns most of the change in family structure to the Pill, see C. Goldin and L. Katz, "Career and Family in the Age of the Pill," *American Economic Review,* May 2000.

7. See Tom W. Smith, op. cit., Table 3, p. 25.

8. Using the standard adjustment for inflation, men in the bottom fifth of income earners went from earning an average of $5,818 in 1979 to earning $3,287 in 1996, a drop of 44 percent. Men in the next-highest fifth went from $22,263 to $16,949, a drop of 24 percent; the middle fifth, from $33,133 to $27,765, a 16 percent drop; the second-to-highest fifth, from $44,102 to $40,561, a drop of 8 percent. Only men in the top fifth gained ground, going from $70,350 in 1979 to $72,893 in the late 1990s, an increase of 4 percent. (The sample represents noninstitutionalized U.S. males aged twenty-five to fifty-nine.) Tabulations are from the March 1980 and March 1997 Current Population Survey files. All wages and income statistics are converted to 1996 dollars. See Gary Burtless, "Effects of Growing Wage Disparities and Changing Family Composition on the U.S. Income Distribution," *Center on Social and Economic Dynamics Working Paper no. 4* (July 1999), Table 2.

9. See Burtless, op. cit.

10. For an analysis, see Barbara H. Wootton, "Gender Differences in Occupational Employment," *Monthly Labor Review,* vol. 120, no. 4 (1997), p. 15.

11. Current Population Survey, op. cit.

12. Goldin and Katz, op. cit.

13. The judge and Mr. Young are quoted in Melody Petersen, "The Short End of Long Hours," *New York Times,* July 18, 1998, p. B1; and in Margaret Jacobs, "Fathers Winning More Child-Custody Cases," *Orange County Register,* July 19, 1998, p. A25.

14. Survey data in Tom W. Smith, op. cit., Table 15, p. 38.

15. See "Births, Marriages, Divorces, and Deaths," historic data, National Vital Statistics Reports, National Center for Health Statistics, Washington, D.C. Note also that some people may want children but are infertile, and unwilling or unable to adopt. Delayed childbearing has increased the rate of infertility.

16. General Social Survey, cited in Tom W. Smith, op. cit.

17. Ibid.

18. Domestic violence is but one of the many consequences of economic stress, and it is not absolutely clear that the causal relationship runs from economic stress to violence and other forms of social deviance; the loss of a job and the social deviance may have a common origin. There is some evidence, but not conclusive, that the incidence of domestic violence increases in the wake of increases in unemployment. See generally Richard Gelles and Murray Straus, *Intimate Violence: The Causes and Consequences of Abuse in the American Family* (New York: Simon & Schuster, 1988); and Robert Burgess and Patricia Draper, "The Explanation of Family Violence: The Role of Biological, Behavioral, and Cultural Selection," in Lloyd Ohlin and Michael Tonry, eds., *Family Violence* (Chicago: University of Chicago Press, 1989), pp. 59–116.

19. Kathryn Edin, "Few Good Men," *The American Prospect,* January 3, 2000, p. 26.

20. Data on illegitimacy in Britain are found in "Key Population and Vital Statistics," Her Majesty's Office for National Statistics, London (December 1997, and subsequent series).

21. Tom W. Smith, op. cit.

22. National Center for Health Statistics, op. cit. Some of these data are summarized in Steven Holmes, "In Climb up the Ladder, Married Blacks Are Choosing Small Families," *New York Times,* July 21, 1998, p. A10.

23. But there's still a puzzle about why the birthrate hasn't fallen faster among unmarried women than among married women, given the large economic costs of having a baby while unmarried.

24. U.S. Census Bureau, *Educational Attainment in the United States* (Washington, D.C.: U.S. Department of Commerce, Economics and Statistics Administration, March 1998), from Current Population Reports, Population Characteristics, Report P20-513, Table 1.

25. "Twelfth Annual Report on Eating Patterns in America" (Port Washington, N.Y.: NPD Group, August 1997). For additional data, see *The Economist,* September 26, 1998, pp. 68–9.

26. *The Economist,* ibid.

27. *New York* magazine, September 28, 1998.

28. Quoted in Monee Fields White and Liz Enochs, "Working Women Spur Economy," *Salt Lake Tribune,* October 26, 1999, p. C6.

29. U.S. Bureau of the Census, Current Population Reports, P70-62, Novem-

ber 1997, Table A: "Primary Child Care Arrangements Used for Preschoolers by Families with Employed Mothers: Selected Years."

30. General Social Survey, cited in Tom W. Smith, op. cit., Table 14.

NINE: PAYING FOR ATTENTION

1. René Spitz, "Hospitalism: An Inquiry Into the Genesis of Psychiatric Conditions in Early Childhood" (1945), reprinted in R. Emde, ed., *The Psychoanalytic Study of the Child,* vol. 12 (New York: International Universities Press, 1983), pp. 53–74.

2. Mary Carlson et al., "Psychological and Neuroendocrinological Sequelae of Early Social Deprivation in Institutionalized Children in Romania," *Annals of the New York Academy of Sciences,* vol. 807 (1997), pp. 419–28.

3. T. Field et al., "Tactile / Kinesthetic Stimulation Effects on Preterm Neonates," *Pediatrics,* vol. 77 (1986), pp. 654–8. See also F. Scafidi et al., "Massage Stimulates Growth in Preterm Infants: A Replication," *Infant Behavior and Development,* vol. 31 (1990), pp. 167–88.

4. Lisa F. Berkman and S. Leonard Syme, "Social Networks, Host Resistance, and Mortality: A Nine-Year Follow-Up Study of Alameda County Residents," *American Journal of Epidemiology,* vol. 109, no. 2 (1979), pp. 186–204.

5. The study is described in John Rowe and Robert Kahne, *Successful Aging* (New York: Random House, 1998), p. 229.

6. Teresa Seeman et al., "Behavioral and Psychosocial Predictors of Physical Performance: MacArthur Studies of Successful Aging," *Journal of Gerontology,* vol. 50 (1995), pp. 177–83.

7. Robert Kraut et al., "Internet Paradox: A Social Technology That Reduces Social Involvement and Psychological Well-Being," *American Psychologist* (September 1998), pp. 1017–31.

8. Both at the start of the study and again at the end, participants took standard tests to gauge their psychological states, and were asked to agree or disagree with statements like "I feel everything I do is an effort" or "I enjoy life." They were also given standard questionnaires used to determine psychological health. Those who were lonelier or more depressed at the start were no more drawn to the Internet than those who were happier and more engaged.

9. Quoted in Amy Harmon, "Sad, Lonely World Discovered in Cyberspace," *New York Times,* August 30, 1998, p. A1.

10. T. Field et al., "Massage Therapy for Infants of Depressed Mothers," *Infant Behavior and Development,* vol. 19 (1996), pp. 109–14.

11. T. E. Seeman et al., "Social Ties and Support as Modifiers of Neuroendocrine Function," *Annals of Behavioral Medicine,* vol. 16 (1994), pp. 95–106.

12. Quoted in Louis Uchitelle, "Gains in Employment, but Not in Productivity," *New York Times,* March 8, 1999, Business, p. 1.

13. Merrill Lynch is hardly the only financial-services company to provide its

elite customers with extra attention. Charles Schwab, the discount broker that has made do-it-yourself stock trading on the Web its stock-in-trade, provides customers who park more than $500,000 in assets with Schwab with "personal" full-time brokers who monitor their accounts and provide ongoing advice. See Joseph Kahn, "Schwab Lands Feet First on the Net," *New York Times,* February 10, 1999, p. C1.

14. Quoted in Charles Gasparino, "Wall Street Has Less and Less Time for Small Investors," *Wall Street Journal,* October 5, 1999, p. C1.

15. Thorstein Veblen, *The Theory of the Leisure Class* (New York: Macmillan, 1899).

16. Nancy Keates, "Coffee, Tea or Massage?," *Wall Street Journal,* November 6, 1998, p. W1.

17. Quoted in Laurence Zuckerman, "Airlines Coddle the High Fliers at Expense of the Coach Class," *New York Times,* April 1, 1998, p. A1.

18. Elizabeth Hayt, "A High Fashion Destination Worth a Detour," *New York Times,* August 23, 1998, section 9, p. 3.

19. Thomas J. Leonard, "Coaching Q&A: What Is Coaching All About?," Coach U. Web site (www.coachu.com/qagrpa.htm), retrieved June 6, 2000.

20. Quoted in Lynette Lamb, "Team Me," *Utne Reader,* January–February 1999, p. 82.

21. Quoted in Todd Purdum, "Where Everyone Drives, Few Deign to Park," *New York Times,* November 28, 1999, p. A1.

22. Natalie Angier, "Among Doctors, Pay for Women Still Lags," *New York Times,* January 12, 1999, p. D7.

23. Timothy Diamond, *Making Gray Gold: Narratives of Nursing Home Care* (Chicago: University of Chicago Press, 1995). For a thoughtful discussion, see Deborah A. Stone, "Care As We Give It, Work As We Know It," unpublished paper, Radcliffe Center on Public Policy, December 1998.

24. For more on the consequences of this rule, see Deborah A. Stone, "Care and Trembling," *The American Prospect* 43, March–April 1999, p. 61.

25. A number of studies suggest that differences in the amount, quality, and consistency of child care can have significant consequences for children later in their lives. See, for example, Ellen Peisner-Feinberg et al., "The Children of the Cost, Quality and Outcomes Study Go to School" (Chapel Hill: University of North Carolina at Chapel Hill, FPG Child Development Center, June 1999). See also H. Goelman and A. R. Pence, "Effects of Child Care, Family, and Individual Characteristics on Children's Language Development: The Victoria Day Care Research Project," in D. A. Phillips, ed., *Quality in Child Care: What Does Research Tell Us?* (Washington, D.C.: National Association for the Education of Young Children, 1987); Cheryl D. Hayes et al., eds., *Who Cares for America's Children? Child Care Policy for the 1990s* (Washington, D.C.: National Academy Press, 1990).

These and related studies tend to use two scales to measure the quality of care of children: The first is the Arnett Scale of Provider Sensitivity, measuring how warm, attentive, and engaged the provider is relative to how critical, threatening or punitive, and detached. See J. Arnett, "Caregivers in Day Care Centers: Does Training Matter?" *Journal of Applied Developmental Psychology,* vol. 10 (1989), pp. 541–52. The second scale is the Adult Involvement Scale, which looks at the degree and kind of caregiving—from ignoring the child, to giving the child routine care (help in blowing her nose, for example), to talking with the child in order to discipline her and answering direct requests for help, to responding to the child's questions positively but briefly, to extending and elaborating on such questions, and, finally, to engaging the child in prolonged conversation, playing interactively, and holding or hugging to provide comfort. See C. Howes and P. Stewart, "Child's Play with Adults, Toys and Peers: An Examination of Family and Child Care Influences," *Developmental Psychology,* vol. 12, no. 3 (1987), pp. 423–30.

26. For more information about the study, see "Early Learning, Later Success: The Abecedarian Project" (Chapel Hill: University of North Carolina at Chapel Hill, February 28, 2000). As of this writing, the study has not appeared in a peer-reviewed journal.

27. While it is true that doctors and professors also tend to work one-on-one or in small groups, and their pay is still relatively good, it should be noted that many of their routine duties are fast being taken over by lower-paid nurse practitioners, interns, graduate students, or itinerant lecturers.

28. See Arlie Russell Hochschild, *The Managed Heart: The Commercialization of Human Feeling* (Berkeley: University of California Press, 1985), for a study of how the caring attention traditionally provided by many women has been turned into a commodity.

29. U.S. Department of Labor, Bureau of Labor Statistics, *Occupational Outlook Handbook,* 2000–01 Edition, Bulletin 2520 (Washington, D.C.: U.S. Government Printing Office, January 2000).

30. Leslie Eaton, "Tourism Is Helping Put Some Back on the Job," *New York Times,* August 30, 1998, p. A29.

31. Todd Purdum, op. cit.

32. Quoted in James Brooke, "Cry of Wealthy in Vail: Not in Our Playground!" *New York Times,* November 5, 1998, p. A18.

TEN: THE COMMUNITY AS COMMODITY

1. For evidence that Americans are joining up less, see Robert Putnam, *Bowling Alone* (New York: Simon & Schuster, 2000).

2. For evidence that Americans are segregating more by income, see Paul Jargowsky, *Poverty and Place: Ghettos, Barrios, and the American City* (New York: Russell Sage, 1997).

3. James Brooke, "Cry of Wealthy in Vail: Not in Our Playground!" *New York Times,* November 5, 1998, p. A18.

4. For one example of this already occurring, see Laurie Flynn, "Georgia City Putting Entire Community Online," *New York Times,* March 17, 2000, p. C4.

5. "Policing for Profit: Welcome to the New World of Private Security," *The Economist,* April 19, 1997, pp. 21–4.

6. On the situation in Chicago, see Bill Dedman, "For Black Home Buyers, a Boomerang," *New York Times,* February 13, 1999, p. A15.

7. Xianglei Chen, "Students' Peer Groups in High School: The Pattern and Relationship to Educational Outcomes," U.S. Department of Education, Office of Educational Research and Improvement, National Center for Educational Statistics, 1997, 1998. On economic mobility as it relates to education, see George J. Orjas, "Intellectual Capital and Intergenerational Mobility," *Quarterly Journal of Economics* (1992), vol. 1, p. 107.

8. D. J. Robertson and J. S. V. Symons, "Do Peer Groups Matter?" Centre for Economic Performance, London School of Economics, Discussion Paper, 1996.

9. L. Katz, J. Kling, and J. Liebman, "Moving Opportunity in Boston: Early Impacts of a Housing Mobility Program," Harvard University, September 1999.

10. Cited in Tamar Lewin, "In Michigan, School Choice Weeds Out Costlier Students," *New York Times,* October 26, 1999, p. A14.

11. Data on school districts funded in part by private foundations are available from U.S. Department of Education, Office of Educational Research and Improvement, National Center for Educational Statistics.

12. "Highlights," Newton Schools Foundation, vol. 13, no. 1 (Fall 1999).

13. Editorial page, August 24, 1998, p. A12.

14. Despite efforts by many states to better equalize school funding, differences still exist. Public school expenditures per pupil (in 1996 constant dollars) in school year 1992–1993 (the most recent date for which such data are available) for districts in which median household income was less than $20,000 was $4,237; in districts where median household income was $35,000 or more, it was $6,661; among the wealthiest school districts, expenditure per pupil ranges up to $9,500. See U.S. Department of Education, National Center for Education Statistics, "National Public Education Financial Survey," yearly issues. See also U.S. Department of Education, National Center for Education Statistics, *The Condition of Education* (1997).

15. Quoted in Michael Janofsky, "Financial Aid Bargaining Drives Admissions Frenzy," *New York Times,* April 5, 1999, p. A12.

16. Caroline Hoxby and B. Terry, "Explaining Rising Income and Wage Inequality Among the College-Educated" (Cambridge, Mass.: National Bureau of Economic Research, Working Paper Series, No. 6873, 1999).

17. Quoted in Frances Perkins, *The Roosevelt I Knew* (New York: Viking, 1946), pp. 282–3.

18. The survey was conducted by the Center for Studying Health System Change. It involved 10,881 physicians in sixty randomly selected communities in 1996 and 1997. Doctors depending on managed-care plans for 85 percent or more of their income spent, on average, 5.2 hours a month caring for indigent patients, while doctors who derived no income from managed care spent nearly twice that amount, or 10 hours a month. The study is reported in Sheryl Gay Stolberg, "Managed Care Squeezes Research Funds and Charity Health Aid, Studies Find," *New York Times*, March 24, 1999, p. A20. See also Diane Rowland, Barbara Lyons, Alina Salganicoff, and Peter Long, "A Profile of the Uninsured in America," *Health Affairs*, vol. 13, no. 2 (Spring II, 1994).

19. Laurence Zuckerman, "Developer of Notes Program to Focus on New Venture," *New York Times*, October 1, 1997, p. D2.

20. Quoted in Deborah Solomon, "As Art Museums Thrive, Their Directors Decamp," *New York Times*, August 18, 1998, Section 3, p. 1.

21. Quoted in David Greenberg, "Small Men on Campus," *The New Republic*, June 1, 1998, p. 19.

22. Ibid.

23. These averages are from data from the U.S. Bureau of the Census, Current Population Survey, P-20 series, various issues.

24. Calculations by Nicholas Johnson and Iris Lav, Center on Budget and Policy Priorities, based on data from the national Conference of State Legislatures. Posted on the Internet at www.cbpp.org/930sttzx.htm.

25. Quoted in Pam Belluck, "Please Stay, We'll Pay You, Nebraska Begs Its Brightest," *New York Times*, February 18, 1998, p. A1.

26. Editorial page, November 30, 1998, p. A22.

27. Calculated from U.S. Bureau of the Census, Annual Survey of Government Finances, op. cit.; National Center for Education Statistics, *Digest of Education Statistics for 1999*; and citations in David Minge, "The New War Between the States," *The New Democrat*, May–June 1999, p. 27.

28. Steve Lopez, "Money for Stadiums but Not for Schools," *Time*, June 12, 1999, p. 54.

29. For a similar comparison in Cleveland, see Melvin Burstein and Arthur Rolnick, "Congress Should End the Economic War for Sports and Other Businesses," *Region*, Federal Reserve Bank of Minneapolis, June 1996, p. 5.

30. Emma Lazarus, "The New Colossus: Inscription for the Statue of Liberty, New York Harbor," 1883.

31. Judith Miller and William Broad, "Iranians, Bioweapons in Mind, Lure Needy Ex-Soviet Scientists," *New York Times*, December 8, 1998, p. A1.

32. Larry Greenberg, "Canadian Professionals' Compensation Trails That of Their U.S. Counterparts," *Wall Street Journal*, December 23, 1998, p. A4.

ELEVEN: PERSONAL CHOICE

1. Freud's *"Lieben und arbeiten"* appears in Erik H. Erikson, *Childhood and Society* (New York: W. W. Norton, 1950), p. 229.

2. *New York Times*/CBS poll, October 1999. Of the 1,038 young people polled, 50 percent of those from households with incomes above $75,000 reported that their lives were harder and more stressful than their parents'; 38 percent of those from households whose incomes were less than $30,000 reported the same.

3. General Social Survey, cited in Tom W. Smith, "The Emerging 21st Century American Family," National Opinion Research Center, General Social Survey Report, no. 42, November 24, 1999, Table 11.

4. See Arlie Russell Hochschild, *The Second Shift* (New York: Avon Books, 1989).

5. Cecile Andrews, *The Circle of Simplicity: Return to the Good Life* (New York: HarperCollins, 1997).

6. From Thoreau's journal, March 11, 1856.

7. Thoreau's *Walden*, "Where I Lived, and What I Lived For" (1854; New York: Signet, 1949), p. 66.

8. *Walden*, "Economy," ibid., p. 14.

9. Poll conducted by Roper Starch Worldwide, April 9 to April 12, 1999, of 1,096 randomly selected visitors to AOL's Opinion Place, reported in "How Much Is Enough?" *Fast Company*, no. 26 (July–August 1999), p. 108.

10. The editor of *Real Simple* states the purpose of the new magazine at the start of its first issue, April 2000.

TWELVE: PUBLIC CHOICE

1. The big choices of the industrial era are nicely chronicled in Robert H. Wiebe, *The Search for Order 1877–1920* (New York: Hill & Wang, 1967). Other useful histories of the era are Morton Keller, *Regulating a New Economy: Public Policy and Economic Change in America, 1900–1913* (Cambridge: Harvard University Press, 1990); Samuel P. Hays, *The Response to Industrialism 1885–1914* (Chicago: University of Chicago Press, 1957); Richard Hofstadter, *The Age of Reform: From Bryan to FDR* (New York: Random House, 1960); and Steven J. Diner, *A Very Different Age: Americans of the Progressive Era* (New York: Hill & Wang, 1997).

2. Frederick Lewis Allen, *The Big Change: America Transforms Itself, 1900–1950* (New York: Harper Perennial, 1969), p. 215.

3. Michael Sandel, *Democracy's Discontent* (Cambridge: Harvard University Press, 1996).

4. From Roosevelt's speech at Osawatomie, Kansas, August 1910.

5. Princeton Survey Research Associates, "People and the Press: 1999 Millen-

nium Survey" (Washington, D.C.: Pew Research Center, conducted April 6 to May 6, 1999), released October 24, 1999. See also International Communications Research, "The Nation's Worries" (Washington, D.C.: *Washington Post,* conducted October 27 to October 31, 1999), released November 7, 1999.

6. The phrase is from Saskia Sassen, *Globalization and Its Discontents* (New York: New Press, 1998).

7. For a fuller discussion of earnings insurance, see Gary Burtless, Robert Lawrence, Robert Litan, and Robert Shapiro, *Globaphobia: Confronting Fears About Open Trade* (Washington, D.C.: The Brookings Institution Press, Twentieth Century Fund, and Progressive Policy Institute, 1998).

8. The idea of a small "transactions tax" on financial transactions was first proposed by economist James Tobin. See his "A Proposal for International Monetary Reform," *Eastern Economic Journal,* vol. 4 (1978), pp. 153–9. The idea was developed more fully by Lawrence and Vicki Summers, "When Financial Markets Work Too Well: A Cautious Case for a Securities Transactions Tax," *Journal of Financial Services Research,* vol. 3 (1989), pp. 261–86.

9. For a thoughtful analysis of a proposal to provide each American, upon reaching eighteen years of age, a financial "nest egg" considerably larger than the one I propose, see Bruce Ackerman and Anne Alstott, *The Stakeholder Society* (New Haven: Yale University Press, 1999).

10. L. Katz, J. Kling, and J. Liebman, "Moving to Opportunity in Boston: Early Impacts of a Housing Mobility Program," Harvard University, September 1999.

ACKNOWLEDGMENTS

I'm indebted to several colleagues and friends (and to many who fit both categories) who read earlier versions of this book and offered useful criticisms. Special thanks to Katharine G. Abraham, John D. Donahue, Janet Giele, Claudia Goldin, Christopher Jencks, Lawrence Katz, Alan Krueger, Lisa Lynch, Martha Minow, Katherine Newman, Richard Parker, Robert Putnam, Michael Sandel, Julia Schor, Jack Shonkoff, Barbara Dafoe Whitehead, and Ralph Whitehead for their valuable insights. Thanks also to Emily Axelrod, Douglas Dworkin, John Heilemann, John Isaacson, Rafe Sagalyn, and my intrepid editor, Jonathan Segal, for their fine suggestions about how to better express all of this. Several of my students helped me track down obscure bits of information and checked their accuracy. I'm especially appreciative of the labors of Roblyn Anderson-Brigham, Lauren Brown, Julia Gittelman, Valerie Leiter, John Lippitt, Debbie Osnowitz, Susan Schantz, and Andrew Sokatch, all of the Heller School at Brandeis University. My assistant, Mary Del Grosso, deserves special thanks for fortitude and good cheer throughout. Research was made possible by grants from the Nathan Cummings Foundation and the Center for National Policy, to which I am grateful. Last, but really first, I want to toast Clare Dalton, a dedicated teacher and scholar as well as community leader, mother of my children, and my partner for three decades, who discussed and debated with me every one of these pages. Whatever is noteworthy in this book I owe to all of the above; its shortcomings I claim as my own.

INDEX

A NOTE ABOUT THE AUTHOR

Robert B. Reich is University Professor at Brandeis University and Maurice B. Hexter Professor of Social and Economic Policy at Brandeis's Heller Graduate School. He has served in three national administrations, most recently as Secretary of Labor under President Bill Clinton. He is a co-founder and national editor of *The American Prospect,* and his writings have appeared in *The New Yorker, The Atlantic Monthly, Harper's,* the *New York Times,* and the *Wall Street Journal.* This is his eighth book. He lives in Cambridge, Massachusetts, with his wife, Clare Dalton. They have two sons.

A NOTE ON THE TYPE

This book was set in Monotype Dante, a typeface designed by Giovanni Mardersteig (1892–1977). Conceived as a private type for the Officina Bodoni in Verona, Italy, Dante was originally cut only for hand composition by Charles Malin, the famous Parisian punch cutter, between 1946 and 1952. Its first use was in an edition of Boccaccio's *Trattatello in laude di Dante* that appeared in 1954. The Monotype Corporation's version of Dante followed in 1957. Although modeled on the Aldine type used for Pietro Cardinal Bembo's treatise *De Aetna* in 1495, Dante is a thoroughly modern interpretation of the venerable face.

Composed by NK Graphics, Keene, New Hampshire
Printed and bound by R. R. Donnelley & Sons, Harrisonburg, Virginia
Designed by Robert C. Olsson